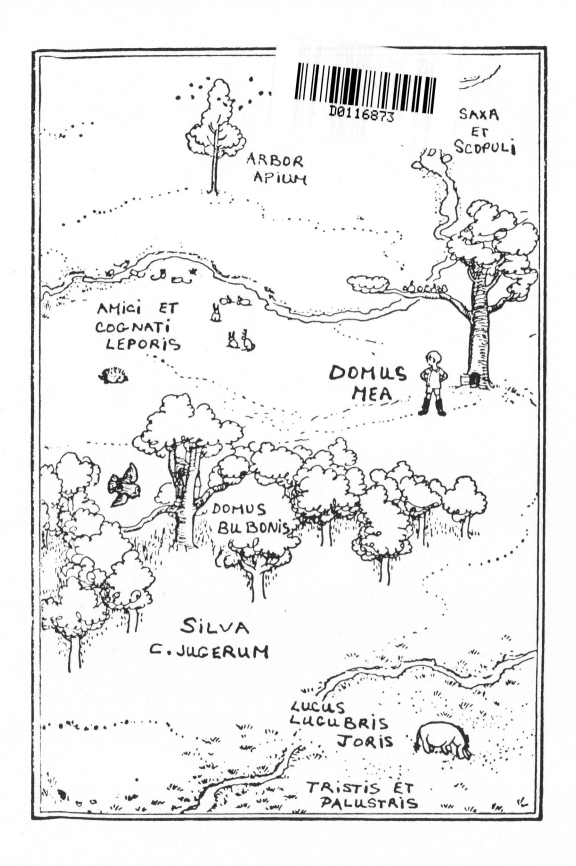

ARBOR
APIUM

SAXA
ET
SCOPULI

AMICI ET
COGNATI
LEPORIS

DOMUS
MEA

DOMUS
BUBONIS

SILVA
C. JUGERUM

LUCUS
LUGUBRIS
JORIS

TRISTIS ET
PALUSTRIS

# The Brilliant Career
## of
## Winnie-the-Pooh

# THE BRILLIANT CAREER OF
# Winnie-the-Pooh

*The story of A. A. Milne and his writing for children*

ANN THWAITE

Methuen

First published in Great Britain in 1992
by Methuen London
an imprint of Reed Consumer Books Limited
Michelin House, 81 Fulham Road, London sw3 6rb
and Auckland, Melbourne, Singapore and Toronto

ISBN 0 413 66710 3
A CIP catalogue record for this book
is available from the British Library

Photoset by Rowland Phototypesetting Limited
Bury St Edmunds, Suffolk
Printed in Great Britain
by BPCC Hazells Limited
Member of BPCC Limited

*For the next generation of Milne readers:*
Jack, William and Maisie, Toby, Matthew and Phoebe

An unfamiliar image of Christopher Robin and the animals carol singing, which was possibly for a Shepard Christmas card, sold at Christie's for £5,280 in December 1990.

# Introduction

During the years when I was working on my biography of A. A. Milne, which was eventually published in 1990, I was very aware of how much interesting visual material I was accumulating: not just photographs, but theatre programmes, newspaper cuttings, certificates, and even menus, cartoons and cigarette cards. There is always a limit to the number of illustrations a thick, expensive biography can carry – and there is never any chance of using colour. I began to have the idea of producing a later version with an edited, abbreviated text and masses of illustrations. I was talking about this to a friend one day when he suggested I provided, not an alternative biography, but a totally new book which would be both a supplement to my biography and a book for other readers who are interested in A. A. Milne's children's books but not inclined to read a 500-page biography of the writer. The next stage was to realize that, although I would include material from Milne's own life, the central focus of the book should be Winnie-the-Pooh, whose extraordinary career certainly deserves attention nearly seventy years after his first appearance in print.

I have many people to thank: first of all the Milne family (especially Milne's niece Marjorie Murray-Rust) for the use of many family photographs and material. Other photographs came from Brian Sibley, editor of *The Pooh Sketchbook*, who had been given them by Milne's widow Daphne when he himself hoped to write a biography. I am grateful to Brian for his appreciation of my work and his selfless generosity in the loan of some rare ingredients. The recent photographs in the book, apart from some of my own, have been specially taken by Bill Sanderson. I am very glad of his contribution. I would like to thank his sons, Jack and William, whose delight in Milne and Shepard has given me so much pleasure. The designer of the book, Christopher Holgate, is also a Milne-and-Shepard fan. I am grateful for the attention he has given to the problems I gave him and for the way he has carried out my intentions. I would also like to thank both Ann Mansbridge and Mary O'Donovan, my editors, for their patience and cooperation. More grateful acknowledgements will be found at the back of the book.

Ann Thwaite

| 273 | *Eighteenth January 1882 Henley House Mortimer Road* | *Alexander Sidney* | *Boy* | *John Vine Milne* | *Sarah Maria Milne formerly Heginbo...* |

Winnie-the-Pooh's brilliant career – though it was not to take off for nearly forty years – began in 1882 with the birth of his brilliant creator. So we start with Milne's own beginnings. The register of births in the Hampstead district of London reveals that his father, John Vine Milne, headmaster of Henley House, a small private school for boys, was slow in registering his third son's arrival. At four weeks old, the child was called Alexander Sidney. How easily Pooh's name might have been linked with other initials: A. S. Milne. The heading of the final column is 'Name entered after registration'.

By an odd coincidence, the other creator of Winnie-the-Pooh, as we know him, had been born two years earlier just round the corner from the school in Mortimer Road. Ernest Howard Shepard was born in Springfield Road. By the time this photo was taken, he and his family had moved to Kent Terrace, nearer Regent's Park. The two never met until, many years later, they were both working for *Punch*. Though Shepard's ancestry was rather grander than Milne's, his drawings from his autobiography can illustrate Milne's childhood as well as his own. H. G. Wells described the Milnes' drawing-room as the most 'drawing-room-like' drawing-room he had ever been in.

| School Master | Jno. V. Milne, Father, Henley House, Mortimer Road, Kilburn Hampstead | Fifteenth February 1882 | Willm. Paan Registrar | Alan Alexander |

Milne disliked the Fauntleroy get-up even more than the uncomfortable starched sailor-suits they also wore. His curls were not cut off until he was ten. In this photograph, probably taken in 1886 (the year of the publication of Frances Hodgson Burnett's *Little Lord Fauntleroy*), Alan is four years old and at the front. Blond and blue-eyed, he was typecast at birth as the brightest and best of the boys. The father has a restraining hand in Barry's (he was cast as the bad boy of the family) and a protective arm round Ken, as if to console him for not being Alan. J. V. Milne was remarkable himself, with the sense of humour his two younger sons inherited. After his death, A. A. Milne called him 'the best man I have ever known'. Ken remained Alan's close friend until his too-early death in 1929. There were only sixteen months between them.

A. A. Milne was born a Londoner, in a part of London which Milne himself described modestly as 'the Kilburn end of Maida Vale'. To London ears this sounds very different from Hampstead, the registration district for his birth, or St John's Wood, as his father and E. H. Shepard called the area. The map shows the streets where the collaborators were born. The Milne boys were allowed a great deal of freedom and Milne's ideal of childhood, which permeates the Pooh books, has much more to do with a love of adventuring than with nannies and nursery tea. Alan and Ken explored London on their own, riding their bicycles daringly in Park Lane, overtaking the horse-buses and darting between hansom cabs. In the other direction, a penny bus ride, or their bicycles, would take them among fields and trees worth climbing. They spent all their summer holidays in the country.

The joyful dog in 'Puppy and I' probably owes more to Brownie, acquired on a Kent holiday in 1889, than to any later pet. He appears here to remind us that Milne's *When We Were Very Young* and *Now We Are Six* often owe as much to his own childhood as to his son's. Reginald Birch's illustration (top right) is from the August 1924 *St Nicholas*, E. H. Shepard's from *When We Were Very Young*. Milne wrote, as all the best children's writers do, 'from a combination of memory, observation and imagination'.

Henley House itself has long since disappeared but this neighbouring house is similar.

This photo of Henley House boys around the time of A. A. Milne's birth shows Alfred Harmsworth, later Lord Northcliffe, on the extreme right.

12  Before his fifth birthday, Alan was competent with the pen. The
address on the first letter is that of his first school, Wykeham
House, where he was taught by Miss Alice and Miss Florence
Budd. Towards the end of his life, A. A. Milne commented: 'This
must have been the first letter which I ever wrote . . . It was
written at the age of four from my kindergarten school. I never
did like collaboration, and it is clear that I spurned it on this
occasion. All around me (I like to think) were other little boys and
girls writing to their dear mammas; asking their companions how
to spell Hampstead Heath, or waiting glassy-eyed for some
suggestion from the mistress as to what constituted "a letter". I
just sailed ahead, tongue out, arms outspread. We had had a

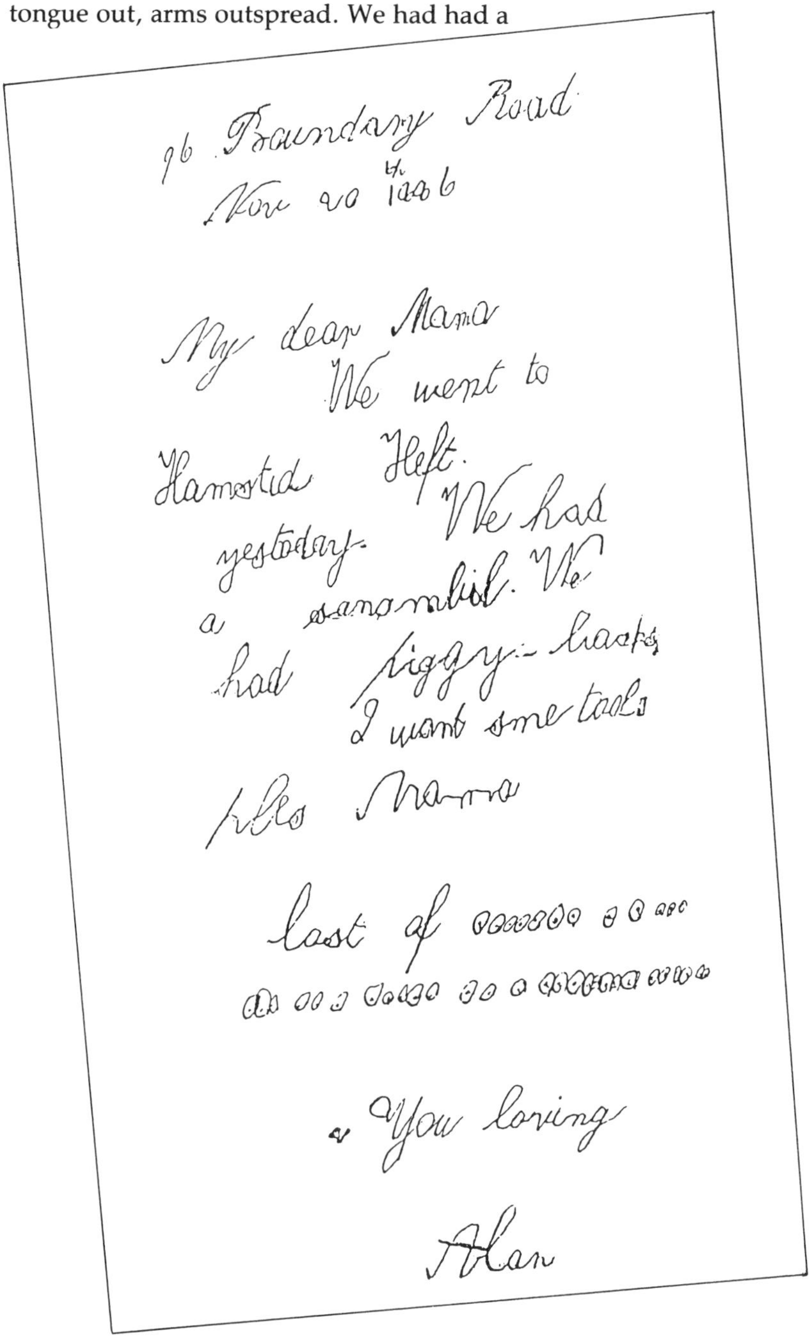

96 Boundary Road
Nov 20 1886

My dear Mama
We went to
Hamstid Heft. We had
yesterday
a ... We
had piggy-backs
I want some tools
Please Mama

last of ...

You loving

Alan

sanambil, and I had decided to be a carpenter. The family would expect to be told.

'If anyone else has ever had a sanambil, I should like him to get in touch with me. The word is clearly written, the "bil" inked over; as if I had played with the idea of some other ending, but realized in time that this combination of letters was the most informative. Could I have meant a "scramble"? One from whose pen "piggy-backs" flowed so faultlessly would surely have made a better beginning of it. Well, we shall never know now; but I like to think of it as one of those pleasant Victorian games, now gone with so much else of those days which was good.'

Dec. 15ᵗʰ 1886

My dear Mama.
   We are not going to have any more lessons after Tuesday Dᵣ Gibson is coming to give away the prizes. We are to come at a quarter to four on Wednesday and I think I shall have a prize...
With love and kisses.
   Your loving
   Alan.

Seldom has an under-five been more prizeworthy. Alan Milne was not five until 18 January 1887.

## MY THREE DAYS' WALKING TOUR.

ON Monday we went out to Oxted to get some waterproof knapsacks, and we were only able to get one. We started on Tuesday—papa, Ken, and myself—and walked to Oxted Station, where we took train to East Grinstead; and when we got there we looked about to get a knapsack, and at last got one. We then walked to Forest Row, where it poured with rain, and we stood under some trees for shelter. After a little while it cleared up, and we walked to Ashdown Forest, where it again poured with rain. As it was so wet, we were not able to go through the forest, which was mostly a common, six or seven miles long and three miles broad. Here we looked on a map which we had brought, and found that we had two more miles to walk and then we should have a lovely dinner at the "Roebuck" inn, at Wych Cross. When we got there we found that it had been turned into a Vicarage! but the Vicar kindly gave us some bread and cheese and milk. We then again started; but it began to rain, and we sat under a furze-bush, with our mackintoshes over us for shelter. After it cleared up we walked to Nutley, and there we had a lovely tea of eggs. As it still poured with rain, we took a waggonette to Buxted Station, and from there we took train home. Altogether, it was only eleven miles' walk.

On Thursday we started again. Rice and Barry joined our party. We then walked to Edenbridge, six miles, and drank out of a pump; and while we were drinking a girl came to us and told us we were drinking river-water, so we went into a shop and bought some ginger-beer. After we had had a good drink, we walked to Hever; and while we were going there we saw some nice butterflies, Tortoiseshells, Peacocks, Blues, large Meadow-browns, &c., and we caught some and kept them. When we got to Hever, a distance of nine miles, we had a good dinner. While we were waiting for dinner we went over Hever Church and Castle, where Queen Anne Boleyn was born. We then had a lovely dinner of ham and eggs. Afterwards, we went two miles across some fields, and ate some lovely nuts, and then into a road which led to Chiding-Stone. When we got there, we bought some biscuits and some ginger-beer, and we went on the Stone and ate them. Then we walked to Cowden. On the road we met a gentleman, who showed us the way (he himself was going to the Isle of Wight). He left us at Cowden Station, which was a mile from the town. We then walked to Cowden, and here we hoped to have a rest. When we got there, we found there was no room at the inn! We then hurried away to the station, a mile off, and took train to Tunbridge Wells.

Here we found a lovely hotel called "Carlton Hotel." We had a tremendous tea of ham and eggs, after a grand wash, and then went to bed. It was nineteen miles' walk that day altogether.

When we got up in the morning, we had a lovely breakfast, and then went over Tunbridge Wells Common, a lovely big common. We then passed the High Rocks (which we did not enter, because it was mostly amusements). We passed through Broadwater Forest, where we played about on the common, and had a battle with fir-cones. Here Ken found a lovely big beetle, which was flying about, and he knocked it down with his hat. We then walked to Eridge Green, where we had some ginger-beer, and went through Eridge Park. Here we saw a yoke of six oxen drawing a waggon, and passed some lovely big water-falls and lakes, where we bathed our feet, which was very refreshing. Here it began to rain a very little, and we stayed under some beech-trees for shelter, and ate some of the nuts. Afterwards, we started and walked to Mark's Cross, where we were not able to have anything but ham and eggs once more, which made Ken feel bilious, and he said he wanted to go home. We then walked to Mayfield, which made fourteen miles altogether, and took train home; which ended my three days' walking tour —forty-four miles of walking altogether.

ALAN A. MILNE,
*Aged 8¾ years.*

---

*The Henley House School Magazine* was founded by Alfred Harmsworth with the encouragement of his headmaster, Alan's father. Alan contributed to it on a number of occasions. This first article is remarkable, for it records Alan's early experiences of Ashdown Forest, later to be the home of Winnie-the-Pooh, who would, like the small Alan, know it was dangerous to 'sit down carelessly' because of the furze or gorse. Pooh would also experience a good deal of weather in 'the forest which was mostly a common'. Alan remained devoted to butterflies, ginger beer and ham and eggs. Many years later a journalist would describe the impression he gave – 'tweeds, dogs, gorse, and a pipe'.

H. G. Wells came to Henley House to teach science and mathematics in January 1889, just a term after Alan himself had joined the school. Wells's influence on Milne was reinforced by the friendship between the young teacher and his headmaster, Milne's father – both of them had had to struggle to educate themselves. Milne would describe Wells, with whom he kept in touch until his death, as 'a great writer and a great friend', though he thought he was 'too clever and too impatient' to be a great teacher. Wells predicted a fine future for young Alan Milne, but as a mathematician rather than a writer. Later he influenced not only Milne's career but his politics.

This description of Alan, aged ten, appeared in the school magazine for Easter, 1892, alongside some portraits of other boys. The heading given was 'SOME SCHOOL CHARACTERS'. Sixty years later Milne would describe his 'disorderly' habits. He continued to find this an extremely interesting world but some of his enthusiasm for learning would die at Westminster School – and he never travelled in France, except en route to Italy. The sport mentioned is football. Milne would play football for his Cambridge college but later his great loves would be cricket and golf.

(D) He does not like French—does not see that you prove anything when you have done. Thinks mathematics grand. He leaves his books about; loses his pen; can't imagine what he did with this, and where he put that, but is convinced that it is somewhere. Clears his brain when asked a question by spurting out some nonsense, and then immediately after gives a sensible reply. Can speak 556 words per minute, and write more in three minutes than his instructor can read in thirty. Finds this a very interesting world, and would like to learn physiology, botany, geology, astronomy, and everything else. Wishes to make collections of beetles, bones, butterflies, &c., and cannot determine whether algebra is better than football or Euclid than a sponge-cake.

Gorse bushes in Ashdown Forest.

# THE PRECOCIOUS CHILD.

## Father Describes Boyhood of A. A. Milne.

## £1000 START.

### Child Whom They Couldn't Stop Working.

As Related

### By JOHN VINE MILNE.

*Father of the humorist and playwright who wrote " Mr. Pim Passes By," " The Dover Road," " The Truth About Blayds " and other plays.*

The most outstanding thing about Alan as a little boy was the extraordinary rapidity with which he absorbed knowledge.

I first noticed this when he was only two and a half years old. His two elder brothers were having a reading lesson from a wall chart with one-syllable words. But the little chap supposed to be playing on the hearthrug was listening too, and presently a baby voice said with much conviction, " I tan do dat, too."

### His First Lesson.

So, just to humour him, I picked him up and said, " Yes, come along, my little man. You can have a lesson, too." I was, however, very much surprised when I found that he actually could " do it, too," just as well and just as quickly as his brothers.

Thus he began his own education, and when scarcely more than three years old he had progressed so fast that he could read quite well. From then on he devoured (no other word expresses it) every book that came near him.

Yet he was not in any sense what is generally meant by studious. He was a jolly, romping child who loved games and enjoyed every minute of life. Often he came in dirty and dishevelled from his play—proof enough of a healthy desire for fun and activity.

His mental activity was even greater than his physical activity. There was never any question of trying to teach him anything. Our one end and aim and his mother's chief anxiety was to keep him back.

A. A. Milne.

Perhaps growing up in a school (I had a school in St. John's Wood, where he and his two brothers were born) helped to stimulate his thirst for knowledge. But his eagerness got no encouragement from me.

Long after he began agitating to attend classes permission was withheld, and when finally it was given his delight was supreme. I remember going up to his bedside one night and asking how he had liked it and what lesson he enjoyed.

The answer to the first question was written all over his face, and to the second he began by saying that he liked them all—the arithmetic, and the reading, and the geography—in fact, there did not seem one lesson he had enjoyed less than the others, and he wound up with " And I love the porridge in the morning."

### Work and Play Time-Table.

He made such strides at school that his mother again became anxious. " Something will have to be done to stop Alan," she used to say to me. " You know how these promising children wear themselves out and end by being dull men."

" Well, my dear," I would answer, " what can I do? He just does everything so well that we can't keep him back."

However, she became so worried and insistent that at last I consented to draw up a time-table specially for him. On it I made provision for an hour's lesson to be followed by an hour's play.

The next thing was to tell Alan. So, being a brave man, I left the room, called him, and said, " You'd better go in to your mother. She has something to say to you." When I thought enough time had elapsed for the painful process to be over I went back and asked her how he had taken it.

" Oh, not so badly. There were no tears or anything, but after studying the time-table carefully for a few minutes he said, in a very disappointed voice. ' But you've taken half my nice lessons away.' "

That was all. But from that day the boy began to pine. He never complained, but he became " mopy " and listless, until finally his health began to suffer. He got pale, lost his appetite, and lost weight. Then I felt it was time to stop the experiment. So one day I called him to me and said, " What is the matter with you lately? "

" Nothing, father."

"Oh, yes, there is, my boy. Now, come, tell me."

"No, there isn't anything, father."

"Is it your lessons that are worrying you?"

"No."

"Do you feel ill?"

"No."

"Is it because you don't go in to lessons?"

"Yes," and the pent-up disappointment of weeks threatened to burst out in tears.

"Oh, well," I answered, "if you feel about it as badly as that, you'd better go back to lessons with the others." After that we had our happy, jolly boy again.

There is one little incident of his childhood which shows how early tact can be developed in a child. He was quite a little boy, probably about three, when one day I picked him up in my arms and said, "Aren't you just the sweetest, dearest, nicest little boy in all the world?"

For a long minute he said nothing. Watching his face, it was obvious he did not want to contradict me, yet his modesty prevented him from agreeing; so he chose a tactful and charming way out by answering, "Well, if you say so——"

We were always a very united family. My only regret was that we had no daughters, but my wife always used to say, "Sons are good enough for me." Certainly, as I once said to a friend, "There is this consolation about a family of boys: your daughter may marry the wrong man, but your daughter-in-law cannot."

"When I was Very Young."
A. A. MILNE as a boy.

## Walking Tours.

The school gave us long vacations which we always spent away from home. Generally we took a house at the seaside or in the country, and had delightful times together.

On one of these occasions Alan came to me in great trouble. "Do you know, father," he said, "there is only one book in this house—such a silly one—and I've read it three times." Even on a holiday he was unhappy without plenty of books to read.

Frequently in those days we used to go on walking tours during week-ends. On one of these we visited Cambridge, which impressed the three boys so much that they expressed the desire to go there themselves.

I explained that it cost a lot of money to send a boy to a public school and then on to the University; that, as there were three of them and I was not a rich man, I should not be able to do so; but that if they worked hard they might win scholarships to take them there.

When the time came two of them did, in fact, win scholarships at Westminster, but Alan, the youngest, won his at 11½ years of age, thereby being the youngest winner of a scholarship in the history of the school—a record he holds to this day.

Before he went to Westminster Mr. H. G. Wells, at that time a master in my school (where, by the way, the late Lord Northcliffe was a pupil), had drawn my attention to the fact that Alan was very good at mathematics. He predicted a brilliant career for him in this branch of learning, saying, if he liked to give his attention to it, he was sure he could one day be Senior Wrangler.

This reputation Alan maintained throughout his schooldays, so that when he did go to Cambridge a career of mathematics had been planned for him.

But fate and Alan had other views.

Much has been said about sparing the rod and spoiling the child. I don't know. The rod may be necessary in some cases. But I can truthfully say that I can never remember an occasion, in school or out of school, when it was necessary to punish him. And I do not think the omission has done him any harm.

This article from the London *Evening Standard* for 6 January 1928, fifteen months after the publication of *Winnie-the-Pooh*, refers mainly to these early years. The italic caption under his father's name shows that A. A. Milne was still in the 1920s regarded mainly as a playwright, as he himself always wished.

Henley House
Mortimer Rd
Kilburn Feb 10th 1892

Dear Ackie

Thank you very much for those crests you sent us
& One of the boys has given us an awful lot, and now we
have got 15 H.M.S. crests. We have had 4 matches this
term and lost 3 and drawn 1

| | | | |
|---|---|---|---|
| Paradise House | "HHS 3" | 8 | (Hot Potatoes) |
| Philological F.C. | 1 | 5 | |
| (all men) Emanuel F.C. | 1 | 4 | (with a lot of muzzling on their part) |
| Kennington Park F.C. | 2 | 0 | (Hot Potatoes) |

We play Kennington Park F.C. on Saturday on Wormwood Scrubbs (an
awful large common about 12 matches going on at once) one which
was rugby.) We watched some of it and it was awfully interesting.
We have not spent at my 10/- already. Behold the Bill

| | | | |
|---|---|---|---|
| Buttledays. | 3/6 | Knife | 16 * |
| Alarum Clock | 1/4 | VERY PRIVATE | -/3 * |
| + Lock with Key | 1/- | Sundries £5 | 4¾ |
| Game | 16 | Gave Barry one farthing | |
| Stationery | -/6 | TOTAL | 10/- |
| Pistol & capsule. | 1/- | + Lock & Key for Sacred Cabinet | |
| Tuck | 1/- | * In Sacred Cabinet | |

+ We are badly in want of Money (I think !). (Smallest contribution thank-
I am doing Greek now and enjoy it very much fully received)
Also mechanics which I like to extremity
I remain
Your loving nephew
Alan
+ P.S. Smallest contributions thankfully received.

Ackie (left) was Alexander Milne, Alan's uncle, his father's younger brother. He had been a teacher at Henley House but by this time had his own school in Hastings and four daughters. Later Ken and Alan would cycle down to the coast to see their cousins. Ackie gave Alan ten shillings for his tenth birthday, a very different matter, of course, from what fifty pence is today. The original thank-you letter does not survive, but Ackie obviously asked his nephew to tell him how he spent the money. The resulting letter is a classic schoolboy document and makes an interesting contrast with his letters written five years earlier.

Alan as a Westminster schoolboy with his father. He started at Westminster in the autumn of 1893 as a Queen's Scholar. The boy had a chequered career at the school, losing his interest in mathematics, though he continued to find the subject easy and it was in maths that he eventually won his exhibition (as a 'sub-sizar') to Cambridge. A poor report aged twelve seems to have turned him to 'the lighter side of life'. He read a great deal, including *Pride and Prejudice*, which was to remain one of his favourite books. He started writing light verse with his brother Ken and his first sight of the Cambridge magazine *Granta* made him vow that he would edit it one day. In 1898, as a Westminster scholar, he attended Gladstone's funeral and walked out of the Abbey behind Sir Henry Irving. Of Westminster, he said, 'If only I had been taught this, that and the other instead!' But he never said, 'If only I had gone to another school.'

THE GRANTA (REGISTERED AS A NEWSPAPER), JUNE 4, 1902.

# THE GRANTA

## May Week Number.

1/=

A. A. Milne went up to Trinity College, Cambridge in the autumn of 1900.

Cast-list for a Shakespeare Society play-reading at Trinity of Acts III to V of *Richard II*. Fellow members of the Society were Leonard Woolf (whose writing this is), Lytton Strachey and Thoby Stephen. Woolf later married Stephen's sister, Virginia. On this particular occasion, Milne (who had been given some unrewarding bit parts) failed to turn up and was fined 2s 6d.

(Left) Milne became editor of *Granta* in January 1902. In the following summer term he enlisted, as co-editor, Hugh Vere Hodge to do all the things he did not want to do, but Milne wrote a good deal of each issue himself. He once said that 'He was a *Granta* man' should be on his memorial. It was his writing in *Granta* which attracted the attention of R. C. Lehmann. *Granta*, with its strong links with *Punch*, was a perfect training-ground for the humorist who would, twenty-five years later, write *Winnie-the-Pooh*.

Trinity College Association Football Team, 1900–1901. Alan Milne is on the right at the end of the back row, without a blazer. He played outside-left in his first year.

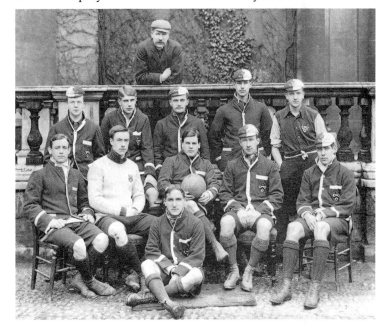

22 On going down from
Cambridge, Milne worked as a
freelance journalist in London
with financial support from his
father and encouragement from
H. G. Wells. His first
contribution to *Punch* appeared
in August 1904. By 1906 he had
made thirty appearances in its
pages and, at twenty-four, was
appointed Assistant Editor.

Milne moved in September
1903 into Temple Chambers, on
the right-hand side of Bouverie
Street, going down from Fleet
Street to the river – convenient,
as Milne said, if he ever
became editor of *Punch* and
near enough to set the Thames
on fire, should he ever get the
chance.

Collections of Milne's *Punch* pieces, such as *The
Day's Play*, *The Holiday Round* and *Once a Week*, were
enormously popular as this list of printings of the
first suggests.

| | |
|---|---|
| *First Published (Crown 8vo)* . . . . . | *September 22nd 1910* |
| *Second Edition* . . . . . . . . | *December* *1910* |
| *Third Edition* . . . . . . . . | *January* *1911* |
| *Fourth Edition* . . . . . . . . | *December* *1912* |
| *Fifth Edition* . . . . . . . . | *December* *1913* |
| *Sixth Edition* . . . . . . . . | *April* *1915* |
| *Seventh Edition* . . . . . . . . | *May* *1919* |
| *Eighth and Cheaper Edition* . . . . | *March* *1921* |
| *Ninth Edition (F'cap 8vo)* . . . . . | *December* *1924* |
| *Tenth Edition (F'cap 8vo)* . . . . . | *May* *1925* |
| *Eleventh Edition (F'cap 8vo)* . . . . | *October* *1925* |
| *Twelfth Edition (F'cap 8vo)* . . . . | *May* *1926* |
| *Thirteenth Edition (F'cap 8vo)* . . . . | *August* *1927* |
| *Fourteenth Edition (F'cap 8vo)* . . . | *October* *1928* |
| *Fifteenth Edition (F'cap 8vo)* . . . . | *1930* |

Milne became a member of the *Punch* 'table' in 1910.
His modestly carved initials can be seen near those
of his editor, Owen Seaman, and of the great
Victorian novelist W. M. Thackeray.

TEMPLE CHAMBERS

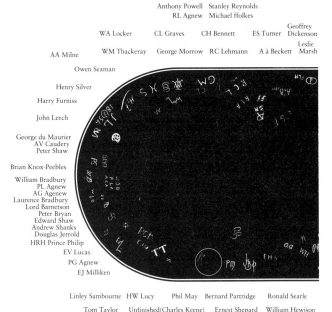

Anthony Powell   Stanley Reynolds
RL Agnew   Michael ffolkes

Geoffrey
Dickenson
WA Locker   CL Graves   CH Bennett   ES Turner
Leslie
AA Milne   WM Thackeray   George Morrow   RC Lehmann   A à Beckett   Marsh

Owen Seaman

Henry Silver

Harry Furniss

John Leech

George du Maurier
AV Caudery
Peter Shaw

Brian Knox-Peebles

William Bradbury
PL Agnew
AG Agenew
Laurence Bradbury
Lord Barnetson
Peter Bryan
Edward Shaw
Andrew Shanks
Douglas Jerrold
HRH Prince Philip
EV Lucas
PG Agnew
EJ Milliken

Linley Sambourne   HW Lucy   Phil May   Bernard Partridge   Ronald Searle

Tom Taylor   Unfinished(Charles Keene)   Ernest Shepard   William Hewison

Russell Brockbank   Alex Atkinson   Peter Dickinson

Kenneth Taylor

These verses appeared seventeen years before Milne's famous praise of butter in 'The King's Breakfast' (see page 60) and long, long before cholesterol and polyunsaturates were part of our everyday language.

Alan and his brother Ken were both working in London and seeing a great deal of each other at this period. Ken was a solicitor and eventually had a distinguished career as a civil servant. He married in 1905. Alan Milne's first close contact with children (and teddy bears) was with Ken's children. The brothers are seen here with Ken's first child, Marjorie.

[The *Mail*, in the course of some remarks on vegetarianism, says that the cow, as a butter-producing animal, has now been entirely superseded by the following vegetable fats: Nutter, Nucoline, Nuttene, Albene, Cocolardo, Vejsu.]

THERE may be some devoted to Nuttene,
    Others who, while admitting choice is hard, owe
Their health, or so they think, to Nicolene,
    With now and then a touch of Cocolardo
Vejsu remains the vegetable fat
That *I* most wonder at.

"Vejsu!"--regard it merely as an oath,
    Conceive it, if you will, a foreign city;
Vejsu--a game, a dramatist (or both),
    Was ever in the world a word so pretty?
Vejsu--some men would find a rhyme, but I
Simply refuse to try.

And what of her, calm-eyed and long of tail,
    Now superseded by this kind of batter,
As truthfully narrated in the *Mail*,
    Making our history a different matter?
I think of MARY, and BOY BLUE, and JACK,
And do not wish her back.

That MARY who, regardless of the tide,
    And urged by fears for the ensuing butter,
Called by the banks of Dee, and calling died
    With not a transitory thought for Nutter;
Would she had known (though calling as desired)
The cattle *weren't* required!

That JACK, whose effort in the building trade
    Was such that, in the end, a tattered waster,
Coming across the lonesome dairy maid,
    Without so much as "By your leave," embraced her—
How innocent the story might have been,
"Bowdlerised" with Nuttene!

That Little Boy who waked to blow his horn,
    Not lovingly as one whose soul is in it,
But lustily—to conjure from the corn
    The cow who drifted thither ev'ry minute—
Vejsu! His case is wild with all regret;
He might be sleeping yet!

A family party at Steeple Bumpstead, on the Essex/Suffolk border, where J. V. Milne retired after selling his school. Alan is sitting on the ground next to his older brother, Barry, and in front of his sister-in-law Maud, Ken's wife.

Marjorie and her mother, Maud. Maud became a close friend of her brother-in-law and found it hard when he married. Alan wrote about Marjorie – as Margery – regularly in *Punch*.

Milne wrote to a fan of the Margery stories: 'Most of the stories about her are founded on fact. Her own share in the conversation is, if not actual, at any rate true to life . . . To get a child properly on to paper one needs to know her by heart.' The talk of a very small child has rarely been more accurately conveyed. Milne celebrates the unembarrassed egotism of children, as he would do much later in such poems as 'Disobedience' and the much-reviled 'Vespers'. 'Afternoon Sleep' is relevant to the brilliant career of Pooh. Milne, writing for adults in *Punch*, can be seen so clearly here as someone who is not sentimental about children (do not be misled by the hypocorisma – child-speak – which would so madden Dorothy Parker), but knows how they work and listens to what they say.

## AFTERNOON SLEEP

'In the afternoon they came unto a land
In which it seemed always afternoon.'

I am like Napoleon in that I can go to sleep at any moment ; I am unlike him (I believe) in that I am always doing so.   One makes no apology for doing so on Sunday afternoon—the apology, indeed, should come from the others, the wakeful parties.

' Uncle ? '

' Margery. '

' Will you come and play wiv me ? '

' I'm rather busy just now, ' I said, with closed eyes. ' After tea. '

' Why are you raver busy just now ?   My baby's only raver busy sometimes. '

' Well, then, you know what it's like ;   how important it is that one shouldn't be disturbed. '

' But you *must* be beturbed when I ask you to come and play wiv me. '

' Oh, well . . . what shall we play at ? '

' Trains, ' said Margery eagerly.

When we play trains I have to be a tunnel. I don't know if you have ever been a tunnel ?   No ;   well, it's an over-rated profession.

' We won't play trains, ' I announced firmly,   ' because it's Sunday. '

' Why not because it's Sunday ? '

(Oh, you little pagan !)

' Hasn't mummy told you all about Sunday ? '

' Oh yes, Maud did tell me, ' said Margery casually. Then she gave an innocent little smile.   ' Oh, I called mummy Maud, ' she said in pretended surprise.   ' I quite *fought* I was upstairs ! '

I hope you follow.   The manners and customs of good society must be observed on the ground floor where visitors may happen ;   upstairs one relaxes a little.

' Do you know, ' Margery went on with the air of a discoverer, ' you mustn't say " prayers " downstairs. Or " corsets ". '

' I never do, ' I affirmed. ' Well, anyhow, I never will again. '

' Why mayn't you ? '

' I don't know,' I said sleepily.

' Say prehaps. '

' Well—*prehaps* it's because your mother tells you not to. '

' Well 'at's a *silly* fing to say,' said Margery scornfully.

' It is. I'm thoroughly ashamed of it. I apologize. Good night. ' And I closed my eyes again.

' I fought you were going to play wiv me, Mr Bingle, ' sighed Margery to herself.

' My name is *not* Bingle,' I said, opening one eye.

' Why isn't it Bingle ? '

' The story is a very long and sad one. When I wake up I will tell it to you. Good night.'

' Tell it to me now.'

There was no help for it.

' Once upon a time,' I said rapidly, ' there was a man called Bingle, Oliver Bingle, and he married a lady called Pringle. And his brother married a lady called Jingle. And his other brother married a Miss Wingle. And his cousin remained single. . . . That is all. '

' Oh, I see,' said Margery doubtfully. ' Now will you play wiv me ? '

How can one resist the pleading of a young child ?

' All right,' I said. ' We'll pretend I'm a little girl, and you're my mummy, and you've just put me to bed ! . . . Good night, mummy dear.'

' Oh, but I must cover you up.' She fetched a tablecloth, and a pram-cover, and *The Times*, and a handkerchief, and the cat, and a doll's what-I-mustn't-say-downstairs, and a cushion ; and she covered me up and tucked me in.

' 'Ere, 'ere, now go to sleep, my darling,' she said, and kissed me lovingly.

' Oh, Margie, you dear,' I whispered.

' You called me " Margie " ! ' she cried in horror.

' I meant " mummy ". Good night.'

One, two, three seconds passed rapidly.

' It's morning,' said a bright voice in my ear. ' Get up.'

' I'm very ill,' I pleaded ; ' I want to stay in bed all day.'

' But your dear uncle,' said Margery, inventing hastily, ' came last night after you were in bed, and stayed 'e night. Do you see ? And he wants you to sit on his chest in bed and talk to him.'

' Where is he ? Show me the bounder.'

' 'Ere he is,' said Margery, pointing at me.

' But look here, I can't sit on my own chest and talk to myself. I'll take the two parts if you insist, Sir Herbert, but I can't play them simultaneously. Not even Irving——'

' Why can't you play vem simrulaleously ? '

' Well, I can't. Margie, *will* you let me go to sleep ? '

' Nope,' said Margery, shaking her head.

' You should say, " No, thank you, revered and highly respected uncle."'

' No *hank* you, Mr Cann.'

' I have already informed you that my name is not Bingle ; and I have now to add that neither is it Cann.'

' Why neiver is it Cann ? '

' That isn't grammar. You should say, " Why can it not either ? " '

' Why ? '

' I don't know.'

' Say prehaps.'

' No, I can't even say prehaps.'

' Well, say I shall understand when I'm a big girl.'

' You'll understand when you're a big girl, Margery,' I said solemnly.

' Oh, I see.'

' That's right. Now then, what about going to sleep ? '

She was silent for a moment, and I thought I was safe. Then—

' Uncle, just tell me—why was 'at little boy crying vis morning ? '

' Which little boy ? '

' Ve one in 'e road.'

' Oh, that one. Well, he was crying because his uncle hadn't had any sleep all night, and when he tried to go to sleep in the afternoon—'

' Say prehaps again.'

My first rejected contribution ! I sighed and had another shot. ' Well, then,' I said gallantly, ' it must have been because he hadn't got a sweet little girl of three to play with him.'

' Yes,' said Margery, nodding her head thoughtfully, ' 'at was it.'

Food was very important at *Punch*,
as it would be in the *Pooh* books.

# THE MAN AS HE IS.

## Mr. A. A. Milne.

Many men become famous by their initials long before their names are widely known to the public. The letters "A.A.M." have appeared in *Punch* week by week for some years, but few readers of that journal know to whom they belong. At the age of 20 Mr. Alan Alexander Milne was already an editor; whilst at Trinity College, Cambridge, he controlled the *Granta*, contributing a good deal to it himself and making it wittier and livelier than it had been for a considerable time. Four years later he was appointed assistant-editor of *Punch*, a position he has filled with considerable satisfaction to himself and great joy to his readers. Though still little more than a youth, he is not overburdened by the responsibilities of his post. He is shy but confident, nervous but by no means silent. His shyness makes him talk hurriedly and with an air of deprecation: he suggests rather than states even his firmest beliefs. He is tall, lean, and athletic. His face is brown, his hair light, his eyes blue. Like nearly all men of great humorous gifts, he is exceedingly sensitive and intuitive. A smile constantly plays about the corners of his mouth, and his eyes light up from time to time. Few men know their limitations better than he does. He knows precisely what is within his powers, and never flatters himself that he can do things just because he would like to do them. In many ways he resembles his work. He is refined, subtle, and elusive. He has little use for the obvious jest, and in conversing with him it is necessary to keep one's wits extremely active if one is to take an intelligent part in the conversation. He has no belief in "hidden" talent—at all events, in journalism. The man with ability, he declares, soon finds his place. He himself is most conscientious in his search for new humorists, and diligently reads the heap of manuscripts that come daily to the office of *Punch* from unknown writers. Humour is rare, but when discovered it is hailed with delight.     X.

From the *Daily Citizen*, 27 August 1913.

A. A. Milne with his parents at Steeple Bumpstead. The dog is Chum, an obstreperous black spaniel Milne would pass on to the Lehmanns, at Fieldhead on the Thames, when the animal became too much for his parents. Chum appeared on several occasions in *Punch* and is undoubtedly partly responsible for Tigger, another bouncy creature.

It seemed a golden time, those years before the First World War. Alan Milne first met Dorothy de Selincourt, known as Daphne, when his editor at *Punch*, Owen Seaman, took him along to her twenty-first birthday dance in November 1910. She was Seaman's god-daughter and it turned out she knew some of Milne's *Punch* pieces more or less by heart. 'She laughed at my jokes,' Milne said as an explanation for what turned out to be a rather ill-matched relationship. Before the War, everything was lovely; they did jolly things together, such as going to Henley. Horace Nicholls's photograph of people arriving at Henley station in 1912 shows how things looked.

In 1913 A. A. Milne went on holiday to Diablerets in Switzerland. In London, a few weeks earlier, buying ski-ing boots, he had run into Daphne de Selincourt. It had turned out that they were both, by an odd chance, going to the same hotel in the same resort. 'I've got a pair of orange trousers,' she said. 'I shall be wearing a red carnation in my button-hole,' he replied. 'We're bound to recognize each other.' They did, and, at eleven o'clock one morning in a snow storm, he asked her to marry him.

Daphne had a 'background of brothers and yachts and riches', as Milne's niece, Angela, would put it.

29

In 1929, he wrote to his brother Ken from Grindelwald: 'Daff is taking to ski-ing bravely. When we did it before, sixteen years ago, I just went down moderate slopes, falling at the bottom, and Daff didn't go down, collapsing at the top. But there appears to be a lot more in it than that. Everybody here is terribly keen, and many of them terribly good. Some of the things they do are beautiful to watch, and I feel, as I feel about anything I can't do, that I would sooner do this one thing than everything I can do (which isn't much).' The combination of ambition and modesty was typical of Milne.

15 Embankment Gardens, Chelsea, seemed the proper place for a writer to live. Milne's London home remained in Chelsea throughout the time he was writing the Pooh books.

Milne spent a good deal of time playing cricket and golf and
watching cricket. Here he is in J. M. Barrie's team, the
Allahakbarries, in a photo taken at Downe House in 1913. Milne
is on the extreme left of the middle row, with Barrie two along
from him. Barrie was an important influence on Milne. Milne
admired *Peter Pan* and it was a hard five acts to follow when he
wrote his own children's play, *Make-Believe*. Milne had written his
first play at Cambridge, but it was not until 1917 that there was a
professional production of one of his plays: *Wurzel-Flummery*,
written after he was invalided home from France. It appeared in a
triple bill with two one-act plays by Barrie. Milne's plays are not
the concern of this book but they were a central part of Milne's
own brilliant career. Long before he published his children's
books, he was extremely famous and rich as a playwright and it
was for his plays (which he continued to write throughout the
1930s) that he wished to be remembered. Also in the photograph
– second from the right in the middle row – is another very
influential person in the career of both Milne and Pooh. E. V.
Lucas was powerful both at *Punch* and Methuen, the publisher
who would eventually bring out Milne's children's books.
Shepard remembered that it was Lucas who first suggested he
should illustrate Milne. The girl is Lucas's daughter, Audrey, a
pupil at Downe House. Her memories of A. A. Milne – at the
house-parties of her childhood – emphasize how good he was
with children, an impression Milne himself often tried to deny.
'Alan, very fair and handsome, knowing exactly how to talk
unpatronisingly to a child, was, with one exception, my favourite
among all the visitors.' The exception was Maurice Hewlett, also
seen in the photo, between Milne and Barrie.

It was before the War, on 26 November 1913, that a bear looking remarkably like Winnie-the-Pooh made his first appearance in the pages of *Punch*. The toy was modelled on a bear called Growler, belonging to Shepard's small son, Graham (left). This was the bear Shepard would always draw even after he had met a toy bear called Winnie-the-Pooh. No photos of Growler seem to have survived but he is thought to have been a Steiff bear. On one occasion, when Shepard was at home and Graham away, Shepard wrote: 'Growler and Puck have been an awful nuisance; they talk and jabber all night.' Puck was a mere 'cork-filled gnome' and not part of this story but it is obvious that Growler ('a magnificent bear', Shepard called him) was a real character and played an important part in the career of Winnie-the-Pooh.

## AN INSULT TO THE PROFESSION.

*Shocked Juvenile.* "Oh, Mother! fairies would never do a thing like that, would they?"

A. A. Milne (left) had been a pacifist since 1910. In 1915 he joined up, under the false impression, as so many were, that he was fighting in the war to end all wars. At least he was able to train as a signals officer and he never fired a shot in anger. In his autobiography, Milne said he would have liked to ignore the four years he spent in the Army. 'I should like to put asterisks here and then write, "It was in 1919 that I found myself once again a civilian." For it makes me almost physically sick to think of that nightmare of mental and moral degradation, the War.'

An American critic reviewed a collection of Milne's *Punch* pieces in 1916: 'Mr Milne is now in the trenches facing German bullets, so this will probably be his last book.' For all its crassness, it makes one realize how easily *Winnie-the-Pooh* might never have been written.

E. H. Shepard (right) was also on the Somme; his brother was killed on the opening day. It seems a miracle that both Milne and Shepard came through. One day their names would be linked as inextricably as Gilbert and Sullivan.

Golden Hill Fort on the Isle of Wight, where Milne was stationed before he went to France.

It was during the War – before he went to France – that A. A. Milne wrote what now seems to be his first children's book: *Once on a Time*. But was it a children's book? Milne himself was never quite sure just what a children's book was. What is sure is that Milne was extremely fond of this particular book. It had its roots in a play, which has not survived, written as an entertainment for troops training on the Isle of Wight and performed by Milne's wife and by his Colonel's five children. The book was described in a review in the *New York Times* as 'an entertaining mockery of war'. Just the stuff to give the troops?

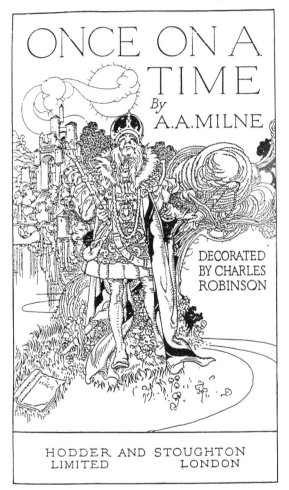

ONCE ON A TIME
*By*
A.A. MILNE

DECORATED
BY CHARLES
ROBINSON

HODDER AND STOUGHTON
LIMITED          LONDON

Once on a Time
A.A. Milne

Paper label (above) on the binding of the first edition, illustrated by H. M. Brock in 1917.

Title page (left) from the edition illustrated by Charles Robinson in 1922.

Illustration by Susan Perl (below) from an edition commissioned by the New York Graphic Society in 1962.

THIS book was written in 1915, for the amusement of my wife and myself at a time when life was not very amusing; it was published at the end of 1917; was reviewed, if at all, as one of a parcel, by some brisk uncle from the Tiny Tots Department; and died quietly, without seriously detracting from the interest which was being taken in the World War, then in progress.

33

# *Winnie as in Winnipeg*

The war brought to England an important character in this story: a bear called Winnie, who got her name from the Canadian town of Winnipeg.

On 24 August 1914 an army officer called Harry Colebourn, who had been born in Birmingham, was travelling by train from Winnipeg, his home at the time, to Valcartier, Quebec. He had been trained at the Ontario Veterinary College in Guelph and before the war was already attached to the 34th Regiment of Cavalry (Fort Garry Horse). Attached now to both the Fort Garry Horse and the Canadian Army Veterinary Corps, Lt Colebourn was on his way to join the 2nd Canadian Infantry Brigade and to embark for England. His train stopped at White River, Ontario and Lt Colebourn bought for twenty dollars a small black female bear cub, from a hunter who had killed her mother. Princess Patricia's Regiment, to which the memorial at the London Zoo refers, was also part of the 2nd Canadian Infantry Brigade. Winnie, as Lt Colebourn named his bear, became a mascot of the Brigade and a pet of many of the soldiers, following them round the camp on Salisbury Plain like a tame dog.

When the Brigade was ordered to France in December 1914, Harry Colebourn took Winnie to the Zoo on a long loan. His diary records that he visited Winnie whenever he was on leave and had the chance. Colebourn survived the war and eventually returned to Winnipeg, presenting the bear to London Zoo in December 1919 (see record card opposite). Winnie, who had settled down happily and become a very popular attraction, did not die until 1934.

White River, Ontario, is planning a huge eight-metre-high statue of Winnie-the-Pooh (Shepard-style, not Disney) to make the most of the connection and attract tourists from the Trans-Canada Highway. Donations towards the cost of the statue have been received from Pooh fans in England, New Zealand, America and, of course, Canada. One of the contributors from England was a man in his eighties called R. W. Coppard, who recalled working on the landscaping of Milne's garden sixty years earlier.

Harry Colebourn with Winnie on Salisbury Plain in 1914.

√√√√ No. 1                    Mappin Terrace HOUSE.

                              Winnie

American Black Bear          SEX. ♀
NAME.

Ursus americanus

HABITAT.
        White River. Ontario Dec. 1. 1919.
HOW ACQUIRED. Presᵈ by Capt. Harry Coleborne, C.A.V.C. F.3ˢ.
Deposᵈ by the 2ⁿᵈ Infantry Brigade
                  Canadian Contingent
DATE OF ARRIVAL.
                              METHOD & DATE OF DEPARTURE.
Dec. 9. 1914
                              Died 12. 5. 34.

32⁷⁄382.

(97—1000—4-19—W. & S.)

The war is over. A. A. Milne has resigned from *Punch*, finding he was not needed and that there was no likelihood that he would ever be editor. To Owen Seaman, Milne remained, as he had always been, 'an unpatriotic Radical'. Milne had realized, even before the war, that as a humorous journalist there was no likelihood of further improvement or ambition. He was already as funny as he would ever be. Now he is on the verge of his first great success in the theatre with *Mr Pim Passes By*. He and Daphne have moved into what Milne called 'the prettiest little house in London'. 11 Mallord Street, Chelsea (later re-numbered to 13) had been built not long before the war in a quiet street just off the King's Road. It was larger than it looked from the street, having been designed rather cleverly round a courtyard. At the top there was a nursery awaiting an occupant.

On 21 August 1920 the child arrived and, not long after, the teddy bear. It is thought that he was made in the factory of J. K. Farrell (est. 1897), who made bears exclusively for Harrods at this time. In profile, a Farrell bear looks rather more like the Pooh of Shepard's drawings.

Even before the astonishing success of Milne's children's books, Christopher Robin was appearing in the newspapers. In this early photo from 1922 (right), the teddy bear makes his first appearance. He had been purchased at Harrods the year before for the boy's first birthday. In 1931 Daphne would say that 'Pooh sheds a tear occasionally when he remembers that he and Christopher Robin were exactly the same size on that day, ten years ago now, when the friendly bear joined the Milne family.' (See page 133.) It seems more likely than some of the things Daphne said. Certainly at this stage the bear had not yet acquired the name of Pooh. Even by 1924, the name Pooh belonged to a swan. See page 58, or the introduction to *When We Were Very Young*. The penguin never appeared in the stories and his fate is uncertain. Perhaps he belonged to the photographer. Another picture, apparently taken on the same occasion, appears on the next page. Both father and son seem uneasy about the publicity.

This letter to a friend of his parents is, typically for Milne, undated, but was obviously written soon after the child's birth. 'We did rather want a Rosemary,' Milne admits. Daphne had found the birth 'a thoroughly traumatizing shock' and was, according to a friend, 'absolutely determined not to repeat the performance'. She had apparently had little idea what was going to happen. Milne was thrilled. He wrote to his friend, editor and fellow author Frank Swinnerton, 'When women can do these things, why do we go on writing, you and I?' By the time the birth was registered, Christopher had been added to the Robin – but he remained Billy and later, with his own pronunciation of his surname, Moon.

38

THE COMEDY THEATRE

# BOOKS AND AUTHO

## CONDUCTED BY ANNA BLANCHE McGILL

### A. A. Milne's Child's Garden Of Verse

A. A. MILNE, HIS WIFE AND LITTLE DAUGHTER.

*"When We Were Very Young,"* by A. A. Milne.

Simple enough request—but surprising, the delays and circumlocutions, as the Queen passed the order

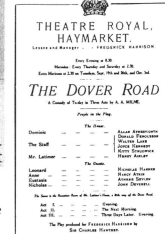

This photo of Christopher Robin and his parents was taken in 1922 and was used in an American newspaper in 1925 to illustrate a review of *When We Were Very Young*. It was not the only time the small boy was taken for a girl. Christopher Milne himself recalls overhearing a woman outside a grocer's in Oakley Street, Chelsea, exclaim, 'Oh, what a pretty little girl!' It was one of his earliest memories at a time when he was small enough to be in a pram. Like his father before him, he had to wait a long time for his first haircut.

Programmes for three of Milne's popular plays, from the years just before the children's books. At one point Milne had five productions on the stage at the same time, on the two sides of the Atlantic.

This photograph of a rather dubious baby Christopher Robin riding on his father's back appeared in many newspapers on both sides of the Atlantic. It was in the *New York Times* on 18 October 1922 with the caption: 'A.A.MILNE CAUGHT WHEN HE WASN'T WRITING A NEW PLAY. The Author of *The Romantic Age*, *The Lucky One* and a Shelf Full of Humor, Teaching His Son Billy the Simple Rudiments of the Safer Kind of Horsemanship.'

In the *Daily Graphic* for 20 November 1922, it appeared on a page headed 'REAL LIFE ROMANCES OF THE LONDON STAGE TODAY'. The caption was: 'Had Mr Pim passed by he would have been delighted with this peep at A. A. Milne in his home at Chelsea. Milne came to Fleet Street years ago in search of a fortune. As a dramatist his income at times ranges from £200 to £500 a week.' This was more than most people at that time earned in a year. But 'a writer wants something more than money for his work: he wants permanence . . . He yearns for immortality,' Milne himself wrote. Titles such as *Mr Pim Passes By* and *The Dover Road* will still sound familiar to some readers, but even *Toad of Toad Hall*, his adaptation of *The Wind in the Willows*, is now rarely performed. True immortality would come not as a playwright but from the children's books, a fact which Milne would live to realize and regret.

A. A. Milne and his wife appeared in *Sphere* in the summer of 1920.

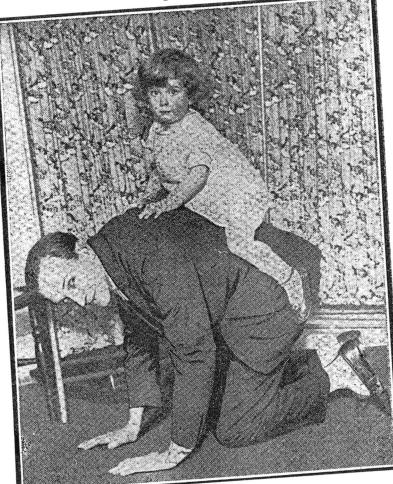

40   A. A. Milne often said he used Kenneth Grahame's *The Wind in the Willows*, first published in 1908, as a test of character. 'One does not argue about *The Wind in the Willows*.' Anyone who does not like it is beyond the pale. E. H. Shepard would report that one of the first questions Milne asked him was whether he had read *The Wind in the Willows*. This was long before Shepard illustrated it and made the link between Grahame and Milne seem even closer. My grandson, Jack, then two-and-a-half, said, 'Winnie-the-Pooh, Grann' one day when we were in a bookshop, but it was actually a poster of *The Wind in the Willows* he was looking at. Jack had recognized Shepard's style uniting the two books. Shepard realized the 'very great influence' *The Wind in the Willows* had had on Milne, as did W. A. Darlington in the *Daily Telegraph* when the play was eventually performed: 'The Wild Wood is quite evidently only a mile or two away

from the forest in which dwell Mr Milne's own creations, Winnie-the-Pooh and the rest.' There is no doubt – though the links are subtle – that *The Wind in the Willows* lies behind *Winnie-the-Pooh*. Without it, Milne's book might never have been written. In November 1921, Curtis Brown, his agent, wrote to Milne to propose that he try to dramatize Grahame's story. Milne responded enthusiastically. 'I shall love doing it . . . and I think I see how it can be done.' It was not an easy task and the production problems Milne's play presented meant that *Toad of Toad Hall* did not appear on the stage until 1929, after the publication of the children's books and at a time, ironically, when Milne was trying to distance himself from children. Its success, during the last part of his life, above his own plays for adults would inevitably cause Milne some very mixed feelings. If Curtis Brown had approached Milne in 1929 rather than 1921, it seems likely that he would have refused the commission.

The court scene in *Toad of Toad Hall* shown in the manuscript (left) was almost entirely Milne's own invention – influenced by Lewis Carroll, another of Milne's heroes.

Other parts of the manuscript show Daphne Milne's handwriting as well as his own. In these early years of their marriage she often acted as his amanuensis and secretary.

This Introduction by A. A. Milne to *Toad of Toad Hall* appeared in the first edition of his play, published on 11 April 1929, eight months before its first appearance on the stage at the Liverpool Playhouse for Christmas. The first London production at the Lyric was at Christmas the following year, 1930.

## INTRODUCTION

THERE are familiarities which we will allow only ourselves to take. Your hands and my hands are no cleaner than anybody else's hands, yet the sort of well-thumbed bread-and-butter which we prefer is that on which we have placed our own thumbs. It may be that to turn Mr Kenneth Grahame into a play is to leave unattractive finger-marks all over him, but I love his books so much that I cannot bear to think of anybody else disfiguring them. That is why I accepted a suggestion, which I should have refused in the case of any other book as too difficult for me, that I should dramatize *The Wind in the Willows*.

There are two well-known ways in which to make a play out of a book. You may insist on being faithful to the author, which means that the scene in the aeroplane on page 673 must be got in somehow, however impossible dramatically, or, with somebody else's idea in your pocket, you may insist on being faithful to yourself, which means that by the middle of Act III everybody will realize how right the original author was to have made a book of it. There may be a third way, in which case I have tried to follow it. If, as is more likely, there isn't, then I have *not* made a play of *The Wind in the Willows*. But I have, I hope, made some sort of entertainment, with enough of Kenneth Grahame in it to appease his many admirers, and enough of me in it to justify my name upon the title page.

Of course I have left out all the best parts of the book; and for that, if he has any knowledge of the theatre, Mr Grahame will thank me. With a Rat and Mole from the Green Room Club, a Baby Otter from Conti, a Pan from Clarkson's, and a wind (off) whispering in the reeds of Harker, we are not going to add any fresh thrill to the thrill which the loveliness of *The Piper at the Gates of Dawn* has already given its readers. Whether there is, indeed, any way of putting these animals on the stage must be left to managers, professional and amateur, to find out. But it seemed clear to me that Rat and Toad, Mole and Badger could only face the footlights with hope of success if they were content to amuse their audiences. There are both beauty and comedy in the book, but the beauty must be left to blossom there, for I, anyhow, shall not attempt to transplant it.

But can one transplant even the comedy ? Perhaps it has happened to you, as it has certainly happened to me, that you have tried to explain a fantastic idea to an entirely matter-of-fact person. ' But they *don't*,' he says, and ' You *can't*,' and ' I don't see *why*, just because—' and ' Even if you assume that—' and ' I thought you said just now that he *hadn't*.' By this time you have thrown the ink-pot at him, with enough of accuracy, let us hope, to save you from his ultimatum, which is this : ' However fantastic your assumption, you *must* work it out logically '—that is to say, realistically.

To such a mind *The Wind in the Willows* makes no appeal, for it is not worked out logically.   In reading the book, it is necessary to think of Mole, for instance, sometimes as an actual mole, some-times as such a mole in human clothes, sometimes as a mole grown to human size, sometimes as walking on two legs, sometimes on four.   He is a mole, he isn't a mole. What is he ?   I don't know. And, not being a matter-of-fact person, I don't mind.   At least, I do know, and still I don't mind.   He is a fairy, like so many immortal characters in fiction ; and, as a fairy, he can do, or be, anything.

But the stage has no place for fairies. There is a horrid realism about the theatre, from which, however hard we try, we can never quite escape. Once we put Mole and his friends on the boards we have to be definite about them.   What do they look like ?

To answer this here is difficult.   To say at rehearsal what they do not look like will be easy.   Vaguely I see them made up on the lines of the Cat in *The Blue Bird* and the Hen Pheasant in *Chantecler*. As regards their relative sizes, Toad should be short and fat, Badger tall and elderly, Rat and Mole young and slender. Indeed Mole might well be played by some boyish young actress.   The ' humans', Judge, Policeman, Usher and the rest, should be as fantastic as possible, with a hint of the animal world about them.   Only Phoebe must keep her own pretty face, but even she must be no mortal. I see her in a ballet skirt or something entirely unsuitable to a gaoler's daughter, pirouetting absurdly about the prison.

But no doubt the producer will see them all differently.   If he is an amateur, I shall congratulate him on his enterprise and wish him luck ;   if he is a professional, I shall be there to watch him, and, no doubt, to tell him enthusiastically how much better his ideas are than mine.

A. A. M.

**LYRIC THEATRE**

**TOAD**
**OF**
**TOAD HALL**

SIX PENCE

---

# LYRIC THEATRE
SHAFTESBURY AVENUE, W.1.

Licensee ... ... A.
Telephones: Gerrard 3686 and 3687

Lessee and Manager ... ... GILBERT

**TWICE DAILY at 2.30 and 8**

BASIL FOSTER and TOM MILLER
PRESENT

## TOAD OF TOAD HALL
BY
A. A. MILNE
From Kenneth Grahame's book "The Wind in the Willows"
Music by
H. FRASER-SIMSON

*Characters in the order of their appearance:*

| | |
|---|---|
| Marigold ... ... ... ... | WENDY TOYE |
| Nurse ... ... ... ... | MONA JENKINS |
| Mole ... ... ... ... | RICHARD GOOLDEN |
| Water Rat ... ... ... | IVOR BARNARD |
| Mr. Badger ... ... ... | ERIC STANLEY |
| Toad ... ... ... ... | FREDERICK BURTWELL |
| Alfred ... ... ... ... | PETER MATHER |
| The Back Legs of Alfred ... | R. HALLIDAY MASON |
| Chief Ferret ... ... ... | ALFRED FAIRHURST |
| Chief Weasel ... ... ... | RONALD ALPE |
| Chief Stoat ... ... ... | WILLIAM McGUIGAN |
| First Field-Mouse ... ... | GORDON TUCKER |
| Second Field-Mouse ... | ROBERT SINCLAIR |
| Policeman ... ... ... | ALBAN BLAKELOCK |
| Gaoler ... ... ... | ALFRED FAIRHURST |
| Usher ... ... ... ... | HUMPHREY MORTON |
| Judge ... ... ... ... | ALFRED CLARK |
| Turkey ... ... ... | GORDON TUCKER |
| Duck ... ... ... ... | ROBERT SINCLAIR |
| Phœbe ... ... ... | JOAN HARKER |
| Washerwoman ... ... | DOROTHY FANE |
| The White Rabbit ... ... | MARIAN WILSON |
| Mama Rabbit ... ... | PHYLLIS COULTHARD |
| Lucy Rabbit ... ... ... | DAPHNE ALLEN |
| Harold Rabbit ... ... | MARCUS HAIG |
| Fox ... ... ... ... | JIM SOLOMAN |
| Barge-woman ... ... | FRANCES WARING |
| A Foolish Ferret (James) ... | SYLVIA GARTSIDE |
| A Brave Young Weasel (Henry) ... | JILL CLAYTON |

---

... ... THOMAS
... ... GORDON TUCKER
... ... WENDY TOYE
... ... STEPHAN MacLAREN
... by MARIAN WILSON.
...ed by FRANK CELLIER.

*Synopsis of Scenery.*

... ... ... Down by the Willows
... ... ... The River Bank

*The Curtain will be lowered for Two Minutes only between Acts I and II.*

| | | |
|---|---|---|
| ACT II. | Scene 1 ... ... | The Wild Wood |
| | Scene 2 ... ... | Mr. Badger's House |
| | Scene 3 ... ... | The Same (some weeks later) |
| ACT III. | Scene 1 ... ... | The Court House |
| | Scene 2 ... ... | The Dungeon |
| | Scene 3 ... ... | The Canal Bank |
| ACT IV. | Scene 1 ... ... | Rats House by the River |
| | Scene 2 ... ... | The Underground Passage |
| | Scene 3 ... ... | The Banqueting-room at Toad Hall |
| EPILOGUE | ... ... | The Wind in the Willows |

Scenery and Dresses designed by
Miss MURIEL STERLING (by permission of Sir Barry Jackson).

The ORCHESTRA under the direction of J. A. de ORELLANA.

Costumes by RUTH FIELD, W. CLARKSON and MORRIS ANGEL & SON, LTD.
Shoes by LILLEY & SKINNER.
Scenery by JOHN BRUNSKILL. Scenery painted by ARTHUR & LE MAISTRE.
Properties by F. A. ELLIOTT.

| | | |
|---|---|---|
| Stage Director ... | | CYRIL CATTLEY |
| Stage Manager ... | For Basil Foster and Tom Miller | R. HALLIDAY MASON |
| Press Representative | | DOUGLAS A. WHISTON |

**Smoking is not permitted in the Auditorium.**

Ladies are earnestly requested to remove Hats, Bonnets, or any kind of Head-dress.
This request being made for the benefit of the Audience, the Management trusts that it will appeal to everyone, and that ladies will assist in having it carried out.

The Management reserves the right to make any alteration in the Cast which may be rendered necessary by illness or other unavoidable causes.

Manager ... (Lyric Theatre) ... A. C. BELSEY

**NEAREST TUBE STATION, PICCADILLY CIRCUS.**

*Extract from the Rules made by the Lord Chamberlain:—*
1.—The public may leave at the end of the performance by all exit doors, and such doors must at that time be open. 2.—All gangways, passages and staircases must be kept entirely free from chairs or any other obstruction. 3.—Persons must not be allowed to stand or sit in any of the gangways intersecting the seating, and standing can only be permitted in the gangways at the sides of the seating where there are no steppings. Sufficient space must be left in gangways where standing is permitted for persons to pass easily to and fro and to have free access to exits. 4.—The safety curtain must be lowered and raised in the presence of each audience.

*Toad of Toad Hall*'s continued performance may be affected by the enormous success of Alan Bennett's play at the National Theatre in London, with Mole at its centre. But without the National's 'technological opportunities' (in Bennett's own phrase), other companies may be better advised to produce Milne's version. Both adapters necessarily lose the lyrical flavour of the book. Bennett has said that his Albert, the carthorse, is 'Eeyore's Wolverhampton cousin' – very lugubrious.

A limited edition of the play, 200 copies on handmade paper signed by both Milne and Grahame, was issued in 1929. These photos of the two writers in overcoats were both taken in 1921, the year Milne adapted Grahame's book – but they did not meet until the play was in production in 1929. Several people have commented that there is something of Mr Toad in the appearance of Grahame himself. Milne and Grahame went to see the play together in London and Grahame enjoyed it, nodding happily when he recognized his own words. He died in July 1932.

In his memoir of his father Christopher Milne described trying at the age of about eight to draw him: 'First the bulging forehead, where all those brains were . . . Then the nose, large, beaky and easy. Noses were easy in profile, not so easy if they came straight at you . . . Now the mouth. "I'm doing your mouth. Could you possibly take your pipe out for just a moment?" The mouth always went wrong and had to be rubbed out several times. It always came too heavy. My father had a thin, delicate mouth, and a lot of the sort of person he was could be seen in it . . . Well, if I failed, at least I failed in good company. Others tried – distinguished professionals – and they did no better. Only Spy in his full-length portrait really – triumphantly – succeeded.' Christopher's attempt can be seen on page 117.

'Spy' was actually an artist called I. L. Ulduardy, who called himself Spy Junior.

46 'Vespers', a poem which Christopher Milne grew to hate, was not written for children. It was written by Milne for his wife and, giving it to her, he said that, if she liked to get it published, she could keep the money. She sent it to *Vanity Fair* in New York; it appeared unillustrated in January 1923 and she received fifty dollars. Over the years, 'Vespers' proved the most lavish present Milne ever gave his wife. In the winter of 1923/24, Milne dutifully copied out the poem for a tiny volume (right) in Queen Mary's Dolls House (E. V. Lucas was helping Princess Marie Louise to form its library). The version of the poem shown here was printed in 1924 in the form of a card to be hung, often framed, in nurseries all over the world – just as the Victoria and Albert Museum reproductions of Shepard's sketches are now. Milne was already, though he did not yet know it, on his way to becoming some sort of poet laureate of the nursery.

This coloured version of the boy saying his prayers first appeared in 1989 after Shepard's death, when Mark Burgess was commissioned to colour the Shepard illustrations to the poems.

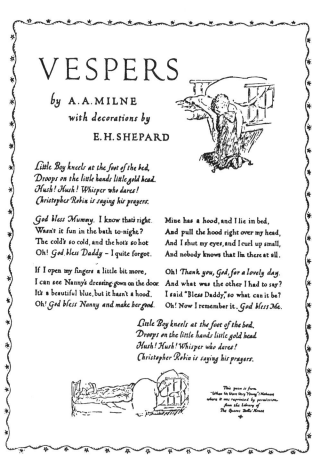

VESPERS

by A. A. MILNE

with decorations by

E. H. SHEPARD

Little Boy kneels at the foot of the bed,
Droops on the little hands little gold head.
Hush! Hush! Whisper who dares!
Christopher Robin is saying his prayers.

God bless Mummy. I know that's right.
Wasn't it fun in the bath to-night?
The cold's so cold, and the hot's so hot
Oh! God bless Daddy – I quite forgot.

If I open my fingers a little bit more,
I can see Nanny's dressing-gown on the door.
It's a beautiful blue, but it hasn't a hood.
Oh! God bless Nanny and make her good.

Mine has a hood, and I lie in bed,
And pull the hood right over my head,
And I shut my eyes, and I curl up small,
And nobody knows that I'm there at all.

Oh! Thank you, God, for a lovely day.
And what was the other I had to say?
I said "Bless Daddy," so what can it be?
Oh! Now I remember it. God bless Me.

Little Boy kneels at the foot of the bed,
Droops on the little hands little gold head.
Hush! Hush! Whisper who dares!
Christopher Robin is saying his prayers.

This poem is from
"When We Were Very Young", (Methuen)
where it was reprinted by permission
from the Library of
The Queens Dolls House

Earlier, J. B. Morton, better known as Beachcomber, penned these memorable lines:

Hush, hush
Nobody cares!
Christopher Robin
Has
    Fallen
        Down-
            Stairs.

Recently, Wendy Cope retaliated:

Little boy dressed in his white judo suit,
Little black belt looking ever so cute.
Hush! Hush! Whisper who dares!
Christopher Robin can throw you downstairs.

In the summer of 1923 there was a wet house-party in Wales. Milne had agreed to share with Nigel Playfair – who had five years before produced his children's play *Make-Believe* at the Lyric, Hammersmith – the cost of renting a house belonging to Clough Williams-Ellis, who would soon develop Portmeirion nearby. It was Plas Brondanw at Llanfrothen near Portmadoc. 'It rains all day in Wales,' Milne wrote gloomily to his friend, Frank Swinnerton. Christopher Robin, aged three that August, shared the nursery wing with the youngest Playfair. As the rain rained, Milne got tired of the company he was supposed to be keeping. One day the post brought him, forwarded from Chelsea, the proof of a poem he had written for Rose Fyleman. It was 'The Dormouse and the Doctor' and it was the first poem he had written deliberately for children. Rose Fyleman (herself best known – rather unfairly – for 'There are fairies at the bottom of our garden!') was editing a new children's magazine, *The Merry-Go-Round*, published by Blackwells, for which she had asked Milne to send her something. She knew Milne wrote apparently effortless light verse for adults. It had been appearing in *Punch* over the years and, most recently, in his collection of both prose and poetry, *The Sunny Side* (1921). Perhaps, though it seems unlikely at this point (when it had appeared only in America), she had seen 'Vespers'. Anyway, she encouraged him to try his hand at writing something for children. At first he said 'No'; he was too busy. Then he thought about what he might have written if he hadn't been too busy, and he sat down and wrote 'The Dormouse and the Doctor', one of the best of all his poems for children.

Plas Brondanw.

Correcting the proof in Wales was the work of moments, but he needed an excuse to remain in the summerhouse, where he had taken himself off with the proof. He was not keen to return to the company of his fellow holiday-makers. His publishers had been urging him to write another detective story. *The Red House Mystery* had come out the year before – a book which has had many admirers – and now he had an offer of no less than £2,000 from Hearst Newspapers for the serial rights of a second one. But Milne always liked the challenge of doing something different. He had a pencil with a rubber on top ('just the thing for poetry') and a reddish marbled quarto exercise book. By the time they left Wales, Milne had written about a quarter of the poems that would form *When We Were Very Young*. 'We are all aware that probably the most hopeless kind of manuscript a publisher expects to receive from his favorite author is that of poetry for children,' his American publisher commented. He could hardly imagine that Milne's verses would take the English-speaking world by storm.

The misguided doctor in the original illustrations by Harry Rowntree is himself a rather large rodent, in top hat and striped trousers, normal wear for doctors in those days. He prescribed milk and massage-of-the-back, and freedom-from-worry and drives-in-a-car, and, above all, chrysanthemums, quite oblivious of the fact that there is nothing really wrong with the dormouse, except for a longing

to be back in a bed
of delphiniums (blue) and geraniums (red).

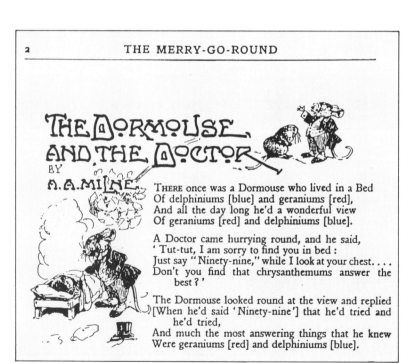

*Os Townsend*
*How about this, my infant made the bright remark*
*quite innocently — EXS Shepard*

*make 'em recognizable as*
*humans*
*Couple under parasol*

*Mary (exploring) Oh, look, mummie, I've found a smugglers cave!*

## The Dormouse and the Doctor

There once was a Dormouse who lived in a bed
Of delphiniums (blue) and geraniums (red),
And all the day long he'd a wonderful view
Of geraniums (red) and delphiniums (blue).

Who was to illustrate the new book?
There were a number of artists appearing
regularly in *Punch* who were possibilities.
Even by 1923 Shepard was by no means
the most obvious choice and the rough of
an early cartoon with the Art Editor's
scribbled remark, 'Make 'em recognizable
as humans' suggests why Milne admitted
to thinking at one stage that Shepard was
'perfectly hopeless'.

The familiar illustrations
by E. H. Shepard
appeared a year later.

In an introduction to a collection of Shepard's drawings in 1927, Milne wrote, 'Perhaps this will be a good place in which to tell the story of how I discovered him. It is short, but interesting. In those early days before the war, when he was making his first tentative pictures for *Punch*, I used to say to F. H. Townsend, the Art Editor, on the occasion of each new Shepard drawing, "What on earth do you see in this man? He's perfectly hopeless," and Townsend would say complacently, "You wait." So I waited. That is the end of the story, which is shorter and less interesting than I thought it was going to be. For it looks now as if the discovery had been somebody else's. Were those early drawings included in this book, we should know definitely whether Townsend was a man of remarkable insight, or whether I was just an ordinary fool. In their absence we may assume fairly safely that he was something of the one, and I more than a little of the other. The Shepard you see here is the one for whom I waited; whom, in the end, even I could not fail to recognize.

'Art is not life, but an exaggeration of it; life reinforced by the personality of the artist. A work of art is literally "too good to be true". That is why we shall never see Turner's sunsets in this world, nor meet Mr Micawber. We only wish we could. But life does its best to keep the artist in sight. Whether sunsets tried to be more Turneresque in the 'fifties I do not remember, but the du Maurier women came in a stately procession well behind du Maurier . . . Kensington Garden children are said to be the most beautiful in the world, but in a little while Shepard will make them more beautiful than ever. . . .

'Every mother prays simply for a little Shepard child, and leaves it to Mr Shepard whether it is a boy or a girl. . . .'

Beautiful Shepard children by the Round Pond in Kensington Gardens, and less beautiful Shepard children (right) at the same place.

*Little Girl (at drawing-room tea and comparing it with nursery fare).* "MUMMY, MAY I TAKE THIS BIT OF BREAD-AND-BUTTER TO NURSE AS A PATTERN?"

A. E. Bestall, who went on to become less famous for another bear, Rupert, was excellent on children. In 1926 he would illustrate Milne's poem 'Forgotten' for *Eve* magazine (below right). The cartoon (above) gives us some idea how he might have replaced Shepard.

> Gold between the poplars
> An old moon shows;
> Silver up the star-way
> The full moon rose;
> Silver down the star-way
> The old moon crept . . .
> And, one by another,
> The pale fields slept.
>
> Lords of the Nursery
> Their still watch keep,
> They hear from the sheep-fold
> The rustle of sheep.
> A young bird twitters
> And hides its head;
> A faint wind suddenly
> Breathes, and is dead.
>
> Slowly and slowly
> Dawns the new day . . .
> What's become of John boy?
> No one can say.
> Some think that John boy
> Is lost on the hill;
> Some say he won't come back,
> Some say he will.
>
> What's become of John boy?
> Nothing at all,
> He played with his skipping rope,
> He played with his ball.
> He ran after butterflies,
> Blue ones and red;
> He did a hundred happy things—
> And then went to bed.

### THE CARNARVON TOUCH.

FOLLOWING THE EXCAVATION OF TUTANKH-AMEN'S TOMB, THE LONG-BURIED TREASURES OF THE ROUND POND AT KENSINGTON, WHICH HAS NOT BEEN CLEANED OUT FOR ABOUT A CENTURY, ARE BEING BROUGHT TO LIGHT.

**52** A. H. Watson, who did
'Sneezles' for Cynthia
Asquith's *Treasure Ship* and
later illustrated Milne's *Gallery
of Children*, was a much less
good artist.

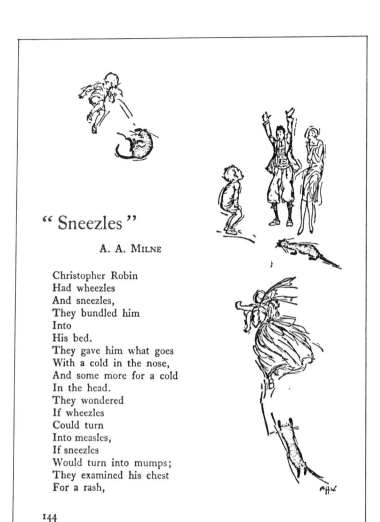

" Sneezles "

A. A. MILNE

Christopher Robin
Had wheezles
And sneezles,
They bundled him
Into
His bed.
They gave him what goes
With a cold in the nose,
And some more for a cold
In the head.
They wondered
If wheezles
Could turn
Into measles,
If sneezles
Would turn into mumps;
They examined his chest
For a rash,

144

As well as the magazine *Merry-
Go-Round*, Blackwells had just
started publishing a lavish
hardback annual, *Joy Street*.
Milne's story *Prince Rabbit*
appeared in No. 2, illustrated
by Hugh Chesterman. In 1966
it came out as a book,
illustrated by E. H. Shepard's
daughter Mary, together with
'The Princess who could not
laugh', which first appeared in
No. 3 *Joy Street*, illustrated by
A. H. Watson.

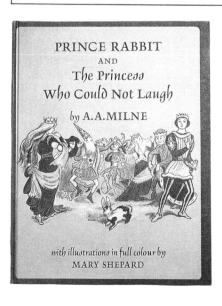

This was the heyday of what Stephen Potter called humour of the 'nice-nice kind'. The innumerable children who made their sweet remarks in the pages of *Punch* in the early twenties were almost invariably upper-class. Pont, Giles and Ronald Searle were still in the future. J. H. Dowd's robust, classless Christopher Robin might have been a very different matter (see page 76). Milne owed a lot to Shepard, but Shepard illustrating non-Milne verses (Drinkwater, Jan Struther, E. V. Lucas) did not survive (see page 69).

Milne considered various titles, including *A Nursery Window-Box* and *Swings and Roundabouts*, but in the end *When We Were Very Young* was agreed. Milne himself realized: 'They are a curious collection; some *for* children, some *about* children, some by, with or from children.' All were written with technical mastery.

When the book was published on 6 November 1924, in England (two weeks later in the States), it carried the following dedication. Originally Milne had written:

TO THE LITTLE BOY
who calls himself
BILLY MOON

but the final version identified the child clearly not only as Milne's own son, but as the character in some of the poems.

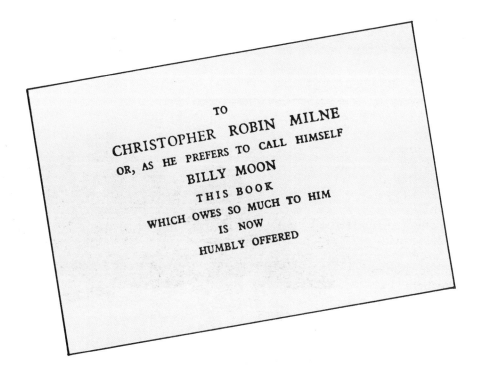

TO
CHRISTOPHER ROBIN MILNE
OR, AS HE PREFERS TO CALL HIMSELF
BILLY MOON
THIS BOOK
WHICH OWES SO MUCH TO HIM
IS NOW
HUMBLY OFFERED

54 In the same letter in which Milne promised to send E. V. Lucas twenty or thirty of the poems, he said, 'I suspect that what you really want is that "Billy Book" you have been urging me to write . . . Fear not. I will do it yet.' As Billy was Milne's name for Christopher Robin, it is reasonable to think of this as the first mention of *Winnie-the-Pooh*. The boy was there; he already had the teddy bear, his first birthday present, and Eeyore, who had arrived for Christmas 1921. Piglet, too, was on the scene, a present from a neighbour in Chelsea.

What was missing in 1923 and 1924, as Milne added to his pile of poems, was the setting, the Forest.

The backgrounds of the poems are mainly domestic and urban, though there are holiday exceptions: the cows in 'The Invaders' and 'Summer Afternoon'; 'The Island', 'Spring Morning' and 'Sand-between-the-toes' – for which Shepard drew a portrait of father and son.

Between their shadows and the sun,
The cows came slowly, one by one,
Breathing the early morning air
And leaving it still sweeter there.

'The Invaders': cows near Poohsticks Bridge.

56 On 20 December 1924, just after the book had been published, Milne inscribed a special copy for his friend Anne, daughter of W. A. Darlington, theatre critic of the *Daily Telegraph*. They lived nearby and Anne attended the same kindergarten as Christopher. Anne – the daughter he never had – would remain extremely important to Milne. *Now We Are Six* was dedicated to her three years later and she would feature in several poems in that book.

(Below) Milne's books appeared in 1965 in i.t.a., the Initial Teaching Alphabet, designed by Sir James Pitman to help children to learn to read. The alphabet was introduced to many schools in the 1960s but has since fallen out of favour.

For Anne Darlington
from her friend Billy Moon
for her birthday
with his love

BUT

(unfortunately)

He has mislaid his pen . . . . . . . . . .

And

as he cannot write with the other one

HE HAS ASKED ME TO DO IT FOR HIM

which I do

A. A. Milne –

December 20th 1924.

## WHEN WE WERE VERY YOUNG

A simple man,
My dearest Anne,
Can only do the things he can:
A year ago
I did not know
Anne Darlington at all, and so
I've been and sung
with luckless tongue
The days when we were very young,
And nothing said
of Anne in bed,
Dementing better for her bread . . .

Forgive me, please. A simple man
Can only do the things he can.
It takes a mother or an aunt
To try and do the things she can't.

A. A. M.:  } in collaboration
C. R. M.:  }

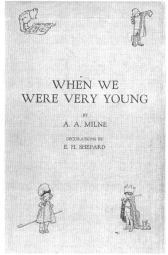

Pooh, who was still known as Edward Bear, appeared on the front of the cream paper dustjacket, together with two small boys and Little Bo Peep.

# WHEN WE WERE VERY YOUNG

Here is a departure from this popular author and dramatist's usual lines. He has always amused and delighted grown-up readers and playgoers; in this gay and frolicsome book he will enchant the nursery too. Mr. Shepard's drawings are in keeping with Mr. Milne's irresistible fun and fancy.

METHUEN & CO. LTD. LONDON

The original blurb.

This title page, with Shepard's signature and some extra pen and ink drawings, is in the Opie collection at the Bodleian Library, Oxford. Pooh seems to be watching the King and Queen offering refreshment to Little Bo Peep.

This Dutton binding uses an illustration from *When We Were Very Young*, the original of which 'now hangs in the nursery of Christopher Robin' according to the *Bookman* in 1925. It comes from a special Holiday Edition in a large format with Christopher Robin's photograph as a frontispiece.

Unnamed in the poem, here is the swan who was the original Pooh. 'This is a very fine name for a swan, because if you call him and he doesn't come (which is a thing swans are good at) then you can pretend that you were just saying "Pooh!" to show how little you wanted him.' This particular drawing, in the Victoria and Albert Museum, is a more elaborate version of the one used in *When We Were Very Young*:

> And there I saw a white
>   swan make
> Another white swan in
>   the lake.

'Teddy Bear' (right) is Pooh's first real introduction to his readers, though he is still called Edward Bear. Apart from 'Teddy Bear', Pooh makes only two very minor appearances in the book. He is at the top of the stairs in 'Halfway Down' and on the end of Christopher Robin's bed in 'Vespers'. Even if the teddy bear is modelled on Graham Shepard's Growler, in habits and habitat he is undoubtedly the Milnes' bear. The ottoman in 'Teddy Bear' was in Christopher Robin's nursery in Mallord Street.

59

## WHEN WE WERE VERY YOUNG.

### IX.—TEDDY BEAR.

A BEAR, however hard he tries,
Grows tubby without exercise.
Our Teddy Bear is short and fat,
Which is not to be wondered at;
He gets what exercise he can
By falling off the ottoman,
But generally seems to lack
The energy to clamber back.

Now tubbiness is just the thing
Which gets a fellow wondering;
And Teddy worried lots about
The fact that he was rather stout.
He thought: "If only I were thin!
But how does anyone begin?"
He thought: "It really isn't fair
To grudge me exercise and air."

For many weeks he pressed in vain
His nose against the window-pane,
And envied those who walked about
Reducing their unwanted stout.
None of the people he could see
"Is quite" (he said) "as fat as me!"
Then, with a still more moving sigh,
"I mean" (he said), "as fat as I!"

Now Teddy, as was only right,
Slept in the ottoman at night,
And with him crowded in as well
More animals than I can tell;

Not only these, but books and things,
Such as a kind relation brings,
Old tales of "Once upon a time,"
And history re-told in rhyme.

One night it happened that he took
A peep at an old picture-book,
Wherein he came across by chance
The picture of a King of France
(A stoutish man), and, down below,
These words: "King Louis So-and-So,
Nicknamed 'The Handsome.'"
There he sat,
And (think of it!) the man was fat!

Our bear rejoiced like anything
To read about this famous King,
Nicknamed "The Handsome." There he sat,
And certainly the man was fat.
Nicknamed "The Handsome." Not a doubt
The man was definitely stout.
Why then a bear (for all his tub)
Might yet be named "The Handsome Cub!"

"Might yet be named." Or did he mean
That years ago he "might have been"?

For now he felt a slight misgiving:
"Is Louis So-and-So still living?
Fashions in beauty have a way
Of altering from day to day;
Is 'Handsome Louis' with us yet?
Unfortunately I forget."

Next morning (nose to window-pane)
The doubt occurred to him again.
One question hammered in his head:
"Is he alive or is he dead?"
Thus nose to pane he pondered; but
The lattice-window, loosely shut,
Swung open. With one startled "Oh!"
Our Teddy disappeared below.

There happened to be passing by
A plump man with a twinkling eye,
Who, seeing Teddy in the street,
Raised him politely to his feet,
And murmured kindly in his ear
Soft words of comfort and of cheer:
"Well, well!" "Allow me!" "Not at all."
"Tut-tut! A very nasty fall."

Our Teddy answered not a word;
It's doubtful if he even heard.
Our bear could only look and look:
The stout man in the picture-book!
That "handsome" King—could this be he,
This man of adiposity?

"Impossible," he thought; "but still,
No harm in asking. Yes, I will!"

"Are you," he said, "by any chance
His Majesty the King of France?"
The other answered, "I am that,"
Bowed stiffly and removed his hat;
Then said, "Excuse me," with an air,
"But is it Mr. Edward Bear?"
And Teddy, bending very low,
Replied politely, "Even so."

They stood beneath the window there,
The King and Mr. Edward Bear,
And, handsome, if a trifle fat,
Talked carelessly of this and that...
Then said His Majesty, "Well, well,
I must get on," and rang the bell.
"Your bear, I think," he smiled.
"Good-day!"
And turned and went upon his way.

A bear, however hard he tries,
Grows tubby without exercise;
Our Teddy Bear is short and fat,
Which is not to be wondered at.
But do you think it worries him
To know that he is far from slim?
No, just the other way about—
He's proud of being short and stout.
A. A. M.

60 One of the most popular poems in *When We Were Very Young* was 'The King's Breakfast'. The design of the whole pages in *Punch* was often more satisfactory than when the poems were transferred to the much smaller pages of the book – but not all the poems had been illustrated on their first appearance.

## WHEN WE WERE VERY YOUNG.

### VI.—THE KING'S BREAKFAST.

THE King asked
The Queen, and
The Queen asked
The Dairymaid:
"Could we have some
    butter for
The Royal slice of bread?"
The Queen asked
The Dairymaid;
The Dairymaid
Said, "Certainly,
I'll go and tell
The cow
Now
Before she goes to bed."

The Dairymaid
She curtsied,
And went and told
The Alderney:
"Don't forget the butter for
The Royal slice of bread."
The Alderney
Said sleepily,
"You'd better tell
His Majesty
That many people now-
    adays
Like marmalade
Instead."

The Dairymaid
Said, "Fancy!"
And went to
Her Majesty;
She curtsied to the Queen
    and
She turned a little red:

"Excuse me,
Your Majesty,
For taking of
The liberty,
But marmalade is tasty if
It's very
Thickly
Spread."

The Queen said,
"Oh!"
And went to
His Majesty:
"Talking of the butter
    for
The Royal slice of bread,
Many people
Think that
Marmalade
Is nicer.
Would you like to try a
    little
Marmalade
Instead?"

The King said,
"Bother!"
And then he said,
"Oh, deary me!"
The King sobbed, "Oh,
    deary me!"
And went back to bed.
"Nobody," he whim-
    pered,
"Could call me
A fussy man;
I *only* want
A little bit

Of butter for
My bread!"

The Queen said,
"There, there!"
And went to
The Dairymaid;
The Dairymaid
Said, "There, there!"
And went to the shed.
The cow said, "There,
    there!
I didn't really
Mean it;
Here's milk for his por-
    ringer
And butter for his bread."

The Queen took
The butter
And brought it to
His Majesty;
The King said,
"Butter, eh?"
And bounced out of bed.
"Nobody," he said,
As he kissed her
Tenderly—
"Nobody," he said,
As he slid down
The banisters —
"Nobody, my darling,
Could call me
A fussy man—
    BUT
*I do like a little bit of
    butter to my bread!*"
            A. A. M.

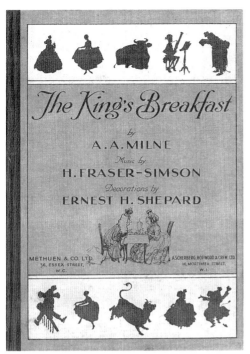

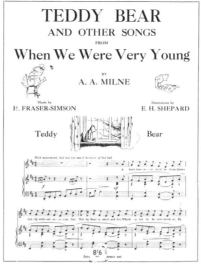

Spin-offs followed immediately. *Fourteen Songs* was published only three weeks after *When We Were Very Young*. By 1928 there were on the market five books of songs with music. In 1929 *The Hums of Pooh* would join them. Milne had been approached by a number of composers while the first verses were appearing in *Punch*. He chose Harold Fraser-Simson, who lived near the Milnes in Chelsea. His settings became very familiar through the wireless where they were always sung, in these early days, by the baritone, Dale Smith.

This order-form for the song books was circulated in 1928. The dedication to Princess Elizabeth (the present Queen, then just a few months old) was in *Teddy Bear*. *Fourteen Songs* was dedicated to the Lascelles boys, Elizabeth's cousins. These dedications were, according to Milne, 'Methuen's idea (E. V. Lucas being thick with Royalty just now).'

In 1974 Vanessa Strong and Andy Ewan celebrated the poem with a curious limited edition (below).

In this introduction to *The King's Breakfast*, A. A. Milne is anticipating the sort of fun Frederick C. Crews, the American academic, would later have in *The Pooh Perplex* (see page 158).

*In which various matters are explained, and the Old English song, " Feed-My-Cow," is now given for the first time.*

BEFORE we start singing *The King's Breakfast*—and I have had a lozenger in my mouth all the morning, in the hope of being in good voice—there is a little matter which has to be settled between us.   You will remember that when the King asked the Queen for butter, the Queen naturally asked the Dairymaid, and that the Dairymaid, having no butter with her, promised to ask the Cow.   So far, so good.   But the Dairymaid, in promising, used a very curious expression,   She said:

> "I'll go and tell the Cow now,
> *Before she goes to bed."*

You will not be surprised to hear that, as the result of these words, the whole world has been asking, *Why did the Cow go to bed at breakfast time ?*

Now in this matter there have been, for many years, two schools of thought. The Grumphiter School (called after Dr James Grumphiter, of Ladbroke Grove) holds that, for reasons as yet unascertained, the Alderney cow was in the habit of having a short nap in the forenoons, probably between the hours of ten and twelve.   At noon she was awakened ;   and, after a drink of water and a couple of health biscuits, was led back into the fields again ; from which point in the day she followed the routine of the ordinary cow.   In other words, Dr Grumphiter thinks that the Alderney was a special kind of cow who required special care in the mornings.

An entirely different view of the matter is taken by the Cadwallader School. ("Cadwallader," I should explain, is pronounced "Calder," and was so spelt until 1903, when the Professor married again ; "School" of course, is pronounced " Scool", the " h " being kept quiet.)   The Cadwallader School, led by Professor H. J. Cadwallader, of Dunstable University, is of opinion that " the transactions narrated in the poem cover a period of, approximately, twenty-four hours, and that actually *two* breakfasts have come within the purview of the historian."   It is a pity he uses such long words, but no doubt you see what he means.

Let us consider this Cadwallader Theory for a moment.   A time-table of events would seem to go something like this :

*Monday,*   9 *a.m.*   King and Queen at breakfast.   King realises that there is only enough butter for that day's meal, assuming (as usual) that the Queen is not hungry.   He helps himself to the last of the pat, saying to her Majesty, " Don't forget the butter for the (to-morrow's) royal slice of bread."   The Queen says, " I won't," but she is thinking of something else.

,, 10 *a.m.*—6 *p.m.*   The Queen attends to her customary royal duties, Monday being a particularly busy day, what with Receptions, Executions, the Washing, and so forth.

| | | |
|---|---|---|
| *Monday*, 6 *p.m.* | | The Dairymaid asks for orders.   The Queen, interrupted in her toilet, says that butter will be wanted for to-morrow's breakfast.   The Dairymaid promises to tell the Cow now, before the latter goes to bed. |
| ,, | 6.15 *p.m.* | Cow suggests marmalade instead. |
| ,, | 6.30 *p.m.* | Dairymaid assures Queen that marmalade is tasty. |
| ,, | 6.31 *p.m.* | Queen says " Oh," and decides to wear the purple after all. |
| ,, | 10 *p.m.* | Their Majesties retire to rest. |

. . . . . . . . . . . . .

| | | |
|---|---|---|
| *Tuesday*, 8 *a.m.* | | Their Majesties rise. |
| ,, | 9 *a.m.* | Their Majesties descend the royal staircase into the Banqueting Hall.   Fanfare of trumpets.   As the last note dies away, Queen says to King, " Talking of the butter for the royal slice of bread, many people think that marmalade is nicer, would you like to try a little marmalade instead ? " |
| ,, | 9.5 *a.m.* | King says " Bother." |
| ,, | 9.6 *a.m.* | King says " Oh, deary me." |
| ,, | 9.7 *a.m.* | King sobs, and goes back to bed. |

After which, it is pretty plain sailing.   The Queen comforts His Majesty, and hurries to the Dairymaid ; in a trice the Dairymaid is with the Alderney ; in a jiffy the Alderney, repentant after a good night's rest, gives the Dairymaid the necessary butter ; and in a brace of shakes the Dairymaid has brought the butter to the Queen.   Whereupon :

> " The Queen took
> The Butter
> And brought it to
> His Majesty . . . "

—and so, calmly, to the long-wished-for end.

Well, that is the Cadwallader Theory.   But why, if these be the facts of the matter, has the poet (to use the local name for this sort of man) not put them more clearly before us ?   Why did he not tell us the truth ?   Thus :

> The King asked
> The Queen, and
> The Queen wasn't
> Listening :
> " Can I have some butter for
> To-morrow's slice of bread ? "
> The Queen said
> " I won't, dear . . .
> *Stockings and*
> *A night-cap—*
> *Or wear the cap another week*
> *And send the shawl*
> *Instead ? "*
> The Queen took
> The washing . . .

But we need not go any further with it.   The Professor suggests that the poet wrote as he did, because he had a long story to tell, *but very little paper to tell it on.*   It was necessary for him, therefore, to squeeze the events of twenty-four hours into a space of five minutes, regardless of historical accuracy. And the Professor adds in a thoughtful foot-note :   "*Poets are like this.*"

We have to decide, then, which of these two schools of thought has found the right explanation of the Dairymaid's words.   And the answer is, " Neither."   The truth of the matter is simply this :   The Alderney had chased the king across two turnip fields the day before, and, *as a punishment,* had been sent to bed immediately after breakfast.   She hadn't meant any harm, as you will know if you have ever read an old song which was sung in those days, and which is supposed to have referred to this adventure of the King's.   Here it is:

## FEED—MY—COW.

**1**
I went down to feed—my—cow,
  (Feed—my—cow,
  Feed—my—cow)
I went down to feed my cow
  At ten o'clock in the morning.

**2**
She looked out and shook—her—head.
  (Shook—her—head,
  Shook—her—head)
She looked out and shook her head
  At ten o'clock in the morning.

**3**
I said bravely, " Here—I—come ! "
  (Here—I—come,
  Here—I—come)
I said bravely, " Here I come,
  At ten o'clock in the morning."

**4**
She looked out and shook-her-horns,
  (Shook—her—horns,
  Shook—her—horns)
She looked out and shook her horns
  At ten o'clock in the morning.

**5**
I said bravely, "Not—so—close ! "
  (Not—so—close,
  Not—so—close)
I said bravely, " Not so close
  At ten o'clock in the morning."

**6**
She come out and shook—her—tail,
  (Shook—her—tail,
  Shook—her—tail)
She came out and shook her tail,
  At ten o'clock in the morning.

**7**
I went back to ask—the—time
  (Ask—the—time,
  Ask—the—time)
I went back to ask the time
  At ten o'clock in the morning.

**8**
She came too, to—ask—the—time
  (Ask—the—time,
  Ask—the—time)
She came too, to ask the time
  At ten o'clock in the morning.

**9**
We both ran, but *I—asked—first,*
  (*I—asked—first,*
  *I—asked—first*),
We both ran, but I asked first :
  'Twas ten o'clock in the morning.

Well, that was how it happened, and in the afternoon, when the King felt rested, he decided to give the cow a very severe punishment.    So it was ordered (and the King wrote it out and sealed it and signed it with his own hand) that on the very next day the Alderney should go to bed " at ten o'clock in the morning."

Now then, having got that off our minds, we can clear our throats.    But before we begin to sing it, I think I ought to tell you how to *say* a poem like this.    It doesn't matter whether you are reciting it, reading it, acting it, or even singing it, there is one way only of doing it, and that is— *on tip-toe*. This story of *The King's Breakfast* is not a walk or a slide or a slither, it is a ballet-dance.    I have heard people recite it :  and I have heard them say, with a great deal of expression, as though they were reading *The Decline and Fall of the Roman Empire* aloud to a sick friend :

"The King asked the Queen (*swallow*) and the Queen asked the Dairymaid . . . "

Now that is not how it was written.    It is always a good idea to suppose that, when somebody writes something in a certain way, this is the way in which he wants it said.

> The King asked—
> The Queen and—
> The Queen asked—
> The Dairymaid—

It is a ballet-dance, in which each step is distinct, not a waltz, where one step slides into the next ;   formal, like a Dutch garden, not a riot in a herbaceous border.    And, above all, it is " expressionless " as far as meaning goes.    All that the speaker has to express is the rhythm and the shape of it : the words have very simple definite meanings of their own, and can take care of themselves quite nicely.    Don't be afraid of saying " and " at the end of the second line ;    the second and third words have the same value, and you need not be alarmed because one is a Royal noun, and the other is a common conjunction.    I know that you are in the habit of saying "'nd "—" Jack 'nd Jill," and quite right too.    But there will be no sort of panic among the guests if, on this occasion only, you say " and ", nor will anybody wonder what the word means.    Only mind that you do say " and," and not " nand." " The Queen nand "—if you say this, you're slithering again, not tip-toeing. What I want you to do is to give each word which you stress a " ting," and then leave it ; touch, and away—as if it were a hot poker.

And again, remember : no " expression." No, not even when " he kissed her tenderly" and " slid down the banisters." If these words are " funny," they will be twice as funny for being said in just the same voice, as if one way were as good as and natural as another for celebrating the appearance of the butter.    Indeed, the more I think of it, the more I am convinced that a Russian who knew the meaning of no word of English, but only how to pronounce it, would be the ideal person to recite *The King's Breakfast*.    So if you like, pretend that you are a Russian. . . .

**66** John Drinkwater's review appeared in the *Sunday Times* on 23 November 1924.

## MR. MILNE'S VERSES.

"When We Were Very Young." By A. A. Milne. Decorations by E. H. Shepard. (Methuen. 7s. 6d.)

Reviewed by JOHN DRINKWATER.

There are two Mr. Milnes in this book, and I hope that the one who has just given me so much delight won't mind if I dismiss the other rather abruptly. The good Mr. Milne, in the prettiest mood of inventive fun, has been making rhymes for a young fellow called Christopher Robin, and, as will be shown, these rhymes are just the very thing for such a person, as right as they can be in design and most happily carried out. But every now and again the bad Mr. Milne has spoken up and said, " If you are going to have a book of poetry you must put some poetry into it," and he (bad Mr. M.) has persuaded him (good Mr. M.) that this is quite an easy thing to do when it occurs to you. And so we get a few pages like this :—

> When the sun
> Shines through the leaves of the apple-tree,
> When the sun
> Makes shadows of the leaves of the apple-tree .

which is in a poem that is called " Twinkle-toes," and has reduced even Mr. Shepard to a level of ordinary fairy inanity, or this :—

> Where the water-lilies go
> To and fro.
> Rocking in the ripples of the water,
> Lazy on a leaf lies the Lake King's daughter.
> And the faint winds shake her,
> Who will come and take her?

We don't want to see him any more, but to be left in undisturbed enjoyment of the good Mr. Milne's company.

And what enchanting company that is !

> What shall I call
> My dear little dormouse?
> His eyes are so small,
> But his tail is e-nor-mouse.

As that falls upon the ears of Alice in her wonderland she must know that a new prophet has arisen. Nor will her friends the White Rabbit and the Gryphon and the March Hare and Bill the Lizard be jealous about a little room in their immortal company when they hear that—

> Ernest was an elephant, a great big fellow,
> Leonard was a lion with a six-foot tail,
> George was a goat, and his beard was yellow,
> And James was a very small snail.
>
> Leonard had a stall, and a great big strong one,
> Ernest had a manger, and its walls were thick,
> George found a pen, but I think it was the wrong one,
> And James sat down on a brick.

What happened further the reader must discover for himself, and it will be worth his while.

**Not Fairydoodleum.**

Mr. Milne's deftness is not to be questioned, but the fortunate thing is that it is, apart from the few lapses, always at work, as Lewis Carroll's was, on a sound common-sense foundation, and not wasting itself on banal vapourings of the fancy. Mr. Milne treats his small companion as a sensible being who, indeed, wants to make up things, as is proper, but wants to make them up about real life and not about fairydoodleum. These two go about in the gayest and most whimsical of tempers, but the things that engage their attention are the soldiers at Buckingham Palace, the three little foxes who didn't wear stockings and didn't wear sockses, the gardener, the king who asked for no more than a little butter for the royal slice of bread, the mouse with the woffelly nose, the dormouse who lived in a bed of delphiniums (blue) and geraniums (red), and such essential problems as waterproof coats, the corner of the street, a penny to spend, and rice puddings. It is all great larks, but I wonder whether the Sterner Critics will realise that it also is a very wholesome contribution to serious literature. A further example of the good Mr. Milne's quality I should like to quote from " Lines and Squares " :—

> Whenever I walk in a London street,
> I'm ever so careful to watch my feet;
> And I keep in the squares,
> And the masses of bears,
> Who wait at the corners all ready to eat
> The sillies who tread on the lines of the street,
> Go back to their lairs,
> And I say to them, " Bears,
> Just look how I'm walking in all of the squares! "

Special marks, by the way, ought to be awarded to Mr. Milne for his preface, which is perfect.

THE ST. PAUL DAILY NEWS    4/11/26

## EVIEWS OF THE NEW I

CHRISTOPHER ROBIN AND HIS DAD.

A. A. Milne, the famous author of "Mr. Pim Passes By," "The Dover Road" and many other stage successes is pictured here with his son, Christopher Robin, to whom he has dedicated his latest work, "When We Were Very Young." This photograph is by Pacific and Atlantic.

Christopher Robin had been drawn into Milne's publicity even before the publication of *When We Were Very Young*. Now he was the centre of attention and sometimes supplied his own four-year-old autograph. Photos of father and son, in more and more uncomfortable poses, continued to appear on both sides of the Atlantic.

*When We Were Very Young* was a huge, immediate success. James Douglas's review was typical of many, and on both sides of the Atlantic the printers could hardly keep up with the ecstatic and continued demand. In the *New York Telegraph* in November 1925, a year after publication, 'Everybody's Talking about this Book' was a headline above a photo of Christopher Robin, and in the following January the *Retail Bookseller* said that the record of *When We Were Very Young* 'is practically without parallel *for any book* in the last ten years'. Milne himself was amazed. 'It is all most odd,' he wrote to his brother, Ken. 'Yellow-faced Anglo-Indian colonels tell me with tears in their eyes how important it is to avoid the lines of the street and thus escape bears.' The book established itself immediately as a classic as this 1927 advertisement (left) in the *New Yorker* suggests, and was read as much by adults as by children.

11 MALLORD STREET
CHELSEA S.W. 3.
TEL. KENSINGTON 2074.

**68** In 1925 Milne would reply to
fan letters and even send
photographs of Christopher
Robin to particularly ardent
requests. Later his mail was too
enormous for this personal
touch.

13, MALLORD STREET,
CHELSEA, S.W.3.
TEL. KENSINGTON 2074.

*[handwritten letter]*

Dear Mr Cortissoz,

Many thanks for your
letter and for what you have
written about Christopher Robin.
It is charming of you. I send
you one or two snapshots of him;
not very good ones, but the best
I have. He isn't always as serious
as he looks in these.

It is delightful of
America to like the book so
much – we have sold 50,000
copies over here, which is a
lot for England.

With again many thanks
to you, Yours sincerely

A A Milne

And, I am prepared to prove, an
even more devoted father than you.

The phenomenal success of Milne's children's poems inevitably produced a spate of other books hoping for similar success. These included Georgette Agnew's *Let's Pretend*, Jan Struther's *Sycamore Square* and E. V. Lucas's own *Playtime and Company*, all illustrated by E. H. Shepard. Decie Merwin illustrated Rose Fyleman's *Gay Go Up* (a Methuen book in a binding very like *When We Were Very Young*). John Drinkwater's *All About Me* was illustrated by H. M. Brock, who years before had worked on Milne's *Once on a Time*. In my own memory Jan Struther's muffin man and Rose Fyleman's Jessica survive but the books themselves are hard to track down. Only Milne stays in print, decade after decade.

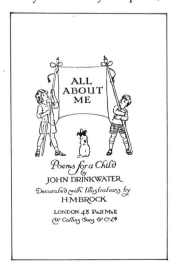

The American publication of *When We Were Very Young* was followed in March 1926 by this volume of parodies, which was itself a great success, being reprinted immediately. Fisher Unwin brought it out in England.

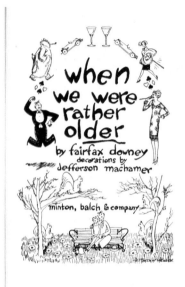

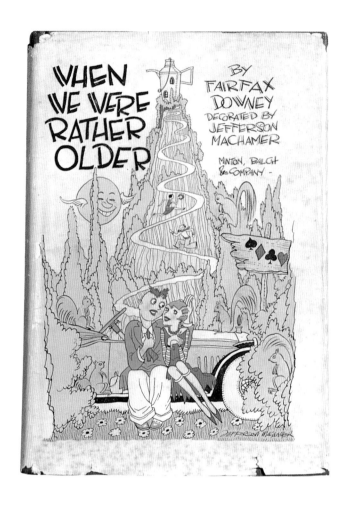

Fairfax Downey was a journalist on the *New York Herald Tribune*. The extract is from his parody of 'Disobedience', called 'The Merry Matron'.

James James
Morrison's Mother's
Had her hair shingled off.
She's late
Home for her dinner,
Being out shooting golf.
Jim says
Somebody told her
That was the modern view,
And since it's the rage not to be your age, well, what can **any** son do?

When my biography of A. A. Milne was published in 1990, I was surprised to receive a letter from a man called James Morrison, who was born in the house next door to the Milnes in Mallord Street, Chelsea. The family lived there when Milne was writing about 'James, James, Morrison, Morrison' in the poem he called 'Disobedience'. The curious thing is that it would seem that Milne was never consciously aware that the boy next door was called James Morrison. Let him tell the story himself: 'I had a pedal tricycle and a hat exactly as depicted by EHS in his drawings while the illustration of my mother is a lookalike. She was six foot tall, had a cloche hat and a fur . . . Her impression of the Milnes in the ten years she lived in Mallord Street was that he was very shy and withdrawn while she (I have to say it) was ''the biggest snob I ever knew''.' The two families had little contact, though 'our nannies and our chauffeurs certainly were friendly with each other'. James Morrison suffered at school from his identification with the boy who told his mother, 'You must never go down to the end of the town without consulting me.' So he had later a particular sympathy with Christopher Robin's much greater suffering.

This photo of Christopher Milne and his mother has never been published before. It was given to Brian Sibley by Daphne Milne.

Shepard updated the mother in a later edition.

This entertaining essay on *When We Were Very Young* by Geoffrey Grigson appeared in his collection *The Contrary View* (1974), so was never seen by Milne himself, who would undoubtedly have wished to correct (as I do) Grigson's assumption that Milne came from a smug, moneyed background. Milne was as worried as Grigson himself by the priorities and attitudes of many of his readers. Grigson cannot enjoy the verse for the sociology. He sees nannies and nurseries *passim* – though in fact the nanny (or 'Nurse') appears in only seven of the forty-five poems, and the children in them are always wanting to break free from the constraints that are constantly imposed on them. In *Winnie-the-Pooh*, of course, there will be no nannies or nurseries.

## When Hoo, Exactly, Was Very Young?

Once, oh once, did not the Public find its voice in the Poet? Once—but now now, O Apollo—weren't new poems sold, in the largest numbers? *Lalla Rookh*, and *Childe Harold*, and *Idylls of the King*, and *Poems and Ballads* (and *Proverbial Philosophy*) ?

Then T. S. Eliot came; and poetry changed to modern; and did not sell.

As such facts are recited (often, if not quite so often as heretofore), how is it that no one remembers Alan Alexander Milne? How is it that no one is asked, in Advanced Level English, even in the Tripos, to estimate the influence upon 'Now I'm engaged to Miss Joan Hunter Dunn' of

Hush! Hush! Whisper who dares!
Christopher Robin is saying his prayers?

A. A. Milne was a poet—he wrote poems, shall I say, no less than John Betjeman, or Eliot; or William Empson. Undeniably *When We Were Very Young*, his most successful book, is filled with poems. Undeniably these poems have sold (and are selling still). Few other poems in English have sold so enormously. They were published—two years after *The Waste Land*—in the autumn of 1924: they have been reprinted (this is the fact) fifty-six times in thirty-four years.

This poet was born to a Scottish prep school master, in London, in 1882, six years before our Mr Eliot was born in St Louis, Missouri. He was educated (nothing 'wrong' about his education) at Westminster School and Trinity College, Cambridge; and soon enough, after editing the *Granta*, the undergraduates' magazine, he was helping to edit *Punch* in its least aggressive and most evasive days. This young man knew the electric fences of the interest in which he was now involved, his master J. M. Barrie, his editor R. C. Lehmann. At what college—let us give an example—should we then have expected something, or someone, so unmanly as a *chess* blue? At an 'inferior' college, to which the better-born sons did not go. 'This is the ballad of Edward Bray', A. A. Milne began a poem, in *Punch*, on the chess match between the universities of Oxford and Cambridge.

Captain of Catharine's, Cambridge Blue.

Exactly so, the 'wrong' college, not King's, not Trinity.

With his own *curriculum vitae*, his own dye of the Poshocracy, in the Squeamish Age (in which St Loe Strachey, editor of the *Spectator*, led a deputation to the Home Secretary asking him to ban *Ann Veronica* by H. G. Wells), Milne's later poems of *When We Were Very Young* were in tune, precisely.

The nature of the best-seller has to do with the nature of a class, its prime interest is one of sociology, not literature; which is the fun of such books. The readers have mattered most of all, and it is not difficult to be sure of the readers who have found a voice in A. A. Milne, to be sure of the readership (and the sociological writership) to which he belonged. From the poems you need only to deduce the keepings of Christopher Robin, and Percy, and John, and Mary Jane, and Emmeline, and James James Morrison Morrison Weatherby George Dupree.

The poems intimate that these children are of good family—at least up to the Forsyte standard. They have nannies and nurseries (*passim*). Maids are also in attendance—though not butlers (see *The Wrong House*).

Their homes, in London, are in the right squares, are not too grand and not too mean. Their families keep dogs, and are kind to uncles, aunts, and animals other than dogs; and display an embryo interest in bird-watching. Their daddies know about trout, mayfly, and expensive rods, their mamas about trugs and delphiniums. When they are not very ill, they are attended by frock-coated white-haired family doctors. They are Church of England—could a dissenting child or a Presbyterian child say 'Thank you, God, for my nice new braces'? They are accustomed, with a full staff, to seaside holidays (I think in North Cornwall), in a rented house:

When we got home, we had sand in the hair,
In the eyes and the ears and everywhere.

Their world is Us, and the Other People. Those of the Other People who sell in shops or work with their hands (Jonathan Jo the gardener) are a little queer, and perhaps need washing (see *Bad Sir Brian Botany*), but they must be treated with consideration; which averts revolution. Bad Sir Brian blipped 'the villagers' on the head with his battle-axe and kicked them into the pond, and into the ditches, and under the waterfall. But observe that the treatment simply made Bad Sir Brian renounce his title, his battle-axe, and his spurred boots, which he threw into the fire; after which he 'goes about the village as B. Botany, Esquire'. He has become one of Us. The class structure is repaired, and improved.

Conclusions? We may now be sure that of these children the males are earmarked for the better schools, then the better colleges, high on the river (*mens mediocris in corpore sano*), at one of the 'two' universities; and that male and female they come of families comfortable, secure, self-certain, somewhat above the middle of the middle class.

Are the poems for other children of such homes? No, rather than yes. Children, in my experience, of every generation since and including the Twenties, have found the poems nauseating, and fascinating. In fact, they were poems by a parent for other parents, and for vice-parental nannies—for parents with a war to forget, a social (and literary) revolution to ignore, a childhood to recover. . . .

Here mamas of the middle way, and fathers, and nannies, those distorting reflectors of the parental ethos, could be sure of finding Innocence Up to Date. Little Lord Fauntleroy – here he was, stripped of frills and velvet (as we can tell by the splendid insipidity of the accompanying drawings) for modern, sensible clothes; heir, after all, to no peerage, but still the Eternal Child. No hint in these poems of children nasty, brutish and short, as *Struwelpeter* or Hilaire Belloc made them (or as they are being re-established in newspaper cartoons).

Are there ever tantrums, as these nice children say 'cos', and 'most', and 'nuffin'', and 'purfickly', and 'woffelly', in their nice accent?

*continued*

*What* is the matter with Mary Jane?
She's perfectly well, and she hasn't a pain.

If there are tantrums, it is rice pudding again; but not the child psyche, not infant sexuality, not Freud, who had now entered the pure English world. (In fairness, though, I must admit a touch of complex in Christopher Robin when he signs off with his prayers—

*God bless Mummy*. I know that's right.
Wasn't it fun in the bath to-night?
The cold's so cold, and the hot's so hot.
Oh! *God bless Daddy*—I quite forgot.

But no doubt this came of independent observation.)

The innocence of *When We Were Very Young*—of course it chimes with the last tinkle of a romantic innocence which by the Twenties had developed to whimsy. Christopher Robin comes trailing the tattiest wisps of a glory soiled by expectation and acceptance. The clouds have gone grey. The Child, in spite of Westminster and Trinity, is all too much at last the Father of the Man. And whenever the Child's impresario allowed an entr'acte, it came in parallel modes of the expected and decayed—daffodowndillies and the last fairies (inherited from the more fanciful—and sinister—inventor of Peter Pan), Twinkletoes upon the apple leaves, the Lake King's daughter on the water-lilies, cave ancients tapping at golden slippers for dainty feet, bluebells, and blackbirds' yellow bills.

For some Poets Who Don't Sell, these poems for people towards the top with children beneath the age of literary consent have the qualities of rhythm, shape, economy, and games with words—good qualities, after all. Would it be too ponderous to say as well that they were poems for a class of middle to top people who had lost their intellectual and cultural nerve, who expected of right things which they had not earned, and who had scarcely looked a fact in the eye for fifty years? It might be too ponderous. But it would be true.

And sometimes out it comes in the charming sick, in the actual stuff, with an ironic unconsciousness. As Christopher Robin says, imagining himself on a desert island instead of his holiday coast of Cornwall, in the land of Betjeman:

And I'd say to myself as I looked so lazily
    down at the sea:
There's nobody else in the world, and the world
    was made for me.

A few days after A. A. Milne died the editor of *The Times* had occasion in his paper (which had just given Milne an obituary not very kind, though much longer, and kinder, than the one it had allowed years before to D. H. Lawrence) to write, in his role as 'Oliver Edwards', on Modern Poetry. He admitted to wondering often, 'heretically, whether, where Mr T. S. Eliot is concerned, Old Possum will not outlive Alfred Prufrock'—hand in hand, no doubt, with Christopher Robin, Hoo, and Pooh. At any rate, more than 745,000 copies of *When We Were Very Young* have been sold. And it is in the bookshops still.

In 1925 Winnie-the-Pooh was still a toy bear and not a book. He was not even in a story until the end of the year – but the name seems by now to have become permanently attached to the bear, who had gone under several other names, as bears often do (Teddy, Edward, Big Bear), if not yet 'under the name of Sanders'. The Milnes had said goodbye to the swan called Pooh and taken the name with them as they did not think the swan would want it any more. The question, 'How did Winnie-the-Pooh get his name?' has often been asked and I go into the subject in some detail in my biography of Milne. When Christopher Milne is asked that question, he simply says, 'I gave it to him.' But there is no doubt that the Winnie part comes from Winnie, the black bear at the London Zoo. The word 'Polar' in Milne's introduction to *Winnie-the-Pooh* seems to be a slip of the pen.

When Christopher Robin goes to the Zoo, he goes to where the Polar Bears are, and he whispers something to the third keeper from the left, and doors are unlocked, and we wander through dark passages and up steep stairs, until at last we come to the special cage, and the cage is opened, and out trots something brown and furry, and with a happy cry of "Oh, Bear!" Christopher Robin rushes into its arms. Now this bear's name is Winnie, which shows what a good name for bears it is.

In 1925, rather than getting on with his 'Billy Book', Milne was distracted by a project for an American publisher who asked him to write some stories for a collection of paintings by H. Willebeek Le Mair. The resulting *A Gallery of Children* has been said to 'intrude like a pale white slug between two butterflies'. It sold on the strength of Milne's name and the stories were later reissued in a cheaper form with illustrations by A. H. Watson. Milne wrote to a friend: 'For God's sake don't buy it,' but there are some things in it that are worth reading.

# The Eveni

London's Predominant Evening Journal.    Larg

NO. 13,745.    Forty-Fifth Year.    LONDON: THURSD

# A CHILDREN'S STO

In December 1925 Milne was asked to write a story for the Christmas Eve issue of the *Evening News*. His wife suggested he wrote down one he had told Christopher at bedtime. Most of the bedtime stories had been stuff about 'dragons and giants and magic rings', designed to send the small boy, now nearly five and a half, off to sleep, but there was just one which was a real story, about his bear. The bold front-page headline gives an impressive idea of Milne's fame and standing at this point. The story eventually became the first chapter of *Winnie-the-Pooh* – but Shepard was busy and it was in drawings by J. H. Dowd that Pooh, not looking quite himself, made his first appearance. Shepard would make the boy's gun more obviously a pop gun, with its cork hanging out, quite incapable of hitting anything – a nicely pacifist touch.

## Christopher Robin.

### Page 7 To-night—To-morrow Night's Broadcast.

A new story for children, "Winnie-the-Pooh," about Christopher Robin and his Teddy Bear, written by Mr. A. A. Milne specially for "The Evening News," appears to-night on Page Seven.

It will be broadcast from all stations by Mr. Donald Calthrop, as part of the Christmas Day wireless programme, at 7.45 p.m. to-morrow.

g News

HOME ED.

LIPTON'S TEA

per 1/8 lb. | per 2/8 lb.

WONDERFUL VALUE | THE FINEST TEA WORLD PRODUCES

ening NET SALE in the World.

ECEMBER 24, 1925.    ONE PENNY.    Other Reliable Blends 2/-, 2/4 & 2/6

# Y BY A. A. MILNE.

This sketch of Pooh from Shepard's notebook was apparently of the Milne bear rather than Growler. He is certainly thinner but the two animals have a good deal in common.

WHEN A. A. Milne wrote "When We Were Very Young" he did more than write a book of adorable nonsense. He became an institution. As quotable, contagious and personal an institution as Lewis Carroll. He sent scores of sedate grown-ups scurrying up the perilous stairway of whimsy, and some of them will never come down again. One has now got quite used to hearing dignified men of affairs confide to their breakfast toast that they are not fussy men. But they *do* like a little butter, etc. When débutantes refer to something as "enormouse," it does not mean that they have been bereft of the educational benefits of the Brearly and Foxcroft. It means they are Milnenomaniacs.

Incurable. Milne began to write when he was an inky little fag at Westminster. At the age of twelve he had completely changed the complexion of the school paper. It looked worse! Later he edited *The Granta* at Cambridge, and later still he was offered the assistant editorship of *Punch*. After four years on the Western front with the Royal Warwickshires, he retired to write for his own pleasure. He has had no financial reason for regretting it. "He's much too busy a'signing things!" And when he is not a'signing things he plays with his possessions, which are quite singular. He has one wife, one son, one house, and one recreation —golf.                                              R. N.

In fact Milne had two houses by the time this piece appeared in an American magazine. In 1925 he bought Cotchford Farm, thirty-five miles from London. From this time on, the family travelled regularly between Chelsea and Hartfield, spending as much time as possible in the country. So now Milne had not only the boy and the toys (Kanga and Roo had now arrived in the nursery) but also the setting. The Billy book which E. V. Lucas wanted was to become the bear's book. After all, as Edward Bear had said in *When We Were Very Young*:

> It really isn't fair
> to grudge me exercise and air.

It would be the juxtaposition between stout toy bear and the natural outdoor scene which was to give *Winnie-the-Pooh* its special charm.

Such was the volume of fan mail and requests for autographs that
Milne not only encouraged his wife to pretend to be 'Celia Brice,
Secretary', but had a special form printed to elicit contributions to
the Authors' Pension Fund. This particular filling-in was a joke
for John Drinkwater.

sept. 15

COTCHFORD FARM,
HARTFIELD,
SUSSEX.

Dear Sir,

Mr. a. a. Milne has signed
your book and thanks you
very much for your subscription
to the Pension Fund.

Yours faithfully
Celia Brice
Secretary

Mr. A. A. Milne will let you have his autograph
if you will send him £5000, which money
will be forwarded to The Pensions Fund of the
Authors' Society.* Mr. Milne does not suggest
that his autograph is worth this or any other
sum, but, obviously, if it has no value for his
correspondent, there is no reason why he
should put himself to the trouble of sending it

\* Or not, as the case may be.

Roo had disappeared long before
this recent photo of Kanga was
taken.

Trees are a very important part of the books. As Russell Davies put it in the *Times Literary Supplement*: 'In the Pooh books, the trees preside: they stand for the real and adult world, while accommodating the fantasy – literally, since everyone lives in a tree-trunk house.' This photo was taken recently near Poohsticks Bridge.

After his success with *When We Were Very Young*, there was no
real doubt that it would be E. H. Shepard, not J. H. Dowd, who
would illustrate the book of Pooh stories. Pooh's appearance was
already decided; Shepard had drawn Christopher Robin's bear on
his bed in the last picture in *When We Were Very Young*. Now he
visited the Milnes to draw the other toys: Piglet, Eeyore, Kanga
and Roo – 'from the living model', as Milne put it. 'They were
what they are for anyone to see; I described rather than invented
them. Only Rabbit and Owl were my own unaided work.' They
had no counterparts in the nursery and Tigger was not yet on the
scene. The family and the toys spent as much time as they could
in the country. Often Anne Darlington went too. The Shepard
drawing of the children at Cotchford illustrates 'Buttercup Days'.

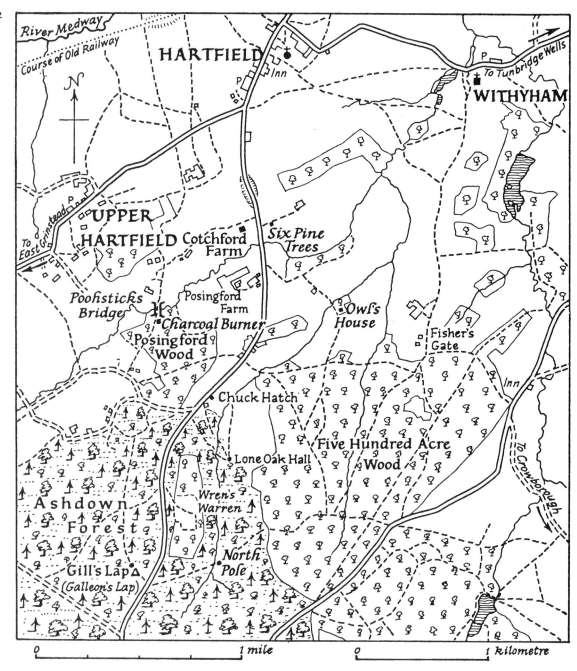

River Medway

Course of Old Railway

HARTFIELD

*Inn*

P

*To Tunbridge Wells*

P

WITHYHAM

N

UPPER
HARTFIELD Cotchford
Farm

*Six Pine
Trees*

To East Grinstead

P

*Poohsticks
Bridge*

*Posingford
Farm*

•Charcoal Burner

*Posingford
Wood*

•Owl's
House

*Fisher's
Gate*

•Chuck Hatch

Inn

To Crowborough

Five Hundred Acre

•Lone Oak Hall

Wood

A s h d o w n

*Wren's
Warren*

F o r e s t

Gill's Lap △

North
Pole

(Galleon's Lap)

0                               1 mile            0                          1 kilometre

Ashdown Forest has passed through some alarming times in the last seventy years, most dramatically in 1987. A threat from BP (keen to drill for oil) and a change of ownership (when East Sussex County Council bought the Forest from Earl de la Warr) preceded the devastating hurricane which brought down large numbers of trees. But today it survives, wild, windswept and undeveloped, miraculously very much as it was in Pooh's day.

84    The manuscripts of the two Pooh books were left to Trinity College, Cambridge, in Milne's will. The stories are very clean and were possibly sent by Milne to a typist – though printers in this period very often did work from handwriting. The versions are exactly as they made their first appearances – seven of them in the *Royal Magazine*. Corrections and alterations for the book were presumably made on the printed texts. In this extract from the sixth chapter of *Winne-the-Pooh* (which in the *Royal* was titled 'Eeyore has a birthday'), it is amusing to see that Owl at Milne's first thought was rather more competent. He wrote: HAPY BTHUTHDA FRUM WOL AND ROO.

never even heard before! An animal who carries her family about with her in her pocket! Suppose I carried my family about with me in my pocket, how many pockets should I want?"

"Sixteen," said Piglet.

"Seventeen, isn't it?" said Rabbit. "And one more for a handkerchief—that's eighteen. Eighteen pockets in one suit! I haven't time."

There was a long and thoughtful silence ... and then Pooh, who had been frowning very hard for some minutes, said: "I make it fifteen."

"What?" said Rabbit.

"Fifteen."

"Fifteen what?"

"Your family."

"What about them?"

Pooh rubbed his nose and said that he thought Rabbit had been talking about his family.

"Did I?" said Rabbit carelessly.

"Yes, you said—"

"Never mind, Pooh," said Piglet impatiently. "The question is, what are we to do about Kanga?"

"Oh, I see," said Pooh.

"The best way," said Rabbit, "would be this. The best way would be to steal Baby Roo and hide him, and then when Kanga says 'Where's Baby Roo?' we say, 'Aha!'"

These extracts from the seventh chapter include the passage which shows that Kanga and Roo were originally father and son. Milne first wrote: 'An animal who carries his child about with him in his pocket . . . ' In the first edition of the book, evidence of Kanga's masculinity survives. Milne forgot to correct the last line of this page. In later editions, it reads: 'Kanga spent the day with her great friend Pooh.'

So Kanga and Roo stayed in the Forest. And every Tuesday Roo spent the day with his great friend Rabbit, and every Tuesday Kanga spent the day with his great friend Pooh, teaching

86   In old age, and after his son's death, Shepard claimed that the drawings of Christopher Robin had been based as much on Graham as on Milne's son. This early drawing of Graham (below left) and Milne's own 1924 photograph of Christopher Robin shows some resemblance between the two. Indeed, a drawing by Shepard, purporting to be of Christopher Robin, which sold for £3,300 at Sotheby's in 1987, could well have been of Graham.

Milne certainly showed Shepard this photograph of his son examining a captured butterfly; indeed he showed it to everyone. Sending it to Irene Vanbrugh, he wrote: 'I bore all the Garrick with it and it is, by general consent, *the* most perfect photograph ever taken. You might think I was become rather an expert with the camera but I have to confess, Madam, that these things are largely a matter of luck.' Milne had taken it on holiday at Poling in Sussex, the summer the boy was four. By the time *Winnie-the-Pooh* was published, he was six and a skilled climber of trees. His favourite place was a hollow walnut tree at Cotchford, now long since fallen. 'There was plenty of room for a "boy and his bear",' Christopher recalled.

Howard Coster's famous photograph of Milne, Christopher Robin and Winnie-the-Pooh was taken in 1926 and is in the National Portrait Gallery in London. The child wrote years afterwards: 'I quite liked being Christopher Robin and being famous.' It was only later, when he had grown out of his part, that he came to resent the books so fiercely.

J. V. Milne with Winnie-the-Pooh and his grandson. He wrote at this time: 'Alan's boy is quite unspoilt.'

Christopher Robin with Pooh, a relation of Piglet, and his nanny, Olive Rand (later Brockwell), who was very different from the 'Alice' of 'Buckingham Palace'.

88 Horses graze now in a field below the house, Cotchford Farm. The Milnes had a donkey called Jessica. 'No connection whatever with Eeyore,' Christopher wrote years later, 'except that she lived in a field a little like Eeyore's.' Christopher used to ride Jessica down the hill into Hartfield where 'It was a pennyworth of bull's-eyes for each of us.' This was in the shop that is now The Shop at Pooh Corner.

'Eeyore has a birthday' (right) appeared in the *Royal Magazine* in August 1926 and in the *New York Evening Post* on 9 October 1926. The book was published by Methuen on 14 October. When the story finally appeared, the mysterious 'baby donkey called Jack-and-Betty' had become 'a box of paints to paint things with'. In the book, the story looks much better, as it is allowed eighteen pages instead of being squashed, with double columns, into seven. Richard Adams has called Eeyore 'the first portrait in English literature of a type of neurotic we all know only too well'. Fortunately, as at the end of this story, Eeyore has moments of happiness which save him from being a caricature.

So he sang " Cottleston Pie."

# EEYORE HAS A BIRTH-DAY.

## By A. A. Milne.

### Illustrated by E. H. Shepard.

*There is no genius like the genius of A. A. Milne. These stories describe further adventures of Christopher Robin and his friend Winnie-the-Pooh, the most attractive bear in fiction. They are among the most charming Mr. Milne has written.*

EEYORE, the old grey donkey, stood by the side of the stream and looked at himself in the water.

"Pathetic," he said. "That's what it is. Pathetic."

He turned and walked slowly down the stream for twenty yards, splashed across it, and walked slowly back on the other side. Then he looked at himself in the water again.

"As I thought," he said. "No better from *this* side. But nobody minds. Nobody cares. Pathetic, that's what it is."

There was a crackling noise in the bracken behind him, and out came Pooh.

"Good morning, Eeyore," said Pooh.

"Good morning, Pooh Bear," said Eeyore gloomily. "If it *is* a good morning," he said. "Which I doubt," said he.

" You seem so sad, Eeyore." "Sad? Why should I be sad? It's my birthday."

Eeyore, the old grey donkey, stood by the side of the stream and looked at himself in the water. "Pathetic," he said. "That's what it is. Pathetic."

" Why, what's the matter ? "

" Nothing, Pooh Bear, nothing. We can't all, and some of us don't. That's all there is to it."

" Can't all *what ?* " said Pooh, rubbing his nose.

" Gaiety. Song-and-dance. Here we go round the mulberry bush."

" Oh ! " said Pooh. He thought for a long time, and then asked : " What mulberry bush is that ? "

" Bon-hommy," went on Eeyore gloomily. " French word meaning bonhommy," he explained. " I'm not complaining, but There It Is."

Pooh sat down on a large stone and tried to think this out. It sounded to him like a riddle, and he was never much good at riddles, being a Bear of Very Little Brain. So he sang "Cottleston Pie" instead.

"Cottleston, Cottleston, Cottleston Pie,
  A fly can't bird, but a bird can fly.
Ask me a riddle and I reply :
'Cottleston, Cottleston, Cottleston Pie.'"

That was the first verse. When he had finished it Eeyore didn't say anything, so he sang the second verse :

Outside his house he found Piglet, jumping up and down trying to reach the knocker. "Hullo, Piglet!" he said. "Hullo, Pooh!" said Piglet.

"Cottleston, Cottleston, Cottleston Pie,
  A fish can't whistle and neither can I.
Ask me a riddle and I reply :
'Cottleston, Cottleston, Cottleston Pie.'"

Eeyore still said nothing at all, so Pooh hummed the third verse quietly to himself :

"Cottleston, Cottleston, Cottleston Pie,
  Why does a chicken? I don't know why.
Ask me a riddle and I reply :
'Cottleston, Cottleston, Cottleston Pie.'"

"That's right," said Eeyore. "Sing. Umty-tiddly, umty-too. Here we go gathering nuts and may. Enjoy yourself."

"I am," said Pooh.

"Some can," said Eeyore.

"Why, what's the matter?"

"*Is* anything the matter?"

"You seem so sad, Eeyore."

"Sad? Why should I be sad? It's my birthday."

"Your birthday?" said Pooh in great surprise.

"Of course it is. Can't you see? Look at all the presents I have had." He waved a foot from side to side. "Look at the birthday cake. Candles and pink sugar."

Pooh looked—first to the right and then to the left.

"Presents?" said Pooh. "Birthday cake?" said Pooh. "*Where?*"

"Can't you see them?"

"No," said Pooh.

"Neither can I," said Eeyore. "Joke," he explained. "Ha-ha!"

Pooh scratched his head, being a little puzzled by all this.

"But is it really your birthday?" he asked.

"It is."

"Oh! Well, many happy returns of the day, Eeyore."

"Same to you, Pooh Bear."

"But it isn't *my* birthday."

"No, it's mine."

"But you said 'many happy returns—'"

"Well, why not? You don't always want to be miserable on my birthday, do you?"

"Oh, I see!" said Pooh.

"It's bad enough," said Eeyore, almost breaking down, "being miserable myself, what with no presents and no cake and no candles, and no proper notice taken of me at all, but if everybody else is going to be miserable too——"

This was too much for Pooh. "Stay there!" he called to Eeyore, as he turned and hurried back home as quick as he could ;

for he felt that he must get poor Eeyore a present of *some* sort at once, and he could always think of a proper one afterwards.

Outside his house he found Piglet, jumping up and down trying to reach the knocker.

"Hullo, Piglet!" he said.

"Hullo, Pooh!" said Piglet.

"What are *you* trying to do?"

"Many a bear—

"I was trying to reach the knocker," said Piglet. "I just came round——"

"Let me do it for you," said Pooh kindly. So he reached up and knocked at the door. "I have just seen Eeyore," he began, "and poor Eeyore is in a Very Sad Condition because it's his birthday, and nobody has taken any notice of it, and he's very Gloomy—you know what Eeyore is—and there he was, and—— What a long time whoever lives here is, answering this door!" And he knocked again.

"But, Pooh," said Piglet, "it's your own house!"

"Oh!" said Pooh. "So it is," he said. "Well, let's go in."

So in they went. The first thing Pooh did was to go to the cupboard to see if he had quite a small jar of honey left, and he had, so he took it down. "I'm giving this to Eeyore," he explained, "as a present. What are *you* going to give?"

"Couldn't I give it, too?" said Piglet. "From both of us?"

"No," said Pooh. "That would *not* be a good plan."

"All right, then, I'll give him a balloon. I've got one left from my party. I'll go and get it now, shall I?"

"That, Piglet, is a *very* good idea. It is just what Eeyore wants to cheer him up. Nobody can be uncheered with a balloon."

So off Piglet trotted; and in the other direction went Pooh, with his jar of honey.

It was a warm day, and he had a long way to go. He hadn't gone more than half-way when a sort of funny feeling began to creep all over him. It began at the tip of his nose, and trickled all through him, and out at the soles of his feet. It was just as if somebody inside him was saying: "Now then, Pooh, time for a little something."

"Dear, dear," said Pooh, "I didn't know it was as late as that." So he sat down and took the top off his jar of honey. "Lucky

—going out on a warm day—

I brought this with me," he thought. "Many a bear going out on a warm day like this would never have thought of bringing a little something with him." And he began to eat.

"Now let me see," he thought, as he took his last lick of the inside of the jar, "where was I going? Ah, yes, Eeyore." He got up slowly.

And then, suddenly, he remembered. He had eaten Eeyore's birthday present!

"Bother!" said Pooh. "What *shall* I do? I *must* give him *something*."

For a little while he couldn't think of anything. Then he thought: "Well, it's a very nice pot, even if there's no honey in it, and if I washed it clean, and got somebody to write 'A Happy Birthday' on it, Eeyore could keep things in it, which might be useful." So, as he was just passing the Hundred Acre Wood, he went inside to call on Owl, who lived there.

"Good morning, Owl," he said.

"Good morning, Pooh," said Owl.

"Many happy returns of Eeyore's birthday," said Pooh.

"Oh, is that what it is?"

"What are you giving him, Owl?"

"What are *you* giving him, Pooh?"

"I'm giving him a Useful Pot to Keep Things In, and I wanted to ask you——"

"Is this it?" said Owl, taking it out of Pooh's paw.

"Yes, and I wanted to ask you——"

"Somebody has been keeping honey in it," said Owl.

"You can keep *any-thing* in it," said Pooh earnestly. "It's Very Useful like that. And I wanted to ask you——"

"You ought to write 'A Happy Birthday' on it."

—like this would never have thought—

"That was what I wanted to ask you," said Pooh. "Because my spelling is Wobbly. It's good spelling but it Wobbles, and the letters get in the wrong places. Would *you* write 'A Happy Birthday' on it for me?"

"It's a nice pot," said Owl, looking at it all round. "Couldn't I give it too? From both of us?"

"No," said Pooh. "That

—of bringing a little something with him."

would *not* be a good plan. Now I'll just wash it first, and then you can write on it."

Well, he washed the pot out, and dried it, while Owl licked the end of his pencil, and wondered how to spell "birthday."

"Can you read, Pooh?" he asked a little anxiously. "There's a notice about knocking and ringing outside my door, which Christopher Robin wrote. Could you read it?"

"Christopher Robin told me what it said, and *then* I could."

"Well, I'll tell you what *this* says, and then you'll be able to."

So Owl wrote, and this is what he wrote:

HIPY PAPY BTHUTHDTH THUTHDA BTHUTHDY.

Pooh looked on admiringly.

"I'm just saying '*A Happy Birthday*,'" said Owl carelessly.

"It seems a long one," said Pooh, very much impressed by it.

"Well, *actually*, of course, I'm saying '*A Very Happy Birthday with love from Pooh*.' Naturally it takes a good deal of pencil to say a long thing like that."

"Oh, I see," said Pooh.

While all this was happening, Piglet had gone back to his own house to get Eeyore's balloon. He held it very tightly against himself, so that it shouldn't blow away, and he ran as fast as he could so as to get to Eeyore before Pooh did; for he thought that he would like to be the first one to give a present, just as if he had thought of it without being told by anybody. And running along, and thinking how pleased Eeyore would be, he didn't look where he was going—and suddenly he put his

foot in a rabbit hole, and fell down flat on his face.

BANG!!!!??? ***!!!

Piglet lay there, wondering what had happened. At first he thought that the whole world had blown up; and then he thought that perhaps only the Forest part of it had; and then he thought that perhaps only *he* had, and he was now along in the moon or somewhere, and would never see Christopher Robin or Pooh or Eeyore again. And then he thought: "Well, even if I'm in the moon, I needn't be face downwards all the time," so he got cautiously up and looked about him.

He was still in the Forest!

"Well, that's funny," he thought. "I wonder what that bang was. I couldn't have made such a noise just falling down. And where's my balloon? And what's that small piece of damp rag doing?"

It was the balloon.

"Oh dear!" said Piglet. "Oh dear, oh dearier, dearie, dear! Well, it's too late now. I can't go back, and I haven't another balloon, and perhaps Eeyore won't mind so *very* much."

So he trotted on, rather sadly now, and down he came to the side of the stream where Eeyore was, and called out to him.

"Good morning, Eeyore," shouted Piglet.

"Good morning, Little Piglet," said Eeyore. "If it *is* a good morning," he said. "Which I doubt," said he. "Not that it matters," he said.

"Many happy returns of the day," said Piglet, having now got closer.

Eeyore stopped looking at himself in the stream, and turned to stare at Piglet.

"Just say that again," he said.

"Many hap——"

"Wait a moment."

Balancing on three legs, he began to bring his fourth leg very cautiously up to his ear. "I did this yesterday," he explained, as he fell down for the third time. "It's

*Owl licked the end of his pencil and wondered how to spell "birthday."*

*Running along, and thinking how pleased Eeyore would be, he didn't look where he was going—*

*—and suddenly he put his foot in a rabbit hole, and fell down flat on his face. BANG!!!*

"I did this yesterday," he explained, as he fell down for the third time. "It's quite easy."

quite easy. It's so as I can hear better. There, that's done it! Now then, what were you saying?" He pushed his ear forward with his hoof.

"Many happy returns of the day," said Piglet again.

"Meaning me?"

"Of course, Eeyore."

"My birthday?"

"Yes."

"Me having a real birthday?"

"Yes, Eeyore, and I've brought you a present."

Eeyore took down his right hoof from his right ear, turned round, and with great difficulty put up his left hoof.

"I must have that in the other ear," he said. "Now then."

"A present," said Piglet very loudly.

"Meaning me again?"

"Yes."

"My birthday still?"

"Of course, Eeyore."

"Me going on having a real birthday?"

"Yes, Eeyore, and I brought you a balloon."

"*Balloon?*" said Eeyore. "You did say balloon? One of those big coloured things you blow up? Gaiety, song-and-dance, here we are and there we are?"

"Yes, but I'm afraid—I'm very sorry, Eeyore—but when I was running along to bring it you, I fell down."

"Dear, dear, how unlucky! You ran too fast, I expect. You didn't hurt yourself, Little Piglet?"

"No, but I—I—oh, Eeyore, I burst the balloon!"

There was a very long silence.

"My balloon?" said Eeyore at last.

Piglet nodded.

"My birthday balloon?"

"Yes, Eeyore," said Piglet, sniffing a little. "Here it is. With—with many happy returns of the day." And he gave Eeyore the small piece of damp rag.

"Is this it?" said Eeyore, a little surprised.

Piglet nodded.

"My present?"

Piglet nodded again.

"The balloon?"

"Yes."

"Thank you, Piglet," said Eeyore. "You don't mind my asking," he went on, "but what colour was this balloon, when it —when it *was* a balloon?"

"Red."

"I just wondered. Red," he murmured to himself. "My favourite colour. How big was it?"

"About as big as me."

"I just wondered. About as big as Piglet," he said to himself sadly. "My favourite size. Well, well."

Piglet felt very miserable, and didn't know what to say. He was still opening his mouth to begin something, and then deciding that it wasn't any good saying *that*, when he heard a shout from the other side of the river, and there was Pooh.

"Many happy returns of the day," called out Pooh, forgetting that he had said it already.

"Thank you, Pooh, I'm having them," said Eeyore gloomily.

"I've brought you a little present," said Pooh excitedly.

"I have had one," said Eeyore.

Pooh had now splashed across the stream to Eeyore, and Piglet was sitting a little way off, his head in his paws, snuffling to himself.

"It's a Useful Pot," said Pooh. "Here it is. And it's got 'A Very Happy Birthday with love from Pooh' written on it. That's what all that writing is. And it's for putting things in. There!"

When Eeyore saw the pot he became quite excited.

"Why!" he said. "I believe my balloon will just go into that pot!"

"Oh, no, Eeyore," said Pooh. "Balloons are much too big to go into Pots. What you do with a balloon is, you hold the balloon——"

"Not mine," said Eeyore proudly. "Look, Piglet!" And as Piglet looked sorrowfully round, Eeyore picked the balloon up with his teeth and placed it carefully in the pot; picked it out and put

"My birthday balloon?" "Yes, Eeyore," said Piglet, sniffing a little. "Here it is" ... And he gave Eeyore the small piece of damp rag.

# Eeyore Has A Birthday.

it on the ground; and then picked it up again and put it carefully back.

"So it does!" said Pooh. "It goes in!"

"So it does!" said Piglet. "And it comes out!"

"Doesn't it?" said Eeyore. "It goes in and out like anything."

"I'm very glad," said Pooh happily, "that I thought of giving you a Useful Pot to put things in."

"I'm very glad," said Piglet happily, "that I thought of giving you something to put in a Useful Pot."

But Eeyore wasn't listening. He was taking the balloon out and putting it back again as happy as could be——

"And didn't *I* give him anything?" asked Christopher Robin sadly.

"Of course you did," I said. "You gave him—don't you remember—a little—a little——"

"I gave him a little baby donkey called Jack-and-Betty."

"That was it."

"Why didn't I give it to him in the morning?"

"You were so busy getting his party ready for him. He had a cake with icing on the top, and three candles, and his name in pink sugar, and——"

"Yes, *I* remember," said Christopher Robin.

*Next month:* "*The Heffalump.*"

But Eeyore wasn't listening. He was taking the balloon out and putting it back again as happy as could be.

# THE CHILDREN'S POETS

## AN INTERVIEW WITH A. A. MILNE

#### THE AUTHOR OF "WHEN WE WERE VERY YOUNG" INTERVIEWED BY ENID BLYTON.

I WENT yesterday to see Mr. Milne of "When We Were Very Young" fame. As I turned into the pretty Chelsea street and came up to his blue front door, I couldn't help thinking he lived in just the right house and just the right street. It's rather a nursery-rhyme sort of street, with latticed windows, coloured doors, and little stiff trees standing about in pots—just the sort of street you would expect the writer of "The King's Breakfast" to live in. And certainly the right street for Christopher Robin!

I sat in a little, long, book-lined room waiting for Mr. Milne. Near by was his writing-desk, and I wondered how many poems had been written there. French windows opened on to the tiniest of tiny gardens. It was paved and set with pots of fuchsias here and there, while creeper hung crimsoning down the steep wall at the back.

### Mr. A. A. Milne.

Then the door opened, and in came A. A. Milne. What is he like, this writer of exquisite child-poems and light-hearted lyrics?

Well, he is just like you would expect him to be. Tall, good-looking, with friendly eyes and a whimsical mouth that often smiles. He is natural and unaffected, and is diffident to an astonishing degree, considering how suddenly and generously fame has come to him.

We began talking about "When We Were Very Young."

"Of course, 'Christopher Robin' is *real*," I said.

"Oh, of course," he answered. "He's six years old. You'll see him in a minute. He's somewhere about."

"Is his name really Christopher Robin?" I said.

"Yes, but we always call him Billy Moon," said Mr. Milne.

"He called himself Moon when he couldn't say Milne, and always refers to himself as Moon!!"

### Christopher Robin.

At that moment in came Mrs. Milne, the poet's charming wife, and Christopher Robin. The latter just like the pictures by Ernest Shepard, except that he has much more hair. He stared at me fiercely and blew tremendously hard, as if he were very much out of breath. He had paper tied all round his legs, and I inquired why.

"So's dragons won't bite me," was the answer, delivered with much panting and snorting.

As he seemed to have turned into a dragon himself I felt a little uncomfortable about my own legs, but mercifully he seemed to have no designs upon them. He carried an enormous Teddy Bear, which he informed me was Pooh. He stood there in his little brown overall, with his great shock of corn-coloured hair, and looked about the room seeking for what he might devour. His bright eyes fell upon his father's fountain-pen, and he immediately took it up and pulled it into as many pieces as possible.

CHRISTOPHER ROBIN.

Photo: Sasha.

Mr. A. A. Milne's little boy, for whom the poems in "When We Were Very Young" were written. He himself is the hero of many of them.

I saw a photo of him dressed in a suit of armour. He has the face of a little knight about to perform his vigil, and then ride forth, sturdy and independent, to rescue fair ladies and fight fearsome dragons.

"He doesn't go to school yet, of course," I said, wondering who would be his teacher.

"Oh, yes," said his father. "He can read and write and do sums—can't you, Billy?"

### Christopher Robin's Problems.

"Billy" said he could, and intimated that he preferred sums. I looked at some of his writing and drawings, and thought if his sums were as good as those, then his father was certainly not the only one in the family with brains!

"He likes problems," said Mr. Milne. "Here's one. There are 500 cows in a field. They go out of a gate at the rate of two a minute. How many are left after two and a-half hours?"

Christopher Robin finds no difficulty with problems of this sort. Nor with the ticklish one about sardines.

"If there are 27 sardines in a tin, how many are laid one way, and how many the other?"

I shall examine my sardines carefully next time, and see. This is the sort of thing that only a Christopher Robin could say off hand!

### Favourite Poems.

I asked Mr. Milne what poem he liked best in "When We Were Very Young."

"I like 'Puppy and I,'" he said.

*"I met a Puppy as I went walking*
*We got talking*
*Puppy and I . . ."*

Mrs. Milne likes Market Square.

*"I had a penny,*
*A bright new penny,*
*I took my penny*
*To the Market Square . . ."*

This interview with A. A. Milne by Enid Blyton (reproduced from an old photocopy as no original could be found) appeared in the *Teacher's World* just before the publication of *Winnie-the-Pooh*. Enid Blyton was then not yet thirty but had already published a dozen books. She had been a teacher herself before her marriage and was a regular contributor to *Teacher's World*. Thirty years or so later, Christopher Milne decided not to stock her books in his Dartmouth bookshop.

She also loves (of course) Vespers, which belongs to her entirely :—

*" Little Boy kneels at the foot of the bed,*

*Droops on the little hands little gold head,*

*Hush! Hush! Whisper who dares!*

*Christopher Robin is saying his prayers."*

Christopher Robin himself, apparently, has no favourites. He likes them all.

### All Sorts of Animals.

Mr. Milne, as anyone who has read his poems will guess, loves children and animals. At his country house ne and Christopher Robin own a donkey, called Jessica, a fox-terrier, a cat called Tattoo, and a three-months old kitten, as well as a pair of kittens three weeks old. Pinkle, the oldest kitten, introduced herself to me—a soft, slinky wee mite. We found her doing her best to put Christopher Robin's sandals on. She had already got her front paws neatly into one.

As Mr. Milne's father was a school teacher, he has a certain interest in the teaching profession. He enjoyed his own schools days at Westminster, and is quite certain his small son so far enjoys his. He spoke with admiration of all teachers, particularly those who spend their days struggling in the poorer districts with terribly large classes. We agreed that they were doing a wonderful work against heavy odds.

### Fame.

As I sat and looked at the author opposite me, smoking his pipe and talking of everything under the sun, it seemed impossible to think that he was a celebrity. There was nothing in his manner to show it—no condescension, not the slightest touch of conceit. I wondered if he liked being famous.

"*Do* you like it?" I asked.

He laughed. "Well, if I *am* famous, then yes, I do like it," he said. "It's all rather thrilling, you know. I suppose it has its boring side occasionally, but so far I like it very much."

It is nice to find someone young enough and natural enough to own that fame is thrilling. It is so damping to find that the great ones are bored with their greatness. They don't deserve their greatness then !

### More A. A. Milne Books.

We shall soon have another book from Mr. Milne. I saw an early copy.

THE CHILDREN'S POETS.

THE aim of this number of " The Teachers World" is to give, in such a form that teachers may use it with children of any age, information about the lives and poetry of popular writers for children.

As a rule the notes deal only with the poetical works of authors who write both prose and poetry, and with such incidents in their lives as may be expected to interest children or to throw some light on the characters of the poets.

As far as possible the articles are written in simple language so that, if desired, they may be read directly to or by the pupils.

It is called by the most exciting title of " Winnie the Pooh," and is the story of the extraordinary adventures of some of the toys in Christopher Robin's nursery. So imperative was it that the toys in the book should be EXACTLY the same as the toys in the nursery that Mr. Shepard, the well-known artist, came to the house especially to draw the very same toys. There they are in the book, just exactly the same—Winnie the Pooh (Christopher Robin's bear), Piglet, Kanga Roo and Little Roo, and a most disconsolate-looking donkey.

### Winnie the Pooh.

"How did you think of ' Winnie the Pooh ' for a title?" I asked, curiously.

"Well, one day we took Christopher Robin to the Zoo," explained Mr. Milne. "And there we went to see a little tame brown bear called Winnie. The keeper unlocked the gate, and we saw the bear inside. Christopher Robin immediately shrieked out, "Oh

Bear ! " and flew to him and hugged him. The bear hugged Christopher Robin, and they had a glorious time together, rolling about and pulling ears and all sorts of things."

"When this new book about the toy bear wanted a title, I thought I would call it Winnie the Pooh-- because that's what Christopher Robin called the Zoo bear."

"I suppose Christopher Robin loves Pooh very much, doesn't he?" I asked.

"Yes, rather," said Mr. Milne. "They hold long conversations together. Pooh calls him Moon. He sits by Christopher Robin's bed all night and guards his handkerchief."

Well, with a boy and a bear like that it is no wonder Mr. Milne writes such attractive poetry, is it?

Soon fourteen more songs called *Teddy Bear and Other Songs* will be out, so that lovers of his work will have a great time

### Christopher Robin and the Dragon.

I must just tell one more anecdote of Christopher Robin. I make no apology for putting him in here so much, for without him we should have had no " When We Were Very Young " poems from Mr. Milne.

It happened that Christopher Robin had been hearing the story of Saint George and the Dragon. Full of inspiration, he rushed upstairs to draw such warlike beings.

Having delivered himself of a masterpiece, he spread it open on the table for his parents to see when they came up, and sat down to his dinner.

As he was finishing, his father and mother came up. They looked at the picture laid out for their admiration. They were not altogether certain which was the dragon and which was the horse.

"That's the dragon," whispered Mr. Milne.

"No, surely not. That's it—can't you see?" said his wife.

"No, *surely* this is the dragon," persisted Mr. Milne.

Christopher Robin regarded them from the end of the table. Then he bent his head to say his grace.

"Thank God for my good dinner," said he, "and *please* let those people understand about the dragon !"

His heartfelt prayer might be echoed by many an artist or poet : " *Please* let those people understand ! "

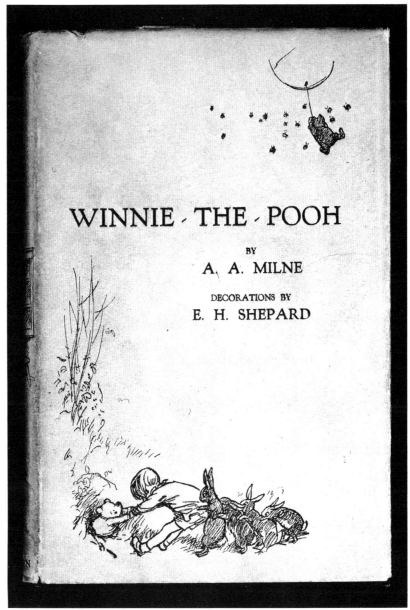

*A. A. Milne: Winnie-the-Pooh, London 1926, original cloth in dustjacket, first edition, inscribed by Milne to Sir James M. Barrie. Estimate: $4,000 to $6,000.*

## Books and Manuscripts from the Estate of John F. Fleming

### Friday 18 November

Enquiries: Stephen Massey or Christopher Coover

A first edition of *Winnie-the-Pooh* inscribed to J. M. Barrie on the London publication (14 October 1926) was sold for $13,200 at Christie's of New York on 18 November 1988. The estimate had been for $4,000 to $6,000. An even higher price was reached at the same sale for a copy of *When We Were Very Young*, inscribed to Milne's nephew Jock with a 'playfully written' letter on the endpapers (see page 169). It was a present for Christmas 1924 and in 1988 sold for $15,400.

Such was the publishers' confidence after the extraordinary success of the first book that the printing in 1926 was seven times the size: 35,000 copies were immediately on sale in England. 150,000 copies were sold in the United States before the end of the year.

The reactions to the first appearances in newspapers and magazines on both sides of the Atlantic, and the initial orders for *Winnie-the-Pooh*, had prepared Milne for the fact that he was about to repeat the success of *When We Were Very Young* – but the reviewers could hardly believe it. The *New York Herald Tribune* said, 'As you read the conviction grows on you that Mr Milne has done it again. There are not so very many books that, sitting reading all alone, you find yourself laughing aloud over. This is one of them. Here is nonsense in the best tradition . . . with the high seriousness about it that children and other wise people love.'

*Vogue* thought it was 'not quite as nice as *When We Were Very Young*, but still it has tremendous charm and is great fun to read aloud.' A St Louis paper also couldn't convince itself that the new book was quite as clever as the first one. But the great majority of the reviewers raved about it. 'Almost never has there been so much funniness in a book.' 'Mr Milne has repeated the rare coup. Once more he has written the perfect book for children.' 'It is even better than *When We Were Very Young*, which is saying much,' said the *Saturday Review*, and a week later May Lamberton Becker wrote in the same place: 'When the real Christopher Robin is a little old man, the same children will find him waiting for them. It is the child's book of the season that seems certain to stay.'

In January 1927 Milne commented: 'In America, by the way, they seem at least twice as keen as they were on WWWVY' – so it seemed, though sales of the poems would keep slightly ahead of *Pooh* for many years. That was also true in England, where the reviews were similarly enthusiastic. 'Another book full of delights for all children under seventy,' the *Nation* said rather strangely. (Why exclude all those over seventy?) In spite of the fact 'that it has not the advantage of demanding that it be learned by heart', it is likely 'to gain quite as many firm and unshakable admirers'. Milne would soon report that Christopher Robin himself 'knows *Winnie-the-Pooh* absolutely by heart', and there would be many like him.

100 *Now We Are Six* (published on
13 October 1927 in both
England and America) was
dedicated to Anne Darlington,
the girl – then seven – to whom
Milne was always devoted.
This is his personal inscription.
Milne's introduction neatly
excuses the varying age-levels
of the poems: 'We have been
nearly three years writing this
book. We began it when we
were very young . . . and now
we are six.'

## NOW WE ARE SIX

Anne and Christopher went to
school together in Tite Street,
Chelsea, and Anne often spent
the weekend at Cotchford too.
The photos of the two children
were taken in both London and
Sussex. The Shepard drawings
illustrate Milne's poem in *Now
We Are Six* called 'The Morning
Walk'. Pooh makes a third.
Long afterwards, Anne's
father, W. A. Darlington,
described the children as
'devoted and almost
inseparable – Anne with a
slight touch about her of the
elder sister'.

Sketch for the End (not used)
for Now We Are Six

The drawing of Christopher Robin, Pooh and Piglet in the hollow tree was apparently suggested as an end-piece for *Now We Are Six* but was never used, perhaps because the boy looks so inactive and wimpish. By now (1927) he was much more like the boy in this illustration from *The House at Pooh Corner*. Just after Christopher's seventh birthday that August, Milne wrote: 'He is mad on tree-climbing, which he really does rather well and pluckily, even after doing the last eight feet (downwards) on his head the other day!'

Milne published a number of children's poems in the period between *When We Were Very Young* and *Winnie-the-Pooh*. One of the earliest (along with 'Busy' and 'The Little Black Hen', which also appeared in 1925) was 'Binker', which made its first appearance as 'Dinkie' in Pears'

PEARS' ANNUAL, 1925

DINKIE   BINKER

*Dinker*

*Binker*

D INKIE—what I call him—is a secret of my own,
And Dinkie is the reason why I never feel alone:
Playing in the nursery, sitting on the stair,
Whatever I am busy at, Dinkie will be there.

Oh, Daddy is clever, he's a clever sort of man,
And Mummy is the best since the world began,
And Nanny is my Nanny, and I call her Nan—
But they can't
See
Dinkie.

*Binker*   Dinkie's always talking, 'cos I'm teaching him to speak :
He sometimes likes to do it in a funny sort of squeak,
And he sometimes likes to do it in a hoodling sort of roar . . .
And I have to do it for him 'cos his throat is rather sore.

*Binker*   Dinkie's brave as lions when we're running in the park;
Dinkie's brave as tigers when we're lying in the dark;
Dinkie's brave as elephants.   He never, never cries . . .
Except (like other people) when the soap gets in his eyes.

Oh, Daddy is clever, he's a clever sort of man,
And Mummy knows all that anybody can,
And Nanny is my Nanny, and I call her Nan—
But they don't
Know
*Dinker*   Dinkie.

This is The poem written by A. A. Milne in 1925 and
Published in "Pear's Annual: The alterations are in Milne's
hand-writing before the Poem was published in "Now we are six"   E. H. Shepard

Annual for 1925. This version (at the Victoria and Albert Museum) was made by Milne himself   103
correcting the Pears' text for publication in *Now We Are Six*. In the book, the child is not a girl
but Christopher Robin.

PEARS' ANNUAL, 1925

63

*Binker*

~~Dinkie~~ isn't greedy, but he does like things to eat,
So I have to say to people when they're giving me a sweet,
"Oh, ~~Dinkie~~ wants a chocolate, so could you give me two?"
And then I eat it for him, 'cos his teeth are rather new.

Well, I'm very fond of Daddy, but he hasn't time to play,
And I'm very fond of Mummy, but she sometimes goes away,
And I'm often cross with Nanny when she wants to brush my hair. . . .
But ~~Dinkie~~'s always ~~Dinkie~~, and is certain to be there.

Oh, Daddy is Daddy, he's a Daddy sort of Man,
And Mummy is as Mummy as anybody can,
And Nanny is ~~my~~ Nanny, and I call her Nan. . . .
But they're not
Like
~~Dinkie.~~

A. A. ~~MILNE.~~

Pooh made a good many appearances in *Now We Are Six*: Shepard and Milne both knew everyone would be looking for him after the enormous success of *Winnie-the-Pooh* the year before. In a whimsical postscript to the Introduction, Milne wrote: 'Pooh wants to say that he thought it was a different book; and he hopes you won't mind, but he walked through it one day, looking for his friend Piglet, and sat down on some of the pages by mistake.' 'Whimsical' was a word Milne came to loathe, but it is difficult not to use it of this sort of thing. It was after *Now We Are Six* that Dorothy Parker first pounced.

As well as the appearances in 'Morning Walk' and the major role in 'Us Two', there are glimpses of Pooh in 'Busy' and 'The Charcoal Burner' and, along with Eeyore, Piglet and Kanga, in 'The Engineer'. He is in 'Furry Bear', 'Knight-in-Armour', 'In the Dark' and 'Forgotten'. Several pictures of him in the *Royal Magazine* were dropped when the poems were published in the book.

Here we have unfamiliar appearances from 'The Friend' and 'Waiting at the Window'.

Dutton produced a new series of covers in 1961.

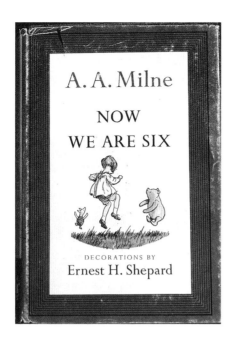

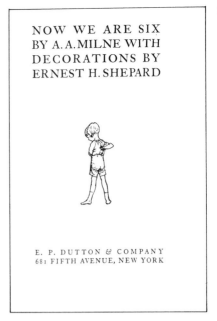

NOW WE ARE SIX
BY A. A. MILNE WITH
DECORATIONS BY
ERNEST H. SHEPARD

E. P. DUTTON & COMPANY
681 FIFTH AVENUE, NEW YORK

Dorothy Parker's review in the *New Yorker*, under her regular pseudonym, appeared on 12 November 1927. Milne himself wrote: 'If I were a critic I should loathe A. A. Milne. How could one help wanting to say that he was falling off, or taking success too easily or whatnot?' By Christmas *Now We Are Six* had sold 94,000 in England alone, overtaking *Winnie-the-Pooh*.

While we are on the subject of whimsies, how about taking up Mr A. A. Milne? There is a strong feeling, I know, that to speak against Mr Milne puts one immediately in the ranks of those who set fire to orphanages, strike crippled newsboys, and lure little curly-heads off into corners to explain to them that Santa Claus is only Daddy making a fool of himself. But I too have a very strong feeling about the Whimsicality of Milne. I'm feeling it right this minute. It's in my stomach.

Time was when A. A. Milne was my only hero. Weekly I pounced on *Punch* for the bits signed 'A. A. M.' I kept 'Once a Week' and 'Half Hours' [she means 'Happy Days' presumably] practically under my pillow. I read 'The Red House Mystery' threadbare. I thought 'The Truth About Blayds' a fine and merciless and honest play. But when Mr Milne went quaint, all was over. Now he leads his life and I lead mine.

'Now We Are Six', the successor to 'When We Were Very Young', is Mr Milne gone completely Winnie-the-Pooh. Not since Fay Bainter played 'East is West' have I seen such sedulous cuteness. I give you, for example, the postscript to the preface: 'Pooh wants us to say that he thought it was a different book; and he hopes you won't mind, but he walked through it one day, looking for his friend Piglet, and sat down on some of the pages by mistake.' That one sentence may well make Christopher Morley stamp on his pen in despair. A. A. Milne still remains the Master.

Of Milne's recent verse, I speak in a minority amounting to solitude. I think it is affected, commonplace, bad. I did so, too, say bad. And now I must stop, to get ready for being ridden out of town on a rail.

CONSTANT READER

106 This essay on A. A. Milne appeared in a book of cartoons called *Lions and Lambs* by Low, with interpretations by Lynx. Lynx turned out to be Rebecca West. On 6 October 1928 Milne reviewed the book in the *Nation*, not knowing this, and showed clearly where he stood, with Low and Lynx 'on the side of the people against privilege'. He makes no comment on the description of his own plays, which cannot have been at all to his taste.

THE children of the past were a pitiful subject people. The tenderness of the mother for her child has always existed; but how little society supported her in her feeling, how often it encouraged her to condemn herself for weakness and insist the child should fit itself into adult society regardless of its own needs and give no trouble. The little princes of Versailles, left in the care of maids and valets, unvisited by their own kin even in sickness; the Wesley children taught by their mother in their very infancy to 'cry quietly'; the innumerable Victorian celebrities who in their reminiscences tell blithely of early hardships that were visited on them not because of poverty but because of the custom of the day, of having to break the ice in their water-jugs to wash in the morning, which forced them to eat coarse and unwholesome food, and submit to the tyrannies of carelessly chosen and unsupervised governesses and tutors. . . . These days do not show such an army of little martyrs. The child is no longer produced in over-large quantities. A mother does not look on her family of eight or nine as so many vultures that preyed on her strength till all was gone, a father does not look on them as so many charges on his estate that will make larger and larger demands as time goes on and cannot even be trusted not to increase in number. In most cases in the English upper-class or middle-class family of to-day the child has not merely been born, he has been invited. He has been asked on a day when it was convenient for his hosts to receive him, at a time when they could afford to entertain him; and they are so conscious of the bravery with which in accepting the invitation their guest has exposed himself to certain perils, that they are resolved to do everything they can to make it up to him. They prepare food for him that will give his body as tranquil an introduction to the digestive problem of life as possible; clothing is planned that if he wants to kick he may, but that neither the ruder airs nor heat shall vex him; and a nursery is made for him, a clear, kind room, not too bright for his eyes, not too dark for them, lacking

Wills's Cigarettes

Rebecca West

A. A. Milne

Low

in any hostile sharp corners, decorated with pictures that show happy visions of the world. There is also kindness as a matrix to the whole, or at least a sense of the duty of kindness towards children which guarantees the child a certain protection. Now that this new attitude of civility towards the child has persisted long enough for those who grew up as its object to be grown men one perceives curious effects in literature. In the old days children's books were written chiefly by women, partly because they are more actually in contact with children than men, and partly because the childishness men imposed on them made them more able to produce the type of imagination required. Children's books written by men were in the main stories which the adult told the child to win its admiration by representing the hero who did all manner of things that only the grown male can do. But now we have another kind of writer of children's books, of whom the most distinguished prototype is Mr. A. A. Milne, which thirsts for childhood as for a lost state of happiness. In his poems and stories that are avowedly for the young he is back in the nursery; his fancies of beasts and woodlands are but fantasies provoked by the nursery frieze. And when he turns to what is professedly his adult work he really does not move out of the nursery. What gives his plays their curious sense of eeriness which exists however matter-of-fact the content may be, and their unaccountably touching quality, is our feeling that somehow the limitations of age have been transcended and we are watching the British child, its fair hair beautifully brushed, its eyes clear, its skin rosy, well trained, sweet-natured, very truthful and knowing no fear at all save that there may perhaps be some form of existence which is not the nursery and will not be kind however good one is, looking at life.

# CHRISTOPHER ROBIN AT HOME.

## An Exclusive Interview With the Hero of "When We Were Very Young."

### By CLAUDE F. LUKE.

THE STREET is one to which married couples move when Greenery Street has frowned upon the bright new pram.

THE HOUSE would be the despair of soulful property agents who, though they might praise it with every cliché in their vocabulary, would yet miss the beauty of Mr. Milne's home. How to describe that sunny house in Chelsea ? To call it a rhapsody in azure and primrose is to risk a charge of flowery fancy; to write merely that its soft carpets are of a heavenly blue, a blue that is picked out in the banisters, cornices, and dadoes, while the walls and curtains give back the light in a flood of yellow, is to convey nothing of that pervading breath of morning, of morning in a very young world, that is a visitor's first impression.

### The nursery door opens.

THE BOY, of course, is Christopher Robin Milne. When, recently, my diary told me that I had to keep an appointment with a certain young gentleman of Chelsea, I knew it for an encounter fraught with many dangers. For my part, I decided firmly, there would be a complete absence of head-patting, and "my-little-manning" to which so many adults are detestably addicted when addressing young gentlemen of seven. It should be a plain, he-man-to-he-man talk with all the rules of the game strictly observed.

But when suddenly the nursery door slipped open and I found myself shaking the small hand, admiring the fair, silky head, and the large grave eyes that were plainly trying to decide whether I was one of the make-believe folk, or merely a tiresome grown-up, I felt myself beginning to weaken. Perhaps it was not so wholly incomprehensible after all, that habit among women of calling curly-haired little boys by endearing names. . . .

### The charm of a child.

You see, Robin, quite unconsciously, affects you like that, struggle against it as you may. He disturbs profoundly anyone who has firmly decided to keep things on a manly plane. I know, for instance, that after the first formalities, I should have been asking him if he liked Rugger, or wanted to be a soldier; I know equally well that no such idea came into my head; that indeed the thought that he would one day in all probability grow hefty calves with which to convert tries, or crop that fair mop because long hair "wasn't done," was not to be borne, so anxious are we poor grown-ups to conceal even from ourselves the tragic ephemerality of such splendid childhood.

And if critics urge that such is dangerous effeminacy, I can only plead that they have not seen that portion of Master Robin's neck where it has risen white and hairless from the light-brown jersey and just before it has drowned itself in the golden shower above.

By great good fortune, Robin accepted me after that preliminary inspection and granted me the Freedom of the Nursery. A delightful room it is, with its light walls and plain, unvarnished furniture; its gay cushions; and the scores of toys; the long shelf of books, and the original Shepherd sketches framed upon the walls; and all the dearly-loved toys that figure in the poems— Piglet (in an absurd green jacket and carrying an umbrella), Poglet, Winnie-the-Pooh, Kanga, and poor old Eeyore ! Robin showed me them all with grave pleasure. He told me how Piglet was not the "'riginal Piglet," which, alas, had been chewed by a dog,

**CHRISTOPHER ROBIN.**

and that poor Eeyore, who nodded so lugubriously, had really "nuthin' to be sad about" !

### The search for knowledge.

On books we talked with shared enthusiasm. He proudly showed me his own tidy shelf, whose contents were the choice of wiser hands. There were children's poems and stories, the Jungle Book, Andrew Lang's "The Blue Fairy Book," several of Howard Pyle's delightful historical romances (" The Story of King Arthur " and " Adventures of Robin Hood " were two I noticed), and a number of the Dr. Dolittle series. Of these Robin is very fond, and is eagerly awaiting the coming of the author, Hugh Lofting, who is making a " speshul visit " to the little boy. The shelf also contains a complete set of the Children's Encyclopædia, and after a moment's thought he gave the last-named as his favourite recreation. "Because," he added, "they tell me things. . . ."

Robin rarely asks any questions; he combs his encyclopædias first, and only when they have failed does he turn to " Blue "—his name for his father. Robin, incidentally, has several names.

" ' Blue ' calls me Moon," he said, shyly, and his nurse explained that this was how the little fellow had first pronounced Milne.

" Then close friends call me Billy Moon," he went on, " and at school I am Christopher Robin, or just Robin."

### To be an explorer.

In a copy of " Now We Are Six " on his shelf there is the following inscription in his father's neat and tiny characters :—

> For my Moon
> From his Blue
> Now I am 45.

On the wall, beside a coloured Spy sketch of his father, hangs a map of Africa, one of those pictorial maps that include the trees, animals, natives, and merchandise to be found in various parts of the country. This, together with a fine Indian feathered head-piece which hangs in a corner, has obviously excited Robin with thoughts of far-off things, for when, with mute apology in my eyes, I asked the inevitable what-was-he-going-to-be, Robin promptly replied :—

" Explorer, I think. But then I change so, you know. One day it's this and the next that. . . ." He frowned slightly as though this career business was an increasing source of worry.

Robin is full of quaint sophistries and delightful simplicities that one would expect from the poems. Whenever I asked him a particularly obvious question, such as " Do you like Blue's books ? " he would gaze at me for a moment, amazed at the immense foolishness of humans, and then turn to his nurse with the expressive remark : " Do I, Nanny ? " as though to say, " Throw out this absurd man ! "

### Poisons.

But when Nanny had gone downstairs to see about luncheon for Robin and Winnie-the-Pooh, the little boy beckoned to me conspiratorially and led me to a secret corner to reveal a row of bottles.

" They're my poisons ! " he whispered, in a voice that would have thrilled Edgar Wallace. I read the labels inscribed in childish scrawl. One was " Salerd dressing for lettus " ; another " Cind of frute salerd —it is good to drink " ; and a third " Loshun for the mouth." He opened one for me to smell.

" I can't face that one," he admitted, wryly, and confessed that it was composed of ipecacuanha wine, flour paste, and—ink ! We agreed it had a deadly odour.

Next he showed me specimens of his sewing and embroidery which Nanny had taught him. They were Easter presents for his friends, little cloth bags with ducks worked in colours; there were powder-puff bags, too, and little powder puffs made from short strands of wool poked through small buttons ! Although they were presents, people like Mummy and Blue would be expected to pay, he admitted.

### A busy day.

Robin's day is a busy one indeed. Up at seven-thirty, he breakfasts at eight; school lasts from nine till twelve and is followed by a walk before lunch; and afterwards away to Kensington Gardens with Nanny and eight-year-old Anne (the Anne Darlington to whom one of Blue's books is dedicated " because she is so speshul " !), where, on their fairy cycles, they race round and round the Albert Memorial. Home again to tea, then a joyous passage of much splashing and wild shouts in the bath-room, and finally at six o'clock there is the " Vespers " scene wherein a little boy, nightgowned and still, kneels beside the tiny bed . . .

" Hush ! Hush ! whisper who dares ! Christopher Robin is saying his prayers."

The last of the four great children's books, *The House At Pooh Corner*, is probably now the most loved and popular of all. It introduces Tigger and the game of Poohsticks, and the underlying theme – of the child growing up and away from his toys, putting away childish things – gives it a particular resonance.

This list of U.S. printings gives an idea of the extraordinary success of the book.

THE HOUSE AT POOH CORNER, COPYRIGHT, 1928, BY E. P. DUTTON & CO., INC. :: ALL RIGHTS RESERVED :: PRINTED IN U. S. A.

|  |  |
|---|---|
| First Printing | Sept., 1928 |
| Tenth Printing | Sept., 1928 |
| Twentieth Printing | Sept., 1928 |
| Thirtieth Printing | Sept., 1928 |
| Thirty-first Printing | Sept., 1928 |
| Thirty-second Printing | Sept., 1928 |
| Thirty-third Printing | Sept., 1928 |
| Thirty-fourth Printing | Sept., 1928 |
| Forty-fifth Printing | Oct., 1928 |
| Fifty-first Printing | Oct., 1928 |
| Fifty-eighth Printing | Jan., 1929 |
| Sixty-first Printing | Nov., 1932 |
| Sixty-fourth Printing | Aug., 1934 |
| New Edition | Aug., 1935 |
| Sixty-sixth Printing | Aug., 1935 |
| Seventy-first Printing | Aug., 1935 |
| Seventy-second Printing | Sept., 1935 |
| Seventy-eighth Printing | Sept., 1935 |
| Eighty-fifth Printing | Oct., 1935 |
| Ninety-second Printing | Nov., 1935 |
| Ninety-ninth Printing | Dec., 1935 |
| 106th Printing | June, 1938 |
| 113th Printing | July, 1939 |
| 120th Printing | Aug., 1940 |
| 127th Printing | July, 1941 |
| 128th Printing | April, 1942 |
| 129th Printing | March, 1943 |
| 130th Printing | June, 1943 |

For many years the poems remained even more popular than the Pooh stories. The British jacket gave the totals for the earlier books:

| | |
|---|---|
| *When We Were Very Young* | 179th thousand |
| *Winnie-the-Pooh* | 96th thousand |
| *Now We Are Six* | 109th thousand |

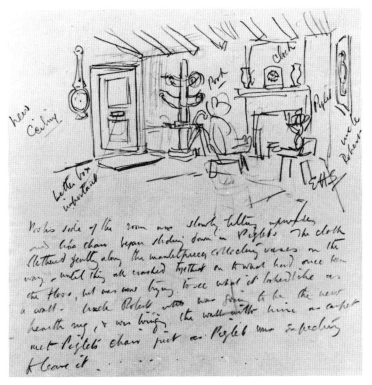

E. H. Shepard's preliminary sketch and notes for the drawing of the Wolery on that blusterous day (when Piglet did a very grand thing) shows the care he gave to getting things right. He needed to see the place as it was before the wind got to work.

110 In the autumn of 1928 (for six weeks from 1 October), *Home Chat* gave away, one each week with each twopenny issue of the magazine, coloured pictures of scenes from the Pooh books. These were Shepard's first colour illustrations for the books, and were apparently never used again.

Christopher Robin gives Extract of Malt all round.

Dorothy Parker as 'Constant Reader' had another go at Milne in the *New Yorker* on 20 October 1928, but otherwise the reviews were almost unanimously enthusiastic. Everyone else lamented the fact that this was the last book. The *Times Literary Supplement* congratulated Milne on resisting 'the temptation to repeat his successful formula mechanically', but said, 'It is sad to see the stories end.' Few realized, let alone Milne himself, that this was a beginning rather than an ending.

It 'seemed to him a Good Hum, such as is Hummed Hopefully to Others.' In fact, so Good a Hum did it seem that he and Piglet started right out through the snow to Hum It Hopefully to Eeyore. Oh, darn – there I've gone and given away the plot. Oh, I could bite my tongue out.

As they are trotting along against the flakes, Piglet begins to weaken a bit.

'"Pooh," he said at last and a little timidly, because he didn't want Pooh to think he was Giving In, "I was just wondering. How would it be if we went home now and *practised* your song, and then sang it to Eeyore to-morrow – or – the next day, when we happen to see him."

'"That's a very good idea, Piglet," said Pooh. "We'll practise it now as we go along. But it's no good going home to practise it, because it's a special Outdoor Song which Has To Be Sung In The Snow."

'"Are you sure?" asked Piglet anxiously.

'"Well, you'll see, Piglet, when you listen. Because this is how it begins. *The more it snows, tiddely-pom* – "

'"Tiddely what?" said Piglet.' (He took, as you might say, the very words out of your correspondent's mouth.)

'"Pom," said Pooh. "I put that in to make it more hummy."'

And it is that word 'hummy', my darlings, that marks the first place in *The House at Pooh Corner* at which Tonstant Weader fwowed up.

In 1939 in his autobiography, Milne allowed himself a brief reply to Dorothy Parker:

The books were written for children. When, for instance, Dorothy Parker, as 'Constant Reader' in the *New Yorker*, delights the sophisticated by announcing that at page 5 of *The House at Pooh Corner* 'Tonstant Weader fwowed up' (sic, if I may), she leaves the book, oddly enough, much where it was. However greatly indebted to Mrs Parker, no Alderney, at the approach of the milkmaid, thinks 'I hope this lot will turn out to be gin', no writer of children's books says gaily to his publisher, 'Don't bother about the children, Mrs Parker will love it.'

The game was originally Poobridge – a logical name as bridge is a game – but Milne crossed it out firmly and substituted Poosticks (sic). Poobridge is just visible in this extract from the manuscript at Trinity College, Cambridge.

Children still play Poohsticks at the bridge today.

If no one has actually put 'Poohsticks' as a recreation in *Who's Who*, it was certainly heard a few years ago on one of those *Miss World* or *Miss Great Britain* TV shows. 'And what is *your* hobby?' 'Playing Poohsticks,' she said. The terrible part of this story is that the competitor defined the game like this, 'You dress up as Paddington Bear and throw sticks in a river.' The interviewer amazingly did not flinch, but thousands, even millions, of viewers did.

The banks under the bridge have now been faced with breeze blocks, because of the erosion caused by fans. Shepard's later views of the bridge show a brick arch, which was never actually there.

THE END OF THE
STORY: Christopher
Robin and Pooh come to
an enchanted place on the
very top of the Forest
called Galleons Lap.

This unused book jacket design illustrates how well designed Milne's two Pooh books were for
endless multiplication. The episodic nature of the books – each chapter is a complete story –
means that Milne had written not two Pooh books but twenty. Many children over the years
would meet Pooh suddenly – not gently introduced to him by Milne – but plunged *in medias res*
in books such as *Tiggers can't climb trees* or *Pooh invents a new game*.

Its real name is Gill's Lap but such
is Milne's influence that his name,
Galleons Lap, now appears on
some maps of the Forest. Whatever
Dorothy Parker might say, for
millions of readers 'a little boy and
his Bear will always be playing'.

# AN INTERVIEW WITH A. A. MILNE, CHRISTOPHER ROBIN AND POOH

### Not Neglecting Mrs. Milne, Kanga, Rabbit, Owl, the Gloomy Eeyore, Piglet and the Bouncing New Tigger.

#### By MAY LAMBERTON BECKER

A long nursery with walls the colour of sunshine; an eminent author crouched in the window-seat, clutching to his breast a fat yellow sofa-cushion; facing him at a convenient distance for attack, a little boy in boxing-gloves, his golden hair tossed back from the brightest and brownest eyes in London, his feet tapping back and forth in the proper professional preparations. This is how I saw Christopher Robin and A. A. Milne again, after two years.

That is, in his own language, I saw "Moon" and "Blue". "Billy Moon" has lately shortened his self-made name by two syllables. The real Christopher Robin still looks like Mr. Shepard's pictures; that is, in moments of comparative repose, as when completing a particularly good tea at the round table in the yellow nursery. But only a cinema, an earnest one up to its business, could deal with Christopher Robin's boxing. It is the real thing and no mistake. Besides his school, he now goes to a famous gymnasium—oh yes, he's still a little boy, but when you say he is, you should stress the second word instead of the first.

As I watched the pillow take punishment, a small, gruff voice—the voice Pooh uses when Mrs. Milne is in the room—cried "Here! hold me up! I mustn't miss this!" and a brown bear came tumbling over my shoulder down into my lap. I had him right-side up directly; I kept my cheek on his good comfortable head for the rest of the bout. I was thinking of the American children whose eyes would shine when I told them. "It was just this way that I held Pooh in my arms so he could watch Christopher Robin boxing."

Pooh came into the Milne family when he was just the size of Christopher Robin, and he still thinks he is. At least, he did a year ago, but I have a notion that he is beginning to have his doubts. Of course, this may be because someone has put back his eye—it was out for ever so long, giving him a rakish and knowing look—and the resultant expression is of a most moving candour, slightly puzzled. But whatever this growing-up business may be, if Christopher Robin does it, it will be quite all right with Pooh. He has grown used to waiting for Christopher Robin to come home from school, sitting with all the animals on the pillow of the little bed in the night nursery, keeping watch. There was a noble company on guard when last I saw them; Kanga and baby Roo—Kanga has a new white-flannel front and looks too tidy for words—the gloomy Eeyore, Piglet with a pocket-handkerchief in his velvet jacket, the bouncing new Tigger. They were all together on the pillow, waiting for Christopher Robin, and Pooh had his arms out, all ready. One was quite sure, looking at Pooh, that Christopher Robin would soon come home.

Pooh has been told that there will be no more books about him after this one that is just coming, "The House at Pooh Corner". I do not know if he has quite taken it in; ideas come rather slowly to Pooh, and he makes no special effort to assimilate unpleasant ideas. What! retire from literature, just when one has performed the unprecedented feat of changing the name of a household institution on the other side of the earth? for this is what happened when almost over night all the Teddy-bears of America became Pooh-bears in the vocabulary of childhood. What! no more books (after this new one) about the house in the hollow tree? no more verses about when we were very young, so young that we tried to buy a rabbit in the Market Square (there is a real rabbit in the new book)? It doesn't seem possible that there are to be no more. For from the time when, under the transparent disguise of "Mr. Edward Bear", Pooh appeared in "When we were very young", to the new volume in which he is still the kind thick-headed little brother of all the world's children, Pooh has been a person for whom to look forward from one season to another. But, it seems, there are to be positively no more Christopher Robin books. Mr. Milne says so, and he ought to know.

It isn't, however, as if Christopher Robin were to drop out of literature. He will be here, waiting for the children of a generation hence, young as he is now, and just as much their companion as he is now the friend of English-speaking children. I wish the bright bachelors who say that the Christopher Robin poems and stories are really for adults and a few exceptional children would try a few of them on just any child at all, and see. It was a little girl not unlike a great many American little girls who when told that she might take but two toys to beguile a long railway journey, tucked a little red book under her arm and said "Now I must choose something to go with Christopher Robin." She did not even say "to go with my book." It was one of the staff of Mr. Milne's American publishers who, when she had completed the advance work connected with the first volume of these stories and was seeking a spot where she would not so much as hear the name of any book, was waylaid on the threshold of her young niece and made to listen to every word of "Winnie-the-Pooh", read aloud in an ecstatic little voice. Oh well, it's not only children who read out this book. When it first appeared, I was living where the floors under mine were occupied by young women, very modern and brilliant; one was a concert pianist, one a painter, one a statistician, and each was engaged to a modern and brilliant young man. One evening as I came upstairs I passed through three layers of "Winnie-the-Pooh", being read aloud by the respective *fiancés*.

"The House at Pooh Corner", which brings the set to a close, closes it on a top note. Or, to say the same thing in another way, it sends the

May Lamberton Becker, an American journalist, visited Mallord Street for the third time in 1928. Her account was published by Dutton in their regular newsletter.

well-beloved creatures marching off into a child's world, safe from all such catastrophes as growing-up, secure from all such calamities as wearing-out. The house in the tree, the house with a bell-pull, ringed about with signs set up by the real Christopher Robin down in Sussex, will be on a firm foundation in that world along with the little house with a top-hat for a chimney, the house that Peter Pan builds anew every London Christmas for delighted children taken to the play. "Billy Moon" made the original "Pooh's House", and in a very real sense he has co-operated with A. A. Milne in the making of "The House at Pooh Corner". The result is that Christopher Robin is the first little child in English literature since Alice to come to children out of their own generation, not out of the memories of the generation before them. These two began without the handicap of being born middle-aged: that may help to explain their vitality. No child could have written the Pooh stories, for no child could put into words what gives them their distinctive charm and special value—the reminder, present in every tale, that the child, to the world so little and so weak, is to his toys tall and powerful. Whenever Christopher Robin comes on the scene all will go well, however, it *may* have been going without him; he is *deus ex machina*, protector, planner. Perhaps the peculiar comfort of toys to a child comes from this compensating sense of power and protectiveness. At any rate, it is a sense distinctly present in these tales, and in no others so distinctly, and no child could get this into words or would try to do so. But the evidence from which Mr. Milne derives the idea and demonstrates it came from Christopher Robin, a real little boy at once reserved and confiding, as little boys are.

This is one of the reasons why this sketch is more about Christopher Robin than about A. A. Milne, as it was supposed to be; another is that Mr. Milne says he told all there is to know about him to the maker of the last leaflet that went out from the house of Dutton in advance of the book-before-this, and doesn't see how he is to provide a brand-new biography for every book. He is tall, slender and sunburned, with blue eyes and a wide sudden smile; Mrs. Milne is tall, slender and brown-eyed; her eyes are indeed just like Christopher Robin's. They all three look very young, and when they look at one another, very happy. They live in a red house off a green square in Chelsea, a house with marvellous old glassware ranged in the windows, catching the light; every week they go in a large blue limousine to their farm in Sussex where stands the tree with the door-plate that marks it for Pooh's house. So far as the new book is concerned, that is all that need be set down here about its author. Everyone knows that he was at one time assistant editor of *Punch*; that he has written plays, all of them favorites with their audiences and half-a-dozen of them distinguished stage successes on both sides of the Atlantic, several volumes of essays, sketches and poems, and one of the best detective stories of our day, "The Red House Mystery". He turned this particular one of his talents to another use this season and produced, in "The Fourth Wall", a comedy truthfully advertised on the bus-boards as "the best murder in London".

This, in a season when no first act can be called complete without a corpse, is strong praise. This should do for a sketch of A. A. Milne; it is well, however, that he should appear through the eyes and pencil of Christopher Robin himself, who lately produced the portrait here reproduced. When "Billy Moon" was the size he is in the very first of Mr. Shepard's pictures he was making portraits of flowers that have kept me wondering ever since what he might do in this line. When I asked his father what he was now doing, he let me see this portrait of "Blue" made by "Moon", now he is past six.

Christopher Robin was peeling off his boxing-gloves. The pillow, much dejected, had taken the count and was now in its corner. I looked back from the doorway; it was two years since I last saw Christopher Robin, and three since the afternoon when, flat on the hearth-rug and with one eye level to the page, he wrote for me upon the fly-leaf of "Fourteen Songs" the first autograph he had produced for anyone outside the family circle. There he stood now, the late level sunshine lighting his hair; it is cut shorter than it was, but he is a little boy still, poised on the loveliest moment of childhood.

"No more Christopher Robin books!" said Mrs. Milne. "Look, Pooh's crying!"

And indeed the brown bear in her arms had his paws over his face.

But between them his candid eyes looked out confidently. Pooh knows that his place in literature is safe.

# BLUE MILNE, AUTHOR OF "THE HOUSE AT POOH CORNER", ETC.

As drawn by his famous son, Christopher Robin, who aspires to be an artist and who calls his father "Blue".

118

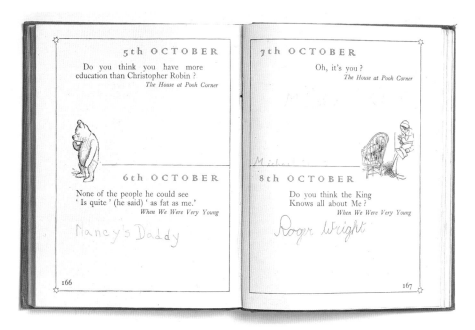

The first *Christopher Robin Birthday Book* was published on 13 November 1930. There have been many since. Milne began his introduction: 'As Eeyore says, "What are birthdays? Here today and gone tomorrow." So let us make a note of them while we can.'

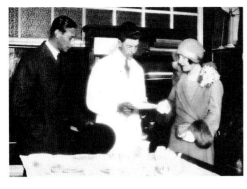

One hundred and two papers reported the visit of the Duke and Duchess of York to the Ashtead Pottery, when they were presented with a nursery teaset for Princess Elizabeth. The *Bradford Argus*, like most of the others, seemed to think all the characters came from *Winnie-the-Pooh* – though many of them are actually from the poems – and said the 'intriguing characters and animals were drawn with such rare skill by the father of "Christopher Robin".' Both Milne and Shepard gave their rights to the Pottery, which employed disabled ex-servicemen. The twenty-four pieces, hand-painted by Albert Robertson, went on general sale but are now extremely rare. Even the Bethnal Green Museum of Childhood does not possess any.

## BABY PRINCESS' NEW FRIENDS.

### CHARACTERS FROM "WINNIE-THE-POOH."

## FROM MAIMED MEN

Christopher Robin, Piglet, Pinkle Purr, and the rest of the quaint characters from Mr. A. A. Milne's book "Winnie-the-Pooh" are to be the meal-time companions of the little Princess Elizabeth

It all happened like this (writes a "Daily Chronicle" representative). Yesterday, when the Duke and Duchess of York visited the factory of the Ashtead Potters, Ltd., they saw a nursery set of plates, cups, and mugs, decorated with quotations and pictures from Mr. Milne's well-known book.

The set, the first of its kind manufactured, had been made by the disabled ex-servicemen who man the factory.

"Oh, these are charming," remarked the Duchess, picking up a piece of the china and calling the Duke's attention to it.

"Here's Kanga and Baby Roo," she exclaimed, "Why! they are all here!"

### CLUES TO A HUSBAND.

"We wish your Highness to accept the set for Princess Elizabeth," said Mr. A. Robertson, a disabled soldier, who had reproduced the quaint figures in colour.

"Baby will be delighted," said the Duchess, with a smile.

Sir Lawrence Weaver, the chairman of the pottery, pointed out to the Duchess a plate bearing a cheery tree in the centre and the figures of the "Tinker, tailor, soldier, sailor," nursery rhyme around the edge.

"Here is a game the Princess will be able to play when she is a little older," explained Sir Lawrence. "By placing her cheery stones in turn against the figures she will find the profession of her future husband."

The Duke and Duchess laughed. "Well, she will not be eligible for that game for a little while," remarked the Duke.

### THE ORIGINAL CHRISTOPHER.

Sir Lawrence told the Royal visitors that Mr. A. A. Milne and Mr. E. H. Shepard, the artist, had given the pottery the sole right of reproducing the Christopher Robin characters on domestic china.

A replica of the baby Princess's set is to be sent to Mr. Milne's little son —the original Christopher Robin.

Before leaving the Duke and Duchess made a complete round of the pottery, pausing to chat and shake hands with the workers. The Duchess fingered the clay and took a lively interest in the various processes.

### "IT IS DELIGHTFUL."

### DUCHESS AND POTTERY GIFT

When the Duke and Duchess of York yesterday visited the Ashtead (Surrey) Potteries, which are run for the benefit of ex-Servicemen, the Duchess was given, for Princess Elizabeth, a dainty nursery set, decorated with characters and quotations from A. A. Milne's nursery book, "Winnie the Pooh."

"I think it is delightful; the animals and characters are all here; there is nothing left out," said the Duchess when Sir Laurence Weaver, chairman of Ashtead Potters Ltd., handed the set to her.

The nineteen pieces in the set were hand-painted by Mr. A. Robertson, one of the ex-Servicemen potters. Before the war he was a printers' machinist, but, like most of the men employed at the potteries, he could not follow his pre-war employment owing to disability.

The Duke and Duchess spent several minutes before a potter's wheel and watched vases take shape. "I should like to work that myself," exclaimed the Duchess. It was explained to her that it takes two years to become expert with the wheel. The Duke, who was anxious to see how pottery was baked, even entered an oven which was still hot to see the process at work.

The Duchess ordered two morning tea sets and a baby's head modelled by Mr. Percy Metcalfe, the sculptor, the original being one of his twin children.

## ROYAL VISIT TO ASHTEAD POTTERIES.

### A TEA SET FOR PRINCESS ELIZABETH.

A nursery tea set was presented to the Duke and Duchess of York as a gift for Princess Elizabeth when the Duke and Duchess visited the factory of Ashtead Potters, Limited, at Ashtead, yesterday. This factory is used for training and employing disabled ex-Service men in the art of pottery.

After inspecting the factory the Duke and Duchess received from Sir Lawrence Weaver, chairman of Ashtead Potters, Limited, a "Christopher Robin" tea set decorated with the illustrations to Mr. A. A. Milne's verses. The Duchess congratulated Albert Robertson, the disabled ex-soldier who had decorated the set by hand. Princess Elizabeth's is the first set made at the factory. The second set will be sent to the original Christopher Robin, and sets will then be made at the factory for general sale.

The Duke and Duchess admired the pottery made by the disabled men, and the Duchess bought a morning tea set and a replica in porcelain of the Academy statuette of Helen Metcalfe, one of the twin daughters of Mr. Percy Metcalfe, the sculptor, who designs most of the shapes reproduced in pottery at the factory. The Duke and Duchess also visited the colony of 23 houses built by Ashtead Potters, Limited, to accommodate the potters.

120 Milne's essay which follows appeared in *By Way of Introduction*, published by Methuen in 1929.

# THE END OF A CHAPTER

I HAVE been asked by an Editor to explain how it comes about that he has printed the last Christopher Robin story. In these cases it is generally the Editor who offers an apologetic explanation to the author; and though I am proud that it is not so now, I feel a little diffident about putting what is really a personal matter before a probably uninterested public. However, one can't go on defying an Editor . . . so here goes.

To begin at the beginning: When Christopher Robin was born, he had to have a name. We had already decided to call him something else, and later on he decided to call himself something still else, so that the two names for which we were now looking were to be no more than an excuse for giving him two initials for use in later life. I had decided on two initials rather than one or none, because I wanted him to play cricket for England, like W. G. Grace and C. B. Fry, and if he was to play as an amateur, two initials would give him a more hopeful appearance on the score-card. A father has to think of these things. So one of us liking the name Christopher, and the other maintaining that Robin was both pleasing and unusual, we decided that as C. R. Milne he should be encouraged to make his name in the sporting world.

'Christopher Robin', then, he became on some legal document, but as nobody ever called him so, we did not think any more about it. However, three years later I wrote a book called *When We Were Very Young*, and since he was much in my mind when I wrote it, I dedicated it to him. Now there is something about this book which I must explain; namely, that the adventures of a child as therein put down came from three sources.

1. My memories of my own childhood.
2. My imaginings of childhood in general.
3. My observations of the particular childhood with which I was now in contact.

As a child I kept a mouse; probably it escaped—they generally do. Christopher Robin has kept almost everything except a mouse. As a child I played lines-and-squares in a casual sort of way. Christopher Robin never did until he read what I had written about it, and not very enthusiastically then. But he did go to Buckingham Palace a good deal (which I didn't), though not with Alice. And most children hop . . . and sometimes they sit half-way down the stairs—or, anyway, I can imagine them doing so . . . and Christopher Robin was very proud of his first pair of braces, though I never heard that he wanted a tail particularly. . . . And so on, and so on.

Well, now, you will have noticed that the words 'Christopher Robin' come very trippingly off the tongue. I noticed that too. You simply can't sit down to write verses for children, in a house with a child called (however officially only) Christopher Robin, without noticing it.

> Christopher Robin goes
> Hoppity hoppity—

Practically it writes itself.
But now consider:

> Christopher Robin had
> Great big
> Waterproof
> Boots on . . .

Hopeless.    It simply must be John.

So it happened that into some of the verses the name Christopher Robin crept, and into some it didn't; and if you go through the book carefully, you will find that Christopher Robin is definitely associated with—how many do you think?—only three sets of verses.    Three out of forty-four!

You can imagine my amazement and disgust, then, when I discovered that in a night, so to speak, I had been pushed into a back place, and that the hero of *When We Were Very Young* was not, as I had modestly expected, the author, but a curiously-named child of whom, at this time, I had scarcely heard.    It was this Christopher Robin who kept mice, walked on the lines and not in the squares, and wondered what to do on a spring morning; it was this Christopher Robin, not I, whom Americans were clamouring to see; and, in fact (to make due acknowledgement at last), it was this Christopher Robin, not I, not the publishers, who was selling the book in such large and ridiculous quantities.

Now who was this Christopher Robin—the hero now, since it was so accepted, of *When We Were Very Young*; soon to be the hero of *Winnie-the-Pooh* and two other books?    To me he was, and remained, the child of my imagination.    When I thought of him, I thought of him in the Forest, living in his tree as no child really lives; not in the nursery, where a differently-named child (so far as we in this house are concerned) was playing with his animals.    For this reason I have not felt self-conscious when writing about him, nor apologetic at the thought of exposing my own family to the public gaze. The 'animals', Pooh and Piglet, Eeyore, Kanga, and the rest, are in a different case. I have not 'created' them. He and his mother gave them life, and I have just 'put them into a book'. You can see them now in the nursery, as Ernest Shepard saw them before he drew them. Between us, it may be, we have given them shape, but you have only to look at them to see, as I saw at once, that Pooh is a Bear of Very Little Brain, Tigger Bouncy, Eeyore Melancholy and so on. I have exploited them for my own profit, as I feel I have not exploited the legal Christopher Robin. All I have got from Christopher Robin is a name which he never uses, an introduction to his friends . . . and a gleam which I have tried to follow.

However, the distinction, if clear to me, is not so clear to others; and to them, anyhow, perhaps to me also, the dividing line between the imaginary and the legal Christopher Robin becomes fainter with each book. This, then, brings me (at last) to one of the reasons why these verses and stories have come to an end. I feel that the legal Christopher Robin has already had more publicity than I want for him. Moreover, since he is growing up, he will soon feel that he has had more publicity than he wants for himself. We all, young and old, hope to make some sort of a name, but we want to make it in our own chosen way, and, if possible, by our own exertions. To be the hero of the '3 not out' in that heroic finish between Oxford and Cambridge (Under Ten), to be undisputed Fluff Weight Champion (four stone six) of the Lower School, even to be the only boy of his age who can do Long Division: any of these is worth much more than all your vicarious literary reputations. Lawrence hid himself in the Air Force under the name of Shaw to avoid being introduced for the rest of his life as 'Lawrence of Arabia'. I do not want C. R. Milne ever to wish that his names were Charles Robert.

Now for the second reason; for I would not have you think that I am a model of unselfishness and parental duty, who never comes to a decision save in the interests of another. No doubt you who read this will remember the occasion when you first met Mr Snooks, the famous author, at a party. He had just published *Woodlice*. You smiled graciously upon him, you said a few nice things about his books . . . and you came away with the feeling that Snooks was the most rude, intolerable and boorish fellow you had ever met. 'My dear,' you said to your friend, 'I simply *fawned* on the man, and he looked as if he wanted to *bite* me!'

Well, that often happens. But authors are not really so vain and so self-conscious as you think. Your fault was not in praising Snooks too little or too much, but in praising him for the wrong thing. If you told Snooks that you adored *Slugs*, I am not surprised that he scowled at you. If you committed the unforgivable sin, and said to him, 'Why don't you write some more books like *Centipedes?*'—then I am not surprised that he looked like biting you. The wonder is that he didn't actually do it. I certainly should have. But if you had praised *Woodlice*, he must have trembled with inarticulate gratitude.

For all an author's hopes and fears and interests are centred in his latest book. As he writes 'The End', he is saying to himself, 'The best thing I have done.' In his heart he may know it is not the best, but he longs to think it is, and will love you for helping him to persuade himself.

Can I go on writing these books, and persuade myself that each is better than the one before? I don't see how it is possible. Darwin, or somebody, compared the world of knowledge to a circle of light. The bigger the circumference of light, the bigger the surrounding border of darkness waiting to be lit up. A child's world of the imagination is not like that. As children we have explored it from end to end, and the map of it lies buried somewhere in our hearts, drawn in symbols whose meaning we have forgotten. A gleam from outside may light it up for us, so that for a moment it becomes clear again, and in that precious moment we can make a copy of it for others. But when the light has gone, to go on making fair copies of that copy—is it worth it?

For writing, let us confess it unashamed, is fun. There are those who will tell you that it is an inspiration, they sing but as the linnet sings; there are others, in revolt against such prig-gishness, who will tell you that it is simply a business like any other. Others, again, will assure you (heroically) that it is an agony, and they would sooner break stones—as well they might. But though there is something of inspiration in it, something of business, something, at times, of agony, yet, in the main, writing is just thrill; the thrill of exploring. The more difficult the country, the more untraversed by the writer, the greater (to me, anyhow) the thrill.

Well, I have had my thrill out of children's books, and know that I shall never recapture it. At least, not until I am a grandfather.

Milne never knew himself to be a grandfather. His only grandchild was born a few months after his death. He might have said it was the end of a chapter but he could never get away from what he had started. The rest of this book will show how Pooh's career continued.

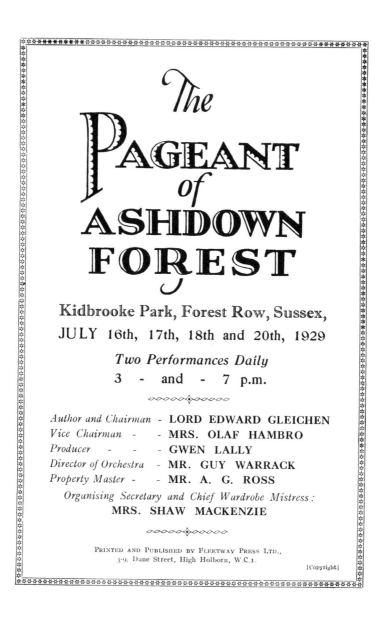

# The PAGEANT of ASHDOWN FOREST

**Kidbrooke Park, Forest Row, Sussex,**
JULY 16th, 17th, 18th and 20th, 1929

*Two Performances Daily*
3 - and - 7 p.m.

| | |
|---|---|
| *Author and Chairman* - | **LORD EDWARD GLEICHEN** |
| *Vice Chairman* - | **MRS. OLAF HAMBRO** |
| *Producer* - - | **GWEN LALLY** |
| *Director of Orchestra* - | **MR. GUY WARRACK** |
| *Property Master* - | **MR. A. G. ROSS** |

*Organising Secretary and Chief Wardrobe Mistress :*
**MRS. SHAW MACKENZIE**

PRINTED AND PUBLISHED BY FLEETWAY PRESS LTD.,
3-9, Dane Street, High Holborn, W.C.I.
[Copyright]

Alan and Daphne Milne went to see Christopher Robin (afternoons only) playing himself in the Ashdown Forest pageant, and the children of Park House School playing 'Winnie-the-Pooh and the other toys'. It was the finale of a pageant which included almost every historical character you could think of: Earl Godwin, Queen Elizabeth, Nell Gwynn, Cromwell, Lady Hamilton, Wellington . . . And then, at the end, a boy and his bear. Christopher rather enjoyed it. He didn't have to speak and there was nothing that could go wrong. 'Exciting without being frightening. . . .It was not like acting in a play or making a gramophone record when your voice might go funny.' The boy had already made a record for HMV, singing 'Down by the Pond', 'The Friend', 'Us Two' and the one about the train brake that didn't work. He had to put on a Poohish voice when he sang, 'Well, *I* say sixpence, but I don't suppose I'm right' – rather a difficult thing to do. He had sung it too at a grand Pooh party for charity in the spring of 1928. On this occasion Pooh was played by a boy with 'a niminy-piminy voice, quite unlike Pooh's gruff voice as inspired by Moon'. The footnote on the opposite page was included in the programme of the pageant.

# FOOTNOTE. By A. A. MILNE.

## CHRISTOPHER ROBIN DISCOVERS THE SOURCE OF THE AMAZON.

For this scene we cross the border-line, not always easy to distinguish, between History and Fiction, and give you something from a story-book. There have been tales told of a little boy called Christopher Robin ; of his adventures in " The Forest " with those fellow-adventurers whom the imagination of a child brings so easily to life. This Forest has been recognised, and indeed there was no secret about it, as our Forest, Ashdown Forest, whose story we are celebrating to-day. There must have been many, and more notable, references to our Forest in story ; but it has been thought that, after all the magnificence, what Pooh would call the Grand History, with which (let us hope) you have been dazzled, and, in one final scene, will be dazzled again, your eyes would find relief in resting for a moment on the simple folk who have wandered through these tales.

So, then, you will see Christopher Robin strolling, as is his casual wont, into the Forest, a few friends under the arm. Just toys, you say to yourself, with whom presently he will play. Wait a little . . . for the ground of the Forest is enchanted ground. See him now coming through the trees. Are they toys ? Is he playing with them ? No, there is more serious work afoot. He is leading an Expotition to the North Pole, or up the Amazon (we cannot be sure till we get there), munching an apple as the Captain of such an Expotition should, and calling words of command over his shoulder. Here come Pooh and Piglet in friendly talk, an admiring distance behind their leader ; here come Owl and Kanga (Roo in her pouch), representative of Learning and Motherliness, so lacking hitherto on the Amazon ; here comes Tigger, bouncing out of the line occasionally to say " Hallo " to a butterfly ; and up and down the line trots Rabbit, trying to give himself the impression that the whole business would go to pieces if he didn't. . . . Then, just when we had thought the tale complete, Eeyore comes gloomily on. He never thought much of Damazons anyhow, or whatever it is they are looking for. Before you know where you are, you have swallowed the stone, and then where are you ? All this Unrest and Going To and Fro, not to mention Rabbit's friends-and-relations Seething all round one. However, if Christopher Robin says the word, well, there it is. . .

So, on this summer afternoon, the Expotition winds its way along, and the Source of the Amazon shrinks in its bed, knowing that all is up with it.

[During the above scene some of Mr. Harold Fraser Simson's settings of the poems in Mr. Milne's "When We Were Young" will be played (by courtesy of Messrs. Ascherberg, Hopwood & Crew, Ltd.).]

In this introduction to *The*    127
*Hums of Pooh* (1929), with
music by Fraser-Simson,
Milne said it might well
be the last time the word
'Pooh' would leave his
nib. It was not.

If you have read (and I don't know why you should, but it will make it very awkward for me if you haven't) two books called *Winnie-the-Pooh* and *The House at Pooh Corner*, then you will need no introduction to this one. For when you see it, you will say (at least, I hope you will) 'Ah, here it is at last!' And here it is.

But if you haven't read these other two books, then, as I say, you have made it very awkward for me. Because what I want to say, and keep on saying, is 'What! You *haven't*? Well! What *have* you been doing all this time?'—and I oughtn't to say this, because (you may as well know; it's bound to come out) I am the author of those two books. I was taught in the nursery (perhaps wrongly) that 'Self-praise is no recommendation'—(one 'c' and two 'm's. Some people do it the other way)—but sometimes I think that if one doesn't praise oneself, and there's nobody else noticing, who *is* going to do it? When I write an Introduction for somebody else's book, I never let go the pen until all my readers are trooping off to the bookshops and saying 'I want two copies of all the books which this man, I've forgotten his name, has written,' but the bother is that I can never get anybody else to write an Introduction to *my* books. They say 'Oh, no, you can do it much better yourself'; and I daresay I can; but I can't Let Myself Go as they could. I did say to Mr. Fraser-Simson, 'Suppose we have two Introductions, and *I'll* tell everybody how good the music is, and *you* tell everybody how good the words are, and then nobody can possibly say we are being conceited,' but he wouldn't. He says he can't write. I suppose he puts two 'c's and one 'm'—a pity.

Very well, then, I've got to do it myself, and this is what I've got to explain. In those two books which you haven't read . . . WHICH YOU HAVEN'T READ . . . no, no, let us hush it up—which you haven't read—there was a bear called Pooh, who lived in the Forest, and hummed as he went about his way. If you had read the books (I am sorry, but I must say it again) you would know all about these hums of his, and just what part of each book each one came in, and what Pooh was doing at the time, and who Tigger and Eeyore and Christopher Robin were. And as you looked through this book, recognizing old friends, you would say of each one, 'I've often wondered what the tune of *this* was, and now I know.' But, as it is, you will be saying, 'Rumpty Tiddle-y tiddle-y tum, rum tiddle-y tum tum—oh, no it's B *flat*—tum *tum*. A very pretty tune, but what's it all *about*?' So at the beginning of each song, I have explained, as quickly as possible, what it *is* all about.

And, turning back to those sensible people, those dear friends, those adventurers, who *have* read the books and know them by heart, perhaps it would be as well if you too, when you sing these songs in public, were first to read aloud these little explanations. For you never know. People are funny; and the old gentleman with whiskers in the middle of the third row *may* take the Pooh books to bed with him every night . . . or he *may* have thought that this was a meeting of the Royal Asiatic Society. So, if the policeman misdirected him at the corner, or he thought it was Tuesday, you can spare him something of the surprise by not sailing into the song until you have given him these few words of warning.

And, finally, to those same dear friends, (since this may be the last time that the word 'Pooh' will leave my nib) may I say, 'Thank you for having loved him.' He will be very proud if you sing his songs, and so keep him for ever in your memory.

The following passage is part of Milne's preface to his play *The Ivory Door*, also published in 1929. Unsurprisingly, he could never escape the 'whimsical' label.

It is always a convenience to have a writer labelled and card-indexed; so that, with the knowledge in front of you that the author is a Realist, you can pull open the appropriate drawer and waste no time in searching for such words as 'meticulous', 'sordid' or 'precision'. The next author is Whimsical, and the 'W' drawer tells you at once that his plays are *soufflés*; 'delicate', if you wish to be polite, 'thin', if you don't; 'charming' or 'nauseating', as you happen to feel; 'tricksy' and what not; but, in any case 'too finely spun out to be a full evening's entertainment'. For these are things you say of 'a whimsical play'. . . but what 'whimsical' means, I, of all people, have the least idea.

And, I suppose, I have the least chance of finding out. For I have the Whimsical label so firmly round my own neck that I can neither escape from it nor focus it. It seems to me now that if I write anything less realistic, less straightforward than 'The cat sat on the mat', I am 'indulging in a whimsy'. Indeed if I did say that the cat sat on the mat (as well it might), I should be accused of being whimsical about cats; not a real cat, but just a little make-believe pussy, such as the author of *Winnie-the-Pooh* invents so charmingly for our delectation.

Here, then, is a whimsical play – or so I was assured by the American critics when Mr. Charles Hopkins gave it its first production. There is a Child in the Prologue; talk of a Magic Door and a Beautiful Princess. . . . Criticism could safely write itself. Even though the Door turns out not to be magic, the Princess not beautiful; even though the child is obtruded on you for little longer than the child in *Macbeth*; yet the name of the author tells you all that you want to know about the thing. Why should you trouble to read it?

However, I hope that you will. For I think (if an author may make these confessions) that it is the best play which I have written; even if it reminds me, not in the least of my favourite *Pooh*, but very much of an earlier play, not noticeably whimsical, *The Truth About Blayds*.

In this piece (right) Milne says he considers *The House at Pooh Corner* his best book, together with his play *Michael and Mary*. He would go through a period later of disliking the children's books for what they would do to his reputation as a writer. On 3 April 1929 C. J. Sisson, the first Lord Northcliffe Professor of Modern English Literature at London University, had written in the *Evening News*: 'Which of our novelists will be read twenty or a hundred years hence? . . . I will tip two certain winners, Conrad and Mr A. A. Milne's *House at Pooh Corner*.' But *Everyman* still gave most prominence to the verses as we can see in this article it published on 15 January 1931. Christopher Robin was then only ten, not twelve as the writer suggests here. Milne was interviewed at the house in Chelsea.

How Writers Work

# A. A. Milne: The Happy Author

*BEFORE* 1924 *Mr. Milne was chiefly known for his light verse in " Punch," of which he was for eight years assistant editor, and for his plays, the most successful of which were " Mr. Pim Passes by " and " The Truth About Blayds." " Toad of Toad Hall," his dramatization of " The Wind in the Willows," is now at the Lyric. But in 1924, with the publication of " When We Were Very Young," he became suddenly famous as a writer of verse for children. In the latter capacity he may be said to have already won immortality in the nursery*

IT is usually impossible to predict immortality for a contemporary writer, no matter how remarkable he seems to us in our generation. But of Mr. Milne we may safely say that his name in one respect at least will be remembered forever. There can hardly be the slightest question but that his children's poetry will be read in nurseries countless generations hence. Whatever may happen to his plays, light verse, essays, novels, and other works, his *When We Were Very Young* has already joined the company of Hans Andersen's *Fairy Tales*, Lewis Carroll's *Alice in Wonderland*, R. L. S.'s *Child's Garden of Verses*, and Sir James Barrie's *Peter Pan* ; and whatever Christopher Robin Milne, now aged twelve, may do in his span of life on earth, his literary immortality is as assured as that of Bevis in Richard Jefferies's *Story of a Boy* and of Mark Twain's Tom Sawyer. The unique thing about Mr. Milne's achievement is that he has created a character in verse, the one being indispensable to the other, both woven into a unity of magic that is irresistible to the child imagination. Christopher Robin moreover is the type of eternal child, not the prodigy born of a temporary vogue like Little Lord Fauntleroy. Children's classics are usually recognized as such during the lifetime of their authors. This is, as Mr. Milne says, because in writing for children the author writes for an audience whose tastes never change. Children are an immortal audience, and it is just possible that R. L. S. may be remembered for his nursery poems when Hardy and all his titanic creations are more or less forgotten.

Considering the small number of classics for children in existence, it obviously takes a rare gift to produce them. The writer for children must remain young, and he must keep also the child's capacity for perfect happiness. Even the bitter Dean, whose *Gulliver's Travels* became a book for children by none of his intention, kept in spite of his miseries a child's heart, as witness his " little language " to Stella. The author of *When We Were Very Young* looks so youthful that it is difficult to believe that he was born in 1882. He is delicate in build, shy in manner, and his smile and twinkle indicate most likely not only his usual mood but his defence against the unhappiness of the world. His face is oval, his colouring sunburned fair, and his expression that of a man very young and very aware of everything, even the smallest detail, that goes on around him. He has a great deal of charm that even the most matter-of-fact social being could take no exception to, and in a way seems to be rather aware of that too ! There is one word which it is impossible to resist using of him, though it has been taboo even in newspaper offices for a long time, and that is the word " whimsical." The final touch to his personality is just that.

It was difficult finding Mr. Milne's front door in the fog, and guided by a flood of light I sought information at what proved to be the kitchen. The cook was large and plump and merry, and her discreet but wholesome mirth over my mistake set the key for my talk with the head of the household.

I asked him, of course, how he came to write the Christopher Robin poems.

" The Vespers poem was first," he said. " I saw him at his prayers, and the poem wrote itself. Rose Fyleman saw it and liked it, and she asked me to contribute more poems for the ' Merry Go Round.' But I said I didn't know how to do it. Then the line,

' There once was a Dormouse who lived in a bed
   Of Delphiniums (blue) and geraniums (red)'

came to me suddenly. I sat down and wrote the poem and sent it to her. Meantime we took a cottage in Wales, with the Nigel Playfairs ; their three boys were there, and mine, who was then 3. We all sat about in one big room. We were always in it. It rained all the time. Finally in complete despair I said ' I must work,' and fled to the summerhouse. At about this time the proof of the poem I had sent to Rose Fyleman arrived. That cheered me up, and I began *When We Were Very Young*. Really, as an excuse for staying in the summerhouse."

" Would you mind telling me how you began to be a writer at the very beginning, before you became successful ? "

" It's always the beginning which is interesting, isn't it ? Anybody can go on, once he has got going. Well, I suppose, it began with writing in the school magazine. Then I went to Cambridge. My father decided that he would spend an equal amount on the education of each of his three sons. Actually what it came to was that each of us was allowed to draw on him for £1,000 after leaving school. I went up to Cambridge, Trinity College, where I spent £700 in three years and got my first taste of journalism editing *The Granta*. Some of the things I did for it received notice in London. I had £300 left, so I decided to go to London and make my fortune as a writer. My father of course didn't like it. No father ever does. That was in 1903. I took some expensive rooms just outside the Temple, and during the first year I spent all the £300 and earned 20 guineas. The latter meant that I got one guinea an article, and 20 of them had been accepted. The second year I came to Chelsea and hired two rooms in a policeman's house for 10s. a week. Breakfast cost me 7d. This year I earned £100 and lived on it. The third year I was on the way to making £200 when I was suddenly asked to join the staff of *Punch*. It was a great piece of luck for me. Among other things, I met my future wife, Owen Seaman's goddaughter. At the time *Punch* was looking for a young journalist as assistant editor ; most of the occasional contributors to *Punch* then were either too old or doing other things for a living. But in time I got sick of it. The prospect of having an idea every Friday morning became too frightful. I decided one day I must get out of it. But I stuck to it until the beginning of the War. After the War I started all over again, as a free-lance. *Mr. Pim Passes By* was my first success, in 1920."

" How did you begin play-writing ? "

" Like everyone else, I wanted to write plays. But the *Punch* work kept me very busy, and knowing how difficult it was to get a play accepted, I felt it was a waste of time to try and write them. So I never really began until the War, when writing was no longer my job, and could be regarded as a recreation. The first one was written at a cottage in the Isle of Wight, where my battalion was training. I dictated it to my wife, and when it was done I sent it to Barrie. I'd known him before the War. He liked it, and sent it to Dennis Eadie. Eadie asked me to come up to London to talk about it and I got leave and went up. But the very next night I was ordered to the Front and had other things to

think about. The next year, when I was back in England, Barrie suggested doing it in two acts, and in this form it was presented with two short plays of his own in a triple bill. That was *Wurzel-Flummery*, and the manager was Boucicault, Irene Vanbrugh's husband. Then Boucicault said, 'Do write one for my wife'. So I wrote *Belinda*. I was still in the Army ; my day began at 6.30 in the morning, and it wasn't until 5.30 in the evening that I was free to write. All the same, I did it in just a week."

" Do you always work rapidly ? "

" I suppose I do, once I am started. But I go through an awful time when I'm waiting for an idea and nothing comes. You feel you're wasting your time. You can't settle down to work and you can't settle down to a holiday. I dread this interval between one idea and another."

Christopher Robin and his pony " Cracker "

" Do you read much ? "

" There are books everywhere in this house. They nearly put us out of house and home until we got the cottage. Now that we have the cottage, there's much more room for them. Yes, I read a good deal ; from *The Corpse in the Cistern* to *The Theory of Relativity*. My wife says I read the very best and the very worst, but not the in-between kind, the sort she calls delightfully twaddly, and reads herself."

" Do you find time to read to Christopher Robin ? "

" He reads for himself now, luckily. *Treasure Island, Phroso, Kidnapped, Bevis, Thy Servant a Dog*, and *The Three Midshipmen* are about the latest."

" I see you keep note-books," I said, observing a pile of exercise books on his desk in purple-mottled paper covers.

" Those are not note-books. I've taken lately to writing in exercise books. I've never taken notes, though I feel more and more that one ought to. But it's seemed to me always such a cold-blooded business."

" Do you revise much ? "

" Not very much in a play. That is because I have already said every speech over and over to myself before it finally goes down on paper. But one is always thinking, and it is difficult to let a manuscript or typescript go. What I detest is the mechanical corrections, which have to be made in typed copies and proofs, probably three or four copies of each. There seems no end to it."

" What do you consider your best work ? "

" *The House at Pooh Corner* and *Michael and Mary*, I think. But probably most people would say *When We Were Very Young* and *The Truth About Blayds*. Of course I'm hoping that the novel—well, we shall see."

" What should you say was the training that helps you most with your writing ? "

" Writing light verse. It was an excellent training for vocabulary, and all the things concerned with style."

" Do you write much journalism nowadays ? "

" I'm wildly keen about certain things, and I can never resist the opportunity to write about them. If I were asked for an article on War, for instance, or the technical side of the theatre, I'd probably rush at it. Anyone who asks me for an article in any kind of shape about the theatre always gets me ! "

" I hoped we'd come back to the theatre again. Can you describe your technique of play-writing ? "

" As I said before, most of the creative time goes to thinking and walking about. An idea at last comes to me. But I begin to think of all the difficulties, and give it up as hopeless. Then, later, I feel that I've *got* to write a play, and again I go through the awful business of trying to think of an idea for one. It's the worst experience one could possibly imagine ! You feel you're simply wasting time, and you envy manual labourers who can just go straight ahead without bothering. Then a new idea comes, and I try to make something of it. But the old idea comes back, and I feel it's not so bad after all. It keeps thrusting itself into the front of my mind until I feel I must get it out of my head somehow, so I begin to write. And then suddenly it seems to be quite a good idea. The dialogue goes fast. Sometimes whole scenes occur to me, and I dash them off in pencil, not knowing where they will come into the play."

" Is your MS. always in pencil ? "

" No, the pencil drafts are all thrown away. I write first in pencil, then in ink, and then have it typed."

He got up and found in a very decorative chest evidently made for the purpose the MS. of the third act of *The Truth About Blayds*.

It was partly in his own thin, swift hand, and partly in another's.

" The second handwriting is my wife's," he explained. " I dictated those parts to her."

" Do you talk over your work with her ? "

" She reads every day's part of it."

" Does she criticize ? "

" No, she just praises ! "

" You would appear to be not only a very lucky but a very happy man."

" Very. But my wife has always had the same sense of humour that I have, and after all, one's work is very much a part of oneself. We don't waste our time criticizing each other. Praise is what an author really wants when he's actually writing."

I commented on his study, which is one that many a man would envy him—a tiny room at the back of the house where it is quiet, with one window, a gas fire, desk, books, MSS. cabinets, and a painting of Christopher Robin by Ethel Walker. One can all but sit in the middle and touch the books and cupboards all round.

" I'm terribly looked after here," he said with his most " whimsical " smile. " I'm given every possible chance. I'm happy, too, in never having written a line I haven't wanted to write."

" Do you work at regular hours? "

" In the mornings, not too early ! From 10 until lunch. Then after tea. I always lunch away from the house, usually at my club, the Garrick. It's a good plan to have a fixed hour for getting out of the house."

I asked about the country cottage, being particularly interested in cottages at the moment, and was taken upstairs to the drawing-room to see a model of it. It stood near one corner of a beautiful red-lacquer Chinese table. The room is in red and yellow, and is thick and shiny with rich woods and tapestries and rugs and enamels. There is in especial a wonderful specimen of Chinese cabinet desk that has a chair made to match out of a gondolier seat. " My wife loves all this sort of thing," said Mr. Milne. We examined the model of the cottage. It is more like a manor-house, built round a central court, the roofs at all angles, including one of the most lovely steep pitches I have ever seen. It is in Sussex, and part of it is fourteenth century. The gardens are wonderful, and it did not in the least surprise me to discover that they are largely the creation and care of Mrs. Milne.

Christopher Milne says the pony shown on the opposite page was not his own. 'It belonged to a man called (I believe) Mr Higgs who lived near Holtye and gave riding instruction.'

A. A. Milne paid his first and only visit to America in 1931. The main purpose was to publicize his adult novel *Two People*, but it was Milne as author of the children's books and father of Christopher Robin in whom the Americans (and everybody else) were most interested. Even his detective story, *The Red House Mystery*, appearing as a paperback would carry the inappropriate addition: 'By the author of *Winnie-the-Pooh*.'

8 THE NEW YORK TIMES MAGAZINE, NOVEMBER 8, 1931.

# MILNE'S HARDEST JOB IS BEING A FATHER

As for the Writing of Children's Books, He Makes It an Art of Pleasing Himself

"A Children's Book Must Be Written Not for Children but for the Author Himself."

*Drawn From Life by S. J. Woolf.*

*By S. J. WOOLF*

A. A. MILNE is in this country and the other day I made this drawing of him in his hotel room. Hotel rooms usually are all alike; their stock engravings and their Louis furniture vary little, whether they are on Broadway or Park Avenue, and whether their occupants are scientists or prizefighters, painters or authors. But somehow or other this room was different, or at least it appeared different when the author of "When We Were Very Young" and a dozen other books opened the door to my ring.

The furniture had been arranged not according to formula but for comfort, and vases of flowers hid the menus and beauty shop announcements that were underneath the glass tops of the tables and bureaus. The flowers did not look as if they had come from a florist's. Perhaps it was the way they were placed in the jars, or perhaps it was the kinds they were; at all events, one felt that Christopher Robin and Winnie the Pooh and Tigger and Kanga were all hiding behind them and at any moment would jump out amid peals of laughter at the consternation of the visitor.

I remember visiting Edgar Wallace at his hotel and how he had changed his room into a combination of a newspaper office and factory. Milne, by contrast, had succeeded in making his resemble an English home, and I was surprised as I looked out of the windows to see the neighboring skyscrapers; Chelsea Bridge would have seemed more nearly in the picture.

But the arrangement of the room played only one part in the transformation. The author himself was the principal factor in the change. Tall and slight, with a tanned face and gleeful eyes, he exudes that spirit of the countryside which seems to thrive amid the gray walls of London and which, like Hyde Park and Kensington Gardens, appears the greener because of its urban surroundings. Though his fine blond hair is beginning to recede from his forehead, about him is the buoyancy of youth.

He breezed the door open and he breezed me into the room. He moves rapidly; he brings to mind, not the roast beef of old England but its hawthorn hedges, its daffodils, its trees—not the staid, steady England of the Athenaeum Club, of Major Pendennis or Mr. Gladstone, but that other lighter England of Master Robert Herrick, or Puck and Peter Pan, that England of Christopher Robin himself when he goes "hoppity hoppity" down the street and sings:

*I went into a house, and it wasn't a house,*
*It has big steps and a great big hall:*
*But it hasn't got a garden,*
*A garden,*
*A garden,*
*It isn't like a house at all.*

We moved the chairs so that there might be a proper light to draw by, and then, with his pipe in his mouth, he sat down and lolled back. He did not do this as a man who is tired; he was keen and tense, yet he breathed the contentment and the joy that one might feel under great elms or on a rug before a fireplace.

It was but a few weeks back that I had seen H. G. Wells, and I mentioned the fact.

"Oh, did you?" he said, his eyes lighting up. "He was one of my teachers. You see, my father was the master of Henley School in London and Wells taught botany there. But if I know nothing of botany, it is not his fault."

The remark was illuminating. It brought up pictures of the patient Wells pouring information concerning calyxes and pistils and stamens into the ears of a boy who was eager to get out of the closed room and rush

*Down to the stream where the king cups grow—*
*Up on the hill where the pine trees blow.*

After leaving his father's school, he told me, he went to Westminster and then to Trinity College, Cambridge, and by the time he was graduated he had decided to become a writer.

"My family was not keen about it," he continued. "My father, with the ideas of a schoolmaster, thought I should go into something where my livelihood would be more secure. However, I had saved a little money from my allowance and I took rooms in London and decided to become an author. My first year's earnings were £20. I think I made about a hundred my second. Then I had a stroke of luck.

"I had been selling some poems and short pieces to Punch. When Burnand, the editor, retired, Owen Seaman, his assistant, was selected to fill the place; he was a Cambridge man, too, and perhaps that was the reason that he picked me as his assistant."

Mr. Milne spoke of the Mahogany Tree, that table which is not made of mahogany at all, around which the editors of Punch meet weekly and on which they have cut their initials. He mentioned Thackeray, one of the original members of the staff, whose tradition still persists, and Sir John Tenniel and his illustrations for "Alice in Wonderland." He recalled that the first dinner he attended was the last one at which Linley Sambourne, who illustrated "Water Babies," was present.

* * *

IT was twenty-five years ago that Mr. Milne became associated with Punch, and for eight years he was its assistant editor. As he spoke of those times he pictured a London that exists no more, a London still filled with the Dickensian spirit, mingled with the ideas of Aubrey Beardsley and Oscar Wilde. He touched on art and declared that it was not life but an exaggeration of it.

"It is life," he said, "colored by the personality of the artist. A work of art is literally too good to be true. We shall never see Turner's sunsets in this world, nor meet Mr. Micawber. As Whistler said, nature tries to keep up with art. Whether sunsets attempted to be more Turneresque in the '50s I do not remember"—here he laughed—"but I do remember that the Du Maurier women came in stately procession after Du Maurier and the Gibson girls followed their creator. The children in Kensington Garden are said to be the most beautiful in the world; they are approaching the beauty that our English artists created for them.

"But I have wandered from my subject. When the war broke out I was on Punch. I joined the Royal Warwickshire Regiment, and my wife came down from London and took a cottage near our barracks. Days were busy for the regiment with drill, but the evenings were long and dreary. My wife and the Colonel's wife put their heads together and planned a concert for the troops. The plans, however, expanded into a sort of fairy pantomime which I was to devise and with parts to be played by my wife and the Colonel's children. The audience appeared so delighted with our little fantasy, which though laid in a fabulous country contained some delicate gibes at those who fiddled while Rome burned, that we decided to expand it into a book. My wife did the harder part; she did the actual writing, while I merely dictated. 'Once On a Time' was the result.

"After the book had been written, however, my wife and I missed the imaginary friends who had kept us company. Why not, we asked, write a real play? Further encouragement came from Sir James M. Barrie. So we wrote 'Wurzel Flummery.'"

* * *

BY the time the war ended, "Wurzel Flummery" had been produced and "Once On a Time" had been published. Both were successes. The result was that when he was mustered out, Mr. Milne decided to leave Punch and become a free lance. Since then he has published books of essays and a detective story and has had numerous successes on the stage, but it is his children's books for which he is best known. "When We Were Very Young," "Now We Are Six" and "Winnie the Pooh" have become classics in the same sense as "Tom Sawyer," "Alice in Wonderland," "Peter Pan" and "A Child's Garden of Verses."

"You know," he told me, "I had heard many stories about America before I left England, some of them not so favorable. But the moment I landed I was made to feel at home because the customs inspector who examined our luggage immediately recognized my name and told me that he had read several of my books. Can you imagine an English customs man who had read the works of an American author? Why, most of them do not read books by Englishmen; I can go around London for days and give my name and nobody recognizes it."

The talk turned to books for young people. He said that the boy that Mark Twain had created was a universal type, that Tom Sawyer and Huckleberry Finn were at heart as much English as American, but that the youngster of the comic strip in this country was not recognized abroad.

The question arose as to what children like in the way of books.

"All uncles," he said, "believe that all babies like to listen to watches. Perhaps they do. At all events children less than a year old make no comment when a watch is held to their ears; so perhaps after all a man with a watch is the ideal baby entertainer.

"In a way the same thing is true of books. Any book for a child is better than no book; and because, I imagine, the first so-called children's writer wrote in a certain way, for the reason that it was the easiest, a certain kind of book came to be regarded as an ideal book for children.

"I have given the matter a lot of thought and I have come to the

(Continued on Page 18)

NEW BOOKS

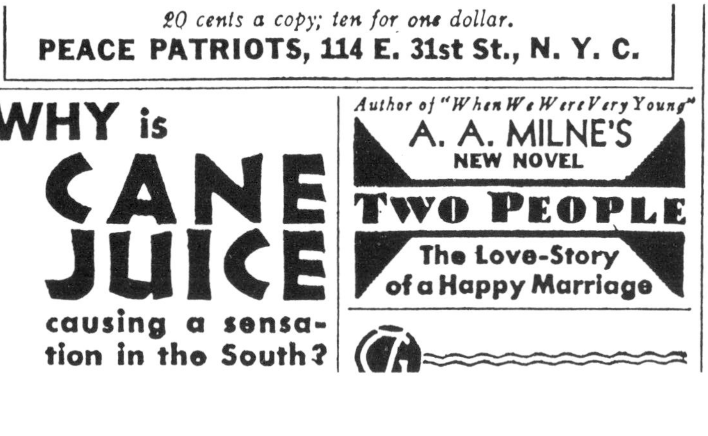

Daphne Milne travelled with her husband and was also a source of interest in America. Sara J. Wardel interviewed her for *Parents Magazine* in April 1931. In May 1933 the magazine would name Christopher Robin one of the most famous children in the world, along with Yehudi Menuhin, Crown Prince Michael of Romania, Princess Elizabeth of England and Jackie Coogan, the child film star.

# NOW WE ARE ELEVEN

## BY MRS A. A. MILNE
## AS TOLD TO SARA J. WARDEL

The mother of Christopher Robin, little boy hero of "Winnie-the-Pooh" and "Now We Are Six", gives an intimate glimpse of him at eleven and contrasts English children with little Americans.

THOUGH CHRISTOPHER ROBIN thought that he wanted to stay six forever and ever, he discovered all sorts of equally nice things about being seven. And eight and nine and ten, too. Now he is eleven and finding it the most fun of all. For he is that sort of little boy. Everything that happens to him he thinks jolly. Boarding school is a lark and he is frightfully keen about cricket. And so when people ask me whether he isn't homesick for his parents, what with a whole ocean temporarily between us, I have to admit quite frankly that he is far too happy living in the moment even to miss us.

All little English boys of his age go away to school, of course. It is a bit hard on Winnie-the-Pooh and Eeyore and those other "Lords of the Nursery" who must wait at home in their time-honored places, to be hugged only surreptitiously during the holidays when no one is looking. For the years have a horrid way of making boys grow up faster than their no-matter-how-cherished playthings. Fortunately these most friendly and agreeable of toys seem to understand. Perhaps they have talked it over among themselves and decided not to hold it against Christopher Robin for growing up. It is one of those awkward things like having to go to bed and eat porridge and brush his teeth that a boy can't help.

But Pooh sheds a tear occasionally when he remembers that he and Christopher Robin were exactly the same size on that day, ten years ago now, when the friendly bear joined the Milne family. It was Christopher's first birthday and from the first the two were inseparable companions. Yet in spite of the dozens of tea-parties they have shared, Pooh hasn't grown a tiny speck bigger while Christopher had been busy putting on extra inches every year. It is all a little puzzling. Pooh shakes his head and frowns. Could it just possibly be, he wonders, because his little playmate has always had to eat all the jam and bread and butter sandwiches for him?

Indeed, Pooh is, if anything, a little thinner, a little shabbier for the years. That is on account of all the hugs and squeezes! So he doesn't mind. His nose has been patched . . . Kisses are hard on a bear's snout ! . . . and he has been to the hospital for new paws. But otherwise he is just the same. It is Christopher Robin who has done all the changing.

Yet, he is younger, I am finding, than most American children of his age. English children seem to belong longer to the nursery than their American cousins. They are less sophisticated, quite babyish really in comparison. It is due, I fancy, to a difference in background and environment.

In England the nursery is not just a casual room of the house where the children play. It is something of an institution, a social custom and a tradition. Occupying usually a whole floor

134 of the house, it is here that the younger members of the family eat, sleep, study and play, living a quite separate existence from the adult life of the home. At tea-time they come downstairs to join the grown-ups and this is the hour sacred to shared confidences, secrets and fun.

The English mother is fortunate in being able to place such full confidence in her children's nurse. Often the trusted and beloved "Nanny" remains in the employ of the family for years, living to love and care for her small charges. She is especially trained for her work which she regards as a real profession, worthy of her pride and deepest interest. (Christopher Robin's nurse is leaving us to be married only now that he has gone away to school and does not need her any longer.)

Inhabiting thus a little world all their own, it is not surprising that English children stay very simple and young. Over here life seems to throw American children into closer contact with the older members of the family. They listen to adult conversations, share adult interests and develop adult points of view at an earlier age. Then, too, life is more stimulating in your large cities. There is so much provided for children to do. They go to matinees, operettas and moving picture performances. Few amusements of this sort exist for English children to attend. Theirs is a very quiet, unexciting existence with walks in the park to feed the squirrels and occasional visits to the zoo their most thrilling diversions.

Incidentally Christopher Robin named his bear for the famous big brown one at the London Zoo, dear to the hearts of innumerable children. But Winnie was a girl's name and Christopher wanted his bear to be a boy! For some inexplicable reason "Pooh" seemed to take care of the requirement. Later the Winnie was largely dropped in the interests of brevity and "Pooh" the cherished comrade remained.

To Christopher Robin the bear was actually alive as were all the rest of his playthings. The rest of the family were always careful to treat them as such, consulting their opinions with great deference. When Christopher came downstairs at tea-time, eyes wide and shining, Pooh must needs walk down a step at a time too. The two indulged in lengthy conversations, Christopher interpolating fierce growls for the bear, feeling thoroughly convinced about it.

For a writer these were ready-made opportunities and in many of the poems his father merely took advantage of actual comments overheard while the inseparable friends were at play on the floor, sometimes hunting wild animals among the chairs that were the jungles of darkest Africa, again content at home across the tea-table, deciding the momentous question of one lump or two !

Christopher's play-life always took him into a dream world peopled by the creations of his own imagination. Progressive modern education, stressing as it does the practical and utilitarian, would protest, I fancy. Our children, it argues, must inherit a machine-age civilization to which steam-engines are more indigenous than fairies. This is an attitude, I think, that may easily be carried too far. For even a steam-shovel must first exist in someone's imagination as a thought, an idea, a fancy before it can be materialized in solid steel to do the world's work. And so the dreamer will always be essential to any civilization no matter how pragmatical. Whimsy, fantasy, dear nonsense of nurseryland! These are the intangible but no less precious gifts of the spirit which, carried over from childhood into maturity, give the world all its beauty, all its wonder and newness of life.

I am not, I fear, a very solemn mother. But children do not ask to be taken like a hard case of the gripe. They love to laugh and play and do all the delightfully silly things we are all too apt to have left behind somewhere as we grew up. It is easier to handle them if one can forget the hand-ling part and just enjoy them instead. Children are not really small adults though we are prone to regard them as such. Quite the contrary. Adults are children, grown to larger stature and a few more years. It is a humbling and vastly salutary thought to remember at times.

People often ask me whether the interest aroused by the poems and stories dealing with his everyday life and little activities has affected Christopher in any way. The answer is simple. He is quite unaware of it. Though immensely pleased with his very own autographed and much thumbed copies of the books, to him they are no more unusual or remarkable than another child might find his baby book or photograph album. As for his father, Christopher Robin thinks him "a good writing man" and lets it go at that !

After all, the moods and fancies captured between covers in the books are only the universal traits of childhood common to your child as well as mine. They represent not only Christopher Robin but all the Jimmys and Billys and Marys. It accounts for their success and the friendly interest with which people have greeted them. Other mothers and fathers recognize in them the quaint and funny little ways of *their* Christopher Robins. Ours merely happened to be fortunate enough to have "a writing man" in the family who could creep up behind a thing and get it down in words.

*The drawings used in connection with this article are reproduced with permission from A. A. Milne's "Now We Are Six" and "Winnie-the-Pooh", published and copyright by E. P. Dutton and Company, Inc., New York. The names "Winnie-the-Pooh" and "Christopher Robin" are registered by Stephen Slesinger, Inc., N. Y.*

The acknowledgements at the end of this article, which was decorated with Shepard illustrations, reveal that 'the names "Winnie-the-Pooh" and "Christopher Robin" are registered by Stephen Slesinger Inc., N.Y.' Later Walt Disney would take over the rights, which explains why even Shepard designs can now carry a Disney copyright notice.

Cotchford Farm, although so closely identified with the Pooh books (from which during the thirties and forties Milne increasingly wished to escape), remained for the rest of Milne's life a cherished haven. Milne was photographed there in the thirties with one of a series of cats. It is still, as can be seen in this recent photograph (below), set in unspoiled country, although so close to London. A car park among trees and new paths encourages Pooh pilgrims to approach Poohsticks Bridge not from what Milne called the Outland, along the lane past the house, but from the other side of the river, through Posingford Wood.

*John Drinkwater*

13, MALLORD STREET,
CHELSEA, S.W. 3.
TEL. FLAXMAN 2074.

29. x. 35

Dear John (to whom all blessings flow)
He tell you now, and then you'll know.
I'd love to come and see you one day
But cannot ever manage Sunday.
In Sussex, that enchanted spot,
I have a little wrick-out-cot
Intended, as one might deduce,
For Saturday-to-Monday use;
Which makes, you see, of Sunday, John
What Latins call a dies non—
A quite non, as far as being present
In Anytime, my favourite Crescent.

—

P.S. Perhaps I might to say
My wife is in the U.S.A.
I trust she also would be sending
Her thanks, apologies, and sending
My letter this November P.M.
Yours jointly A.A.M. and D.M.

### MRS. A. A. MILNE

Auburn-haired Mrs. A. A. Milne, wife of the novelist and playwright, arrived on the Aquitania today for what she called "my annual autumn vacation from my husband."

Smiling she told ship news reporters: "Sometimes I act as his secretary and do all sorts of tasks for him—so he thinks I ought to have a rest from him once a year. I'll stay a month, go to the theatres—and see his producers! Still working for him, you see."

*A. A. Milne*

A. A. Milne was firmly established by now as a 'Famous British Author', as this set of W.D. & H.O. Wills cigarette cards confirms. Milne, though never part of any literary group, and rather unsociable in temperament, knew many fellow writers. H. G. Wells, Milne's old teacher, was of course another in the set. P. G. Wodehouse's good opinion of Milne's writing for adults survived a rupture in their friendship after Wodehouse's 1941 broadcasts from Germany. But he made fun of the children's verse both in *The Mating Season* (1949) and in a short story called 'Rodney has a Relapse' in *Nothing Serious* (1950). R. C. Sherriff, who wrote *Journey's End*, the most successful play to come out of the First World War, also thought Milne's plays would survive. 'I am quite sure all his work will live,' he wrote in 1956. 'Those of his plays which have been broadcast of recent times are as fresh as when they were written.'

This cutting (left) from the *New York Post* for 26 October 1937 recorded one of Daphne's regular visits to America during the 1930s. At this period the Milnes were leading rather separate lives. Daphne was interested in the American playwright, Elmer Rice, and Milne in an actress, Leonora Corbett, who appeared in several of his plays. Christopher and his father remained close. This snap (right) was taken in Dorset, where father and son spent a number of holidays with the family of Milne's brother Ken, who had died in 1929. When this photo was taken, Christopher was just about to start at his public school, Stowe, where 'Christopher Robin' would become, as he himself put it, 'a sore place that looked as if it would never heal up'. The break between father and son was not until after the war, when Christopher returned from service overseas, married a cousin and determined on independence as a bookseller in Devon.

R. C. Sherriff

H. G. Wells

P. G. Wodehouse

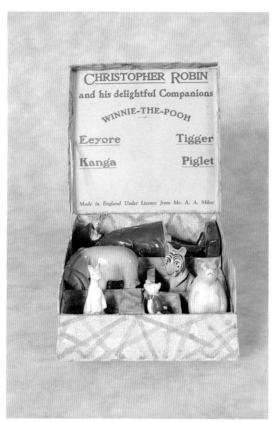

Already in the 1930s a Pooh industry was developing and representations of the characters appeared in various materials. Many of us remember, before the war, Chad Valley soft toys of the animals and even Christopher Robin dolls, most of which have long since disappeared. Here are two pre-war sets, one in ceramic and one in wood (from which Pooh and Piglet have gone missing). Also shown is an early example of a board game.

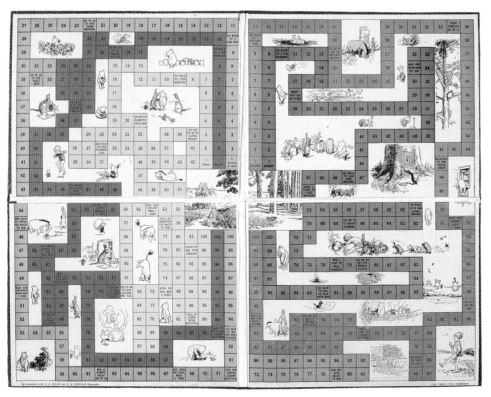

This garden 'statuary', similar in form to the ceramic figures on the opposite page, is in the Dorset garden of Milne's niece Marjorie.

The paper dolls were American and made by Queen Holden, 'the most famous paper doll artist in the U.S.' They were reproduced in the 1980s by Merrimack, N. Y.

The patents for the bookend designs (there were two others besides the ones shown) were taken out on 27 March 1930 by Constance Stella Watson of Ockley in Surrey.

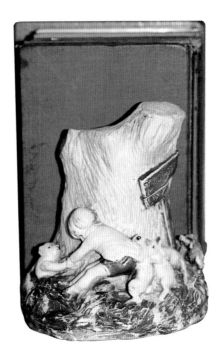

140 In 1934, Milne, who generally tried to keep his distance from writing for children, made an exception when he introduced the first English translation of *The Story of Babar*. We can easily see why the Babar books appealed to Milne, with their gentle satire of French bourgeois and colonial life, their confident mixture of reality and fantasy.

The first cheap editions of Milne's four books came out in England this same year and in America a year later, 1935. The first paperbacks did not appear in England until 1965 and in America not until 1970.

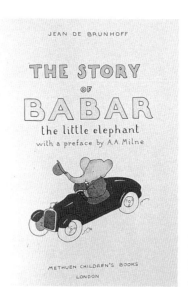

## Introduction

Two years ago at a friend's house I was introduced to Babar and Celeste. They spoke French then, but they spoke it with a charming simplicity which saved me from all embarrassment. With a little trouble I managed to get them into my own house; and with no trouble at all they settled down at once as part of the family.

Since then I have been insisting that my publishers should take out naturalization papers for them, and let them settle down at once in everybody else's family.

So here they are.

If you love elephants, you will love Babar and Celeste. If you have never loved elephants you will love them now. If you who are grown-up have never been fascinated by a picture-book before, then this is the one which will fascinate you. If you who are a child do not take these enchanting people to your heart; if you do not spend delightful hours making sure that no detail of their adventures has escaped you; then you deserve to wear gloves and be kept off wet grass for the rest of your life.

I can say no more. I salute M. de Brunhoff. I am at his feet.

A. A. Milne

IT'S  TOO  LATE  NOW
*The Autobiography of a Writer*

*by*
A. A.  MILNE

*With a frontispiece*

SECOND  EDITION

METHUEN & CO. LTD., LONDON
*36 Essex Street, Strand, W.C.2*

Milne published his autobiography just after the outbreak of the Second World War, in September 1939. Both in England, as *It's Too Late Now,* and in America, where it was called simply *Autobiography,* it sold extremely well for such a book at such a time. Most of Milne's emotional energy had gone into writing about the early part of his life, though he could not bring himself to say that he was most interested in childhood – that would have been playing into the hands of those who were eager to label him finally as a children's writer, a label he relished less and less as the years went by. He devoted more than half of his autobiography to his own beginnings – child, schoolboy, undergraduate – and, in a book of more than two hundred and fifty pages, only seven to the children's books, though he must have been well aware that that was the section a great many people would read with particular interest. He lamented the fact that he could not escape from them and their amazing success. 'As a discerning critic pointed out: the hero of my latest play, God help it, was "just Christopher Robin grown up". So that even when I stop writing about children, I still insist on writing about people who were children once. What an obsession with me children are become!'

Sales of the books continued to rise during the war. In England it was in 1941 that for the first time sales of *Winnie-the-Pooh* for a six-month period were almost exactly the same as for *When We Were Very Young,* with *The House at Pooh Corner* not far behind and *Now We Are Six* a poor fourth, though even that sold 8,554, several thousands more than in the corresponding period of the previous year. In neutral Sweden, sales soared until in 1946 *Winnie-the-Pooh* was selling nearly 5,000 copies a year. It was not only children, of course, who loved and read the books. The American writer, Randall Jarrell, called *When We Were Very Young* 'the perfect book for the soldier, this soldier anyway'.

# WINNIE-THE-POOH

## AND FRIENDS

## VISIT AMERICA

A world famous group of distinguished visitors from England is making an extended tour of the United States.

They are finding a warm welcome wherever they go, for they are Mr. Edward T. Bear, better, and more affectionately known as Winnie-the-Pooh, and his inseparable companions, Kanga, Piglet, Eeyore and Tigger.

Their visit was arranged by Mr. Elliott B. Macrae, President of E. P. Dutton & Co., who succeeded in persuading them to make the journey when he visited them in Sussex,

In 1947 the original toys themselves – Pooh, Piglet, Eeyore, Kanga and Tigger – made a triumphant tour of America. Milne provided a 'birth certificate' (see next page) and they were insured for fifty thousand dollars, an even vaster sum of money in those days. They then travelled around America for ten years or so, visiting libraries and department stores and occasionally coming to rest in the offices of their American publisher, Dutton, in New York. There were inevitably stories of Pooh fans travelling hundreds of miles through snowdrifts to catch a glimpse of the beloved bear.

Dutton sent Milne reports and he eventually agreed that the animals should stay in America. 'We like to say that Pooh became an American citizen,' Elliot Graham, publicity director at Dutton, said fondly. Eventually (and we rush ahead a bit here) Pooh became permanently a New Yorker, as a headline in the *New York Times* put it in September 1987. After a brief visit to England in 1969 (flying as a VIP in Concorde) for a Shepard exhibition at the Victoria and Albert Museum, Pooh moved from Dutton to the Children's Room of the New York Public Library on West 53rd Street, together with his faithful old friends. 'POOH AND COMPANY GO PUBLIC' was the headline in the *Daily Telegraph* in London. The *New York Times* said: 'Ultimately they will occupy a climate-controlled case that some might think of as a shrine.'

## BIRTH CERTIFICATE

HEN the first stories of WINNIE-THE-POOH were written there were three animals in the nursery: stuffed animals to the visitor, but to the resident very much alive. They were Pooh, Piglet and Eeyore. Pooh had been the first birthday present, Eeyore was the Christmas present of a few months later. Piglet was an undated arrival at the hands of a stranger, who had often noticed a little boy walking in the street with his nurse and sometimes stopped and talked with them.

With these three friends, and an imaginary Owl and Rabbit, the stories began; and as they went on, additions to the family were made in the persons of Kanga (with Roo in her pouch) and Tigger. It must be confessed that the newcomers were carefully chosen, with the idea of not only giving pleasure to the reader, but also fresh inspiration to the chronicler of their adventures.

Five of these animals are paying a personal visit to America in the hope that some of those who have read about them will now be pleased to meet them. Anyone who does so will recognize them at once, for they were drawn from life for the illustrations in the books. The sixth one, Roo, is believed to be somewhere in Sussex, but no details are available. A subsequent dog, who became part of the establishment, took him for a walk once and left him in a hollow tree, from which he was extracted a year later. But the spirit of adventure was now strong upon him, and soon afterwards he was off again—whether or not with the co-operation of the dog this time is not known. The latter was one of those friendly but unbalanced young things who must have company; and if Piglet's face now gives the impression of having seen better days, they were the days before the dog joined the party. But no explanation is needed for the world-weariness of Pooh and Eeyore. Time's hand has been upon them since 1921. That was a long time ago.

Signed
A. A. Milne

*A. A. Milne*

The last fresh image of Pooh which appeared in Milne's lifetime decorated the beginning of his last book, a series of monthly jottings called *Year In, Year Out* (1952).

The feature on A. A. Milne at home at Cotchford (right) comes from *Weldon's Ladies' Journal*, January 1950.

# A. A. MILNE

# AT HOME

This month we take you to the home of a famous author and playwright, whose latest book, "A Table Near the Band," has recently been published.

Here you are looking into the bedroom-study where Mr. Milne does all his writing at this small, unpretentious desk. Yellow walls, yellow-flowered chintz curtains, a rust carpet, and one of those gay Indian rugs all make for bright simplicity.

Oak panelling and ancient beams in the dining-room look well with a plain fawn carpet, gold curtains and a handsome antique Italian chest-of-drawers, painted green, which the Milnes use as a sideboard.

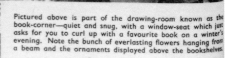

Pictured above is part of the drawing-room known as the book-corner—quiet and snug, with a window-seat which just asks for you to curl up with a favourite book on a winter's evening. Note the bunch of everlasting flowers hanging from a beam and the ornaments displayed above the bookshelves.

(Left) Main view of the drawing-room, a large and pleasant room, with bright yellow walls, pale amber carpet, and curtains and covers of amber, tobacco-brown, yellow and oyster. Mrs. Milne's hobby is doing patchwork, and the cushion covers she has made for this room give a gay splash of colour.

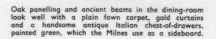

Photographs by Humphrey Joel.
Captions by Jeanne Heal

Cotchford Farm, in the heart of the Sussex countryside, is a little old farmhouse set in a delightful garden. With tall chimneys and quaint, irregular roof, it is a mixture of red tiles and ancient brickwork and stone. Here, at the back of the house, a terrace looks out over the garden, the meadows and copses.

A peep into what used to be Christopher Robin's bedroom, with its painted furniture and gay chintz, and the original oak characteristic of the whole house. Now it is a spare room, for Christopher Robin is grown up and married.

In this garden Christopher Robin played, surrounded by the characters his father created for him. As you wander round, from time to time you come upon statues by famous sculptors of the well-loved animals from the Pooh books. Come closer to this sundial, and you can read: "This warm and sunny spot belongs to Pooh, And here he wonders what it's time to do."

The main bedroom glows with bright, warm colours. Mrs. Milne's home-made patchwork bedcover is in lovely silks of all shades of red, pink, yellow and green. All the furniture is painted, some of it antique and priceless, some done at home. For instance, the wardrobe is Venetian and very valuable; the corner cupboard was painted for his mother by Christopher Robin.

25

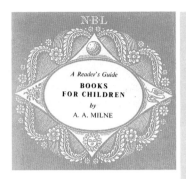

Milne's essay appeared as an introduction to a *Reader's Guide* published by the National Book League in 1948. The wood-engravings which illustrated it are by Joan Hassall.

Reader's Guides in the past have been based on the object sought: biography, bibliography, poetry, books about this or that; and it was easy, when making the selection, to decide whether any particular book was within the category. To-day's Guide is subjective. It is the reader, not the book, that determines the choice, and the reader is that most indeterminate of all creatures, the Child.

How shall we define a child? For we must know for whom we are catering before we start to cater. *The Concise Oxford Dictionary* begins with 'Unborn or newborn human being', goes from there to 'boy or girl', and ends with 'childish person'. One way and another we have now got half the population of Britain clamouring for our Guide. All we have to do is to jot down a list of books likely to appeal to an unborn human being, a little girl in a perambulator, a boy just getting into his House XV, Bertie Wooster, and an old woman in her second childhood. But how do we do that? How can a Guide be planned along these lines? Fortunately *Chambers's Twentieth Century Dictionary* is more helpful. Chambers, the crossword-solver's friend, is once again a friend, and gives us the perfect definition. A child, he says, is 'one intimately related to one older'.

Now I think that when we talk of Children's Books, as if they were an easily identifiable article, all in the same box and possessing some common property, we have, or ought to have, this definition at the back of our minds. Remembering that the young of the human species vary more than the old: that it is when adult that they leave the by-paths and settle into their tram-lines: I shall say boldly that the only common denominator of a 'children's book' is the fact that it is a book chosen by an older person for someone in intimate relationship with him—or, more often, her. It is, in short, a book which the giver thinks the receiver ought to like, the receiver, from lack of experience or pocket-money, being unable to buy the book for himself.

This does not necessarily mean that a children's book must make a grown-up appeal to the giver before it is given to the child. Very often it is given because it had made a childish appeal many years earlier. That is why (if I may divagate for a moment) the writing of children's books is even more of a gamble, whether one is doing it for art's sake or the butcher's, than the writing of a novel. On the one hand they have the insistent competition of their forerunners to meet, as novels have not; on the other hand, if once they join their competitors on equal terms, then they too are 'portions and parcels of the dreadful past', and will outlive many a better novel of the same season.

Children's books, then, are books chosen by us for others; either because they pleased us when we were young; or because we have reason for thinking that they please children to-day; or because we have read them lately, and believe that our adult enjoyment of them is one which younger people can share. Unfortunately, none of these reasons is in itself a sure guide.

As children many of us read *Alice in Wonderland*. We have read it a dozen times since with pleasure and can place any quotation from it;

but are we sure that the enjoyment of it which we attribute to our childhood is not the enjoyment which we have experienced since? I know that in my own case *Alice* meant little to me when I was young, and that all my delight in her has come since I left school. I am prepared to say now that *Uncle Remus* was my favourite nursery book. But it was read aloud to us by a much loved father with a genius for reading aloud. How much of my happy recollection of it is a nostalgic memory of happy evenings round a happy fireside in a happy home?

The books which other children like, what of them? The book which your friend gave to her little girl, or somebody else's little girl, and 'My dear, she simply loves it'. Well, a book is a book and a possession is a possession, and children are taught to be polite. 'You must write and thank Aunt Mary, darling, and tell her how much you enjoyed the lovely book she sent you. *Wasn't* it kind of her?' And so Aunt Mary recommends the book to her friends. Children, she says, simply love it.

And the 'children's book' which you have just read, and enjoyed, and are sure that children will enjoy too: have we anything against that one? It is always a temptation to choose such a book, for we may be called on to read it aloud, and it is torture to read anything aloud with which we ourselves are bored. I used to think that a good test of any book, but certainly of a book for the young, was its ability to keep the interest of the reader-aloud. From my own experience the *Doolittle* books failed lamentably to do this, but they passed triumphantly the test of personal appeal to the child. I had an equal failure when I tried to read aloud a favourite book of my own youth: *The Three Midshipmen*, by W. H. G. Kingston. It was quite unreadable; but its unreadability somehow conveyed pleasure to the listener, and less impatient readers were mobilized to relieve me.

It begins to look as if there were no safe guide to a child's taste in books. But then there is no safe guide to a child's taste in sweets—other than the assurance that it will accept gratefully any sort of sweet. A child who likes reading is prepared to read anything. I suppose I was about nine when I read *Oliver Twist*. In those days children were usually given this first unfortunate introduction to Dickens, doubtless for the absurd reason that it alone of his works could be hopefully described as 'a book about a child'. The young can assimilate a good deal of blood-letting in their romances, but they should be spared the realism which lets the wolfish faces at the window into their innocent dreams. The night-thoughts of a child, waking or sleeping, can be terrifying, and we should be careful not to provide it with any such substance for its fears. In comparison with a tale which I read when young of gypsies kidnapping a child, all the corpses of *Hamlet* would have been subject for a pleasant reverie. One cannot imagine oneself being poisoned or stabbed in Buckingham Palace, but one can easily imagine oneself being carried off by the gypsies on the common.

Assuming that the right sort of child of whatever age will read any book with eagerness, but an occasional one with ill-effect, can we say that there are certain books which it should be encouraged to read? I think that we can; particularly in these days when comic strips and films are spreading one sort of illiteracy, the bureaucrats another, and broadcasting tends to seduce us all from studying the English language for ourselves. There are certain standards of good writing with which the young should become acquainted, for if they accept them now they are more likely to appreciate them in later life. It is not altogether true to say that we needs must love the highest when we see it, but we are unlikely to love it when we never do see it. Contact with beauty creates an awareness of beauty; beauty becomes something felt rather than something learnt. Children should not be forcibly fed with what are called 'the classics', even the classics of their own favourite form of reading; but they should be given every encouragement to assimilate them.

When we hear talk of the classics, we think, perhaps, of some Victorian library, with rows of beautifully bound books in it which nobody ever reads. In those days, it was said, one could order forty feet of literature from a house-furnisher, as one ordered a mahogany what-not or an uneasy chair, and there they stood, silent witnesses to the culture of the owner. A Scotsman was quoted the other day as saying 'Never a year passes but I think of taking down my Burns from its shelf', and this may be as near as many of us get to reading some of the classics.

But it is not only snobbery—the snobbery of dreading to be 'out of it'—which makes us feel that we should do well to read them. Just as the sentimental lover (so I have been told) looks up at the moon and is wafted happily nearer to the absent one by the knowledge that it is shining on her too, so we can take comfort from our common heritage of the great books which have been part of the lives of so many people over so many years. For to share an author with another is to double one's pleasure in him.

The list which follows, then, gives a selection of well-written books, most of which have brought happiness to two or more generations of book-receivers. Anybody can say that this or that book is not worth its place, and, with more assurance, that some other favourite of his own should certainly have been included. You who are guided by it, whether Parent, Teacher or Librarian, will recognize that it is a direction post leading to open country, not to a one-way street. Some of the books are merely a sample of a particular author. *The Light Princess* and *At the Back of the North Wind* have at least equal rights with *The Princess and The Goblin*; and the books chosen to represent Beatrix Potter and E. Nesbit speak not only for themselves but for all Potters and all Nesbits. You can take your choice between *The Children of the New Forest* and *Masterman Ready*, though only one of them is given here, and if they lead you on to *Midshipman Easy*, so much the better. It may be felt that *Tom Brown's Schooldays* will not make the appeal to-day of any of Charles Turley's or P. G. Wodehouse's school stories. Probably not; but it is a little bit of English history and English literature; and, being no more 'out of date' than a penny-black English stamp, it should be added to the collection. If a child shall have read all these books, and any others for which they have created an immediate demand, it will have formed a habit of good reading and a love of good English which will never be taken away from it; no, not even if it grows up into a world in which the writing industry finds itself nationalized and the tongue that Shakespeare spake has been put on points.

Milne's last phrase may be lost on younger readers; 'points' were a form of food rationing at the time Milne was writing.

In 1952 Milne was seventy. The *New York Herald Tribune* asked him to contribute a short autobiography. On 12 October it appeared under the headline:

# A. A. Milne—Always Time for a Rhyme

BORN in 1882:
(Small, of course, but slowly grew)
Educated, so to say,
In the customary way—
School and college: at the latter
Wrote as madly as a hatter,
Wrote, and used to wonder "Can't a
Man who runs the Cambridge Granta
Satisfy for life his creditors
By cajoling London editors?"

So to London, and collected
Divers forms for the rejected:
£20 the year's reward,
Not enough for bed and board.
Two more years went lightly by
Editors still rather shy.
"Punch," however, kept its head,
Made me its Assistant Ed.
There I stayed until the war . . .
(Married He; the year before).

Training in the Isle of Wight

Had a little time to write;
Wrote a play which got a laugh
From my so much better half
(Reason One: Why Men Should Marry):
Sent the play to J. M. Barrie.
Barrie like the thing, so
Sent it on to Boucicault;
And in the ensuing summer he
Staged it (title: Wurzel Flummery):
Which, because it wasn't hissed
Changed me to a dramatist. . . .

Found, and no one more surprised,
War could end. Demobilized.
Peaceful days succeeded days
Mostly spent creating plays.
Wife's supreme creation, son,
Took the stage in '21.
(That's poetic license. I'm
Hampered by the need for rhyme.
And by "21" I meant he
First appeared in 1920).

If a writer, why not write
On whatever comes in sight?
So—the Children's Books: a short
Intermezzo of a sort:
When I wrote them, little thinking
All my years of pen-and-inking
Would be almost lost among
Those four trifles for the young.

Though a writer must confess his
Works aren't all of them successes,
Though his sermons fail to please,
Though his humor no one sees,
Yet he cannot help delighting
In the pleasure of the writing.
In a farmhouse old by centuries
This so happy an adventure is
Coming (so I must suppose,
Now I'm 70) to a close.
Take it all, year in, year out,
I've enjoyed it, not a doubt.

*"Year In, Year Out" will be published in the middle of November.*

Three days after the verses had appeared in New York, A. A. Milne was rushed to East Grinstead hospital after a stroke. In December he was operated on but he was never able to walk again. He lived for three more years.

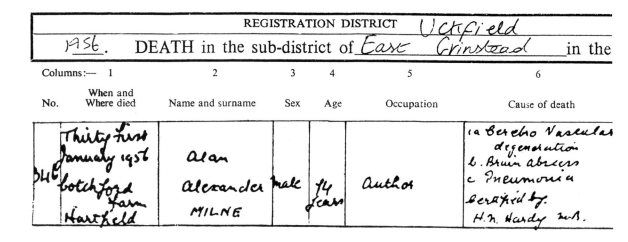

| | REGISTRATION DISTRICT | *Uckfield* | | | |
|---|---|---|---|---|---|
| *1956.* | DEATH in the sub-district of *East Grinstead* | | | | in the |

| Columns:— 1 | 2 | 3 | 4 | 5 | 6 |
|---|---|---|---|---|---|
| No. | When and Where died | Name and surname | Sex | Age | Occupation | Cause of death |
| 346 | *Thirty first January 1956 Cotchford Farm Hartfield* | *Alan Alexander MILNE* | *male* | *74 years* | *Author* | *1a Cerebro Vascular degeneration b. Brain abscess c. Pneumonia Certified by H. R. Hardy m.B.* |

Many years before, Milne had written the following lines in Shepard's copy of *Winnie-the-Pooh*. In December 1990 the book was sold at Christie's in London for £16,500.

When I am gone,
Let Shepard decorate my tomb,
And put (if there is room)
Two pictures on the stone:
Piglet, from page a hundred and eleven,
And Pooh and Piglet walking (157) . .
And Peter, thinking that they are my own,
Will welcome me to Heaven.

A. A. Milne

*Life* published a photograph of Christopher Milne and Anne Darlington walking together out of All Hallows-by-the-Tower, where the memorial service was held. Norman Shelley had sung Pooh's song, 'How sweet to be a cloud', and recited 'Vespers' to an organ accompaniment. What Christopher felt is best not imagined.

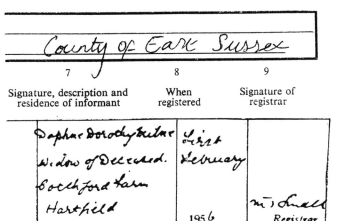

There were long obituaries on both sides of the Atlantic. *Punch* alone managed to mention the children's books only in passing. More typical was that in *Time*.

## A Man Who Hated Whimsy

"If I write anything less realistic, less straightforward than 'the cat sat on the mat,'" A. A. Milne (rhymes with kiln) once complained, "I am [called] whimsical." To Alan Alexander Milne, whimsical was the most "loathsome adjective," but it was one that he could never escape. No matter how many adult plays and novels he wrote, he was forever the biographer of Christopher Robin and Winnie-the-Pooh. On starting one of his children's books, Critic Dorothy Parker once reported that on page five "Tonstant Weader fwowed up." Milne's other readers had an entirely different reaction—and they could be counted in the millions.

The third and youngest son of a London schoolmaster, Milne remained throughout his life fascinated by childhood. "When I read the biography of a well-known man," he wrote, "I find that it is the first half of it which holds my attention." His own childhood was unusually happy. He knew how to read at two, was confident that his parents loved him, learned his first smatterings of science from an awkward young teacher named H. G. Wells. Though he had trouble with Greek, he breezed into spartan Westminster School, and in spite of the fact that there was not a single bath in the place ("It was enough that it was built by Christopher Wren"), he enjoyed himself thoroughly. He went on to Cambridge and to the fulfillment of his first literary ambition: the editorship of the undergraduate *Granta*.

**What's My Line?** After graduation, his father made up his mind that A. A. should be a schoolmaster, for he "was convinced now that I was not good enough for the Civil Service." But Milne had already decided to become a writer. He took the £300 coming to him and moved into his own flat.

Though he managed to sell a few articles to *Punch*, his first book, *Lovers in London*, received such notices as: "The only readable part of this book is the title." Milne became an assistant editor of *Punch*, got married, and while serving as a signaling officer in World War I, wrote a play called *Wurzel-Flummery*. By 1923, he found himself a success. Then one day the lady editor of a new children's magazine asked him to write some verses. "I said that I didn't and couldn't, it wasn't in my line." As it turned out, it was.

**Heffalumps & Wallaboos.** The verses and stories that were to be *When We Were Very Young, Now We Are Six, Winnie-the-Pooh* and *The House at Pooh Corner*, were based on the doings of his three-year-old son, Christopher Robin Milne,* who insisted on calling himself Billy Moon. As Christopher Robin, Billy eventually became a fixture in thousands of nurseries in England and the U.S. If he went to the zoo or to see the changing of the guard at Buckingham Palace, his father put it all into rhyme. Even his evening prayers ("Oh! God Bless Daddy —I quite forgot") and the tantrums of his little friends ("What is the matter with Mary Jane?") worked their way into the repertory of mothers, nannies and children on both sides of the Atlantic. Billy's stuffed animals came to life as Pooh, Piglet, Tigger, Eeyore, Kanga and Roo. As if these animals were not enough, Milne invented some others, *e.g.*, the Heffalump and "a sort of a something which is called a wallaboo."

A reserved, debonair man with "one wife, one son, one house, one recreation— golf," A. A. Milne tried in vain to make the playwright and the novelist keep up with the author of *Winnie-the-Pooh*. He insisted that he did not even like children very much, that they had become merely "an obsession with me." His obsession sold more than 2,500,000 copies in the U.S. alone, brought him a fortune in royalties from records, toys, stationery, pop-up books. Last week, when he died at 74, the books that he had written so lightheartedly had become nursery classics. In the closing words of his last children's book, A. A. Milne unintentionally summed up his own claim to immortality. "Wherever they go," he said of Pooh and Christopher Robin, "and whatever happens to them on the way, in that enchanted place on the top of the Forest, a little boy and his Bear will always be playing."

* A graduate of Cambridge and a World War II veteran, Christopher Robin, now 35, owns a bookshop in Dartmouth, England.

**TIME, FEBRUARY 13, 1956**

In 1960 editions of a Latin version of *Winnie-the-Pooh* by a Hungarian doctor, Alexander Lenard, appeared in both London and New York. The extraordinary story of how that came about was told by Lenard in his book *The Valley of the Latin Bear* (1965).

The relatively peaceful times in Rome finished abruptly in September, 1943. Overnight a situation developed which not even prophets of the rank of Nostradamus could have foreseen. Rome was defended by the arch-enemy, the Germans, and attacked by her friends, the Anglo-Americans.

Meanwhile, I had to live on something, and as times were far too dramatic for people to be sick, I taught English. "They will come in a fortnight," was the watchword of all who waited, and learning English seemed to hasten liberation. Rich people even offered a piece of bread and cheese for a lesson!

On a particularly hungry autumn day I got a new pupil. He spoke the melodious accent of Venice and said, "I know no English at all. We had it in school and you know what schools teach. I hate grammar. I do not want to memorize words. But I have to talk to Allied authorities, once they are in Rome."

"When do you think they will come?" I asked.

"In a month or so."

"Yes, sir," I said, surprised to find a pessimist. Actually the Allies did not get to Rome until more than eight months later.

"We start tomorrow at eight."

"Yes, sir."

"And you choose me a book."

"Yes, sir."

I chose. My choice was greatly facilitated by the fact that I had only one—namely, Alan Alexander Milne's *Winnie-the-Pooh*. I loved that book so much that I had even forgotten who had lent it to me. I dived into it to see if I could use it.

Soon I was relieved to see that I could. The book contains remarks about the present and expected weather, a subject which I felt would be a perfect introduction to conversation with British staff officers, though I was not quite sure about the American attitude in this matter. The book contained information about the transmission of messages by air, by means of bottles, or by whistling in a particular way. It contained a plan, pure General Staff style, for capturing someone or something by means of deception. Finally there was a banquet with an appropriate speech one might deliver if honored in a particular way.

"Here is the book I have chosen from among many," I lied next morning at eight o'clock sharp.

We started with the chapter on the Heffalump, as I held the conversation between Pooh and Piglet as essential, in case my friend made contact with senior officers: "Piglet said, 'If you see what I mean, Pooh,' and Pooh said, 'It's just what I think myself, Piglet,' and Piglet said, 'But, on the other hand, Pooh, we must remember,' and Pooh said, 'Quite true, Piglet, although I had forgotten it for a moment.'" We made speedy progress. When we reached the Cunning Trap, I already knew that my pupil had been sent by the underground of Venice in order to obtain arms from the Allies. The day Piglet took his bath Monty left the command of the Eighth Army. The Allies seemed stuck at Cassino very much like Pooh in Rabbit's door. My pupil's English improved rapidly, although it was I who was getting slenderer and slenderer. Eeyore's balloon exploded and the island of Leros fell to the Germans. Roo took a swim and Leipzig went up in flames. When finally Pooh received his pencil-case my friend said, "No more lessons."

"The irregular verbs . . . ," I objected.

"I have to leave. Besides, I think my English is good enough by now."

I did not meet Pietro Ferraro again until after the war, after the ending which was a happy one for all of us who had not already been shot. He had received the arms, and had been parachuted back into Venice, where he had led the insurrection and prevented the Germans from carrying out their sabotage plan. He had been awarded the highest Italian decoration, the Medal of Gold.

"I had no difficulty in treating with the British," he said. "On the contrary. They complimented me on my English."

So Winnie-the-Pooh had helped Winnie Churchill to win the war.

# WINNIE ILLE PU

A LATIN VERSION OF A. A. MILNE'S
'WINNIE-THE-POOH'

TRANSLATED BY ALEXANDER LENARD

Half of the mine belonged to a French company and there were three French engineers. Two of them had daughters, and the daughters needed somebody to teach them Latin, English, mathematics, and history. Besides being a doctor with the salary of an orderly, I became a well-paid professor of philology and science. I hadn't wasted my time reading French novels for a lifetime and Latin medical books for fifteen years. . . .

My former teaching experience having been limited to expounding and commenting on the deeds, poems, and adventures of Edward Bear, better known as Winnie-the-Pooh, I started with Milne's book, still the only volume representing English literature in my scanty library. The young ladies, having passed their early life in a lead mine in Argentina, had not known the book and were curious and enthusiastic.

They were far less curious, let alone enthusiastic, about Latin grammar. They found that five declensions were far too much and cases like the ablative entirely useless. Eeyore, who had lost his tail, touched them more deeply than their compatriot Vercingetorix, who had lost a battle and his life.

"Is there no Latin book like *Winnie-the-Pooh?*" asked Anne, the prettiest of them all.

I could have told them about Petronius and Apuleius, but I realized that their lovely fables were not the ones I was expected to recommend to *jeunes filles en fleur.*

"I'll try to find one," I promised vaguely.

That night I sat down and tried to translate the story of the Heffalump, which we were just then reading, into the old, old doctors' Latin.

I do not dare to say that my translation was brilliant, but it worked. The mademoiselles were ready to follow the events around the Cunning Trap even in spite of ablatives and gerunds. Even the Chief Engineer, a splendid humanist himself, and thanks to his education in Greek lead mines a far better Grecist than myself, liked both the Bear, which had helped him to live when a prisoner of the Boches, and the translation. When he left for Paris he sent me Quicherat's great and massive French-Latin dictionary.

Now I felt under obligation to continue. The short spells between knifings and accidents belonged to classical philology.

This idyllic life came to a sudden end when the manager who had hired me on the island fired me, apparently on a quick decision. I cannot reproach him. I had obstinately suggested to the lead-poisoned miners that they get the hell out of the place, although he had repeatedly warned me that the mine was not a welfare institution and that it was a hard job to find new personnel. Sadly I said *"Au revoir"* and left for São Paulo, the immigrants' hope city.

Here I soon discovered that it was I who could not get out of the "Cunning Trap". The Latin Pooh—or *Pu*—had started as a necessity, had become a hobby, and was by now an obsession. I had asked myself a question that only years could answer: Is it possible to find all the phrases in the story of Pooh and his friends in the extant Latin literature?

Knowing the book by heart, I started to read my way first through Horace, later Livy . . . and obstinately, like a dope addict, through more and more. The text slowly became a mosaic of fragments, ever more similar to those texts Gutenberg's invention had poured all over Europe, or at least the Republic of Humanists.

Here I am now with the manuscript of the Latin bear, the manuscript I always consider finished until a new old author lands on my desk. I send the text to faraway friends and I keep receiving touching, discouraging letters. "Children read no Latin, grown-ups do not read children's books," a wise publisher wrote. "Maybe you have too much spare time, but we have not," was the reaction of another.

I tried to write a letter to a few publishers. I considered it a masterpiece of argumentation. "The parents of good students will buy the book for their children as a gift. The parents of bad students will buy it so that their children will develop a liking for Latin. People who have studied Latin will buy it so that they will finally have a use for their Latin. People who did not study Latin will buy it to find out what Latin is like." I got only one simple, very short reply: "I am not crazy."

On long Sunday afternoons I browse through my Latin authors, correcting the text here and there, replacing a line with one I think more suitable, hoping that there will be, among the countless publishers the world over, a crazy one.

The opportunity to print my Latin bear came with an Inter-American Congress of Pathology. Translating medical congress proceedings is a strange job, as it calls for very different skills and is therefore well paid. It is very much as with riding a bicycle: you do not get real money for it. Nor are you paid for playing "Home, Sweet Home" on the violin. Blowing smoke rings from a cigar is also a hopeless skill if you want to make money. But if you ride your bike, play the violin, and blow smoke rings at the same time any good circus will hire you and pay you good money. If you are able to translate into English a Portuguese paper on ganglia cell changes, as quickly as one who has ten minutes to report about ten years of research reads it, you may go—at least for a week—into the publishing business.

That was exactly what I did, when an old friend remembered my past experiences and achievements in this particular field and called me to the city for a short while.

To have money means to be tempted to spend it. Even states possessing printing presses are tempted to spend more money than they can print. How should I have resisted the temptation to print my translation and see my name on the title page of a Latin book? I recalled the years in Roman libraries: reading Latin books only meant being a visitor in the Republic of Humanists. To have written a Latin book meant full citizenship. A stateless refugee is always longing for some sort of citizenship, even of a state which is not issuing passports.

Is the Republic of Humanists really unreal? The Knights of Malta have lost their island long ago, but still send ambassadors to courts of kings . . . A representative of Goa is still in Lisbon, claiming the colony has not been lost. The difference between reality and fiction is a matter of definition.

In order to enter the fictive Republic (this is where we feel a common border between reality and fiction) one has to pay—to pay real money. The rights to *Winnie-the-Pooh*, or, as I preferred to call him, *Winnie ille Pu*, belonged to the estate of his author. I obtained the address of the agents and boldly asked them to sell me the rights. Even relatively small amounts of money, when carried close enough to one's skin, are capable of overcoming certain inhibitions against which psychotherapy would fight in vain.

The agents were—that's evidently what they are paid for—concise, cool, and objective. They said, "No."

"No" is an excellent position to start bargaining from. I did what they had expected me to do: I asked if I could buy permission to print about three hundred copies, one single edition.

They considered my offer, quite rightly, a sort of unconditional surrender. They said, "Yes," and added, "but you must pay ten guineas and are not allowed to sell your translation. You may give it away free of charge. And you must send us ten copies."

Only a madman—they evidently thought—could think about translating a children's book into Latin. Moreover it must be a wealthy madman, with lots of spare time, bored with golf playing and Caribbean cruises, a man living for his hobbies.

This last supposition being the only right guess of the series, I tried to bargain.

"Do I not possess already the right to give my translation away, printed or handwritten, free of charge?" I timidly asked.

"You have," they admitted. "But pay three guineas anyhow."

I was tempted to ask if three pounds wouldn't do, but I liked the term "guinea" too much. Do not tailors and doctors still count in guineas? Is not the guinea a nonexistent, dreamlike, fictive coin? I found it was right to enter a fictive Republic paying my dues in fictive units. I paid.

Now I had the right of printing three hundred copies, but lacked the funds to do so. The rest of my riches could not pay for more than one hundred copies.

I had read years ago a Swedish essay about the chances of finding an old book. "You can find old books," the author, a librarian, said, "only if they were printed in sufficiently small numbers." Very small editions are treasured in libraries and private collections. They are listed in handbooks for book lovers. Books printed by the millions disappear without leaving a trace because nobody cares for them. Old copies of newspapers vanish; not one of a million survives. Thrillers disappear by a mysterious mechanism the authors of thrillers cannot solve.

A hundred copies, I thought, will make an edition small enough to assure me immortality.

My position was definitely more agreeable than that of the average publisher. I did not have to bother about publicity, retail orders, profit or loss. All I had to do was to find somebody who was willing to set a Latin book in type.

Printing Latin books in São Paulo, in Brazil, I am tempted to say, is a typical Hungarian business. I soon found a Hungarian typesetter willing to do the job by night on the machines of an Italian daily . . . the machines had certain technical imperfections, but these he promised to repair. He started right away.

In saying that printing Latin—or translating into Latin in Brazil—is typical Hungarian business, I may be wrong. Many Hungarians were forced into emigration by prewar and postwar persecution and had to earn a living. In exile one cannot live on diplomas, privileges, acquired rights, or inherited property. One has to rack one's brain and invent a trade for himself. If one's genius helps one, so much the better. I think it was despair and determination which made Hungarians invent electronic calculating devices, hydrogen bombs, gadgets for the atomic pile, and theories about the structure of the atom nucleus. The same factors prompt a simpler spirit to smuggle needles across the border or to print Latin books by night.

It took some time to transform a number of sheets of cheap paper into a hundred copies of *Winnie ille Pu*. My friends helped me pass this time by explaining to me what I should have done instead. They pointed out that shoes were useful even where social conventions do not necessarily call for their use, and that I would have more social prestige in town as the owner of a hat. I had no arguments. How should I have explained to persons living simply in South America that I wanted to become a citizen of the Republic of Humanists? I confess I did not really listen to useful advice. I was busy figuring out the list of persons I wanted to surprise with the Latin bear.

Ancient authors sent their works to kings and queens. The method has much to recommend it. Johann Sebastian Bach, for example, sent six concertos to the Elector of Brandenburg. They were neither acknowledged nor performed, but two hundred years later they were found untouched in the same drawer royalty used to bury gifts of well-educated subjects. So I destined copy number one to His Royal Highness, the Prince of Wales. . . .Kings are scarce nowadays, so I destined one to an old friend who happened to be the Royal Danish Librarian. . . .As to princes of literature, I thought about Robert Graves, still able to write Latin verse if he felt like it. The Republic of Humanists is in certain respects like the Noble Guard of the Pope: an army in which lieutenant is the lowest possible rank.

It may be hard to sell a hundred copies of a Latin book; it is easier to give them away—and certainly more exciting.

I had sent a few to newspapers and periodicals. Only one mentioned it as "the oddest of all odd gifts ever received." No compliment, but at least a superlative, I thought. Oddly enough, a letter from the editor followed. "Could you send us another copy?" it read. "After several attempts were made to pinch it, we had to lock up the existing copy in our safe."

That sounded far more encouraging.

Every letter which crosses a continent, an ocean, and finds its way through the intricate channels of the Brazilian mails (letter writing is considered a pastime for foreigners in a country of illiterates) is a wonder no less miraculous than those letters the *Legenda Aurea* reports as having been brought by ravens to hermits in the Egyptian desert.

One of the letters certainly fell into the category of miracles. It was the one from the Royal Danish Librarian, short and matter of fact. It said: "Winnie is known and loved in Sweden under the name of

Nalle. The great Swedish publishing house Svenska Bökforlaget has decided to accept your Latin version which I submitted to them. They are going to publish two thousand copies this Christmas. Half of it will be distributed free and they'll try to sell the rest—if you don't mind and agree."

Of course I did not mind and agreed.

For one who lives among plants, nothing seems more difficult than to realize the speeding up of events. Plants have a steady rate of growth. Every tree knows exactly how slowly it should stretch. But once the trees become pulp and paper they lose their innate sense of time. Books may sleep for centuries; sometimes they grow and multiply with incredible speed.

*Winnie ille Pu* was one of them. The little white-covered booklet with its uncounted misprints and displaced letters made a career. The Swedish edition was followed by British and American ones. . . .It seemed the Republic of Humanists was wider than we had surmised. Not hundreds, not thousands, but tens of thousands of *Winnies* were printed, and—I could hardly believe it—read.

Figures are unexpressive. Even weeks on the best-seller list do not tell anything about the real fate of a book. It is nice to collect favorable reviews, but they do not tell the whole story either.

Fragments of the story can only be pieced together from letters. Perhaps one out of a thousand readers sits down to tell me his impressions, ask his questions, give his advice; that makes a hundred and fifty for 150,000—quite a lot of mail for a post office which seldom handles such an amount of correspondence in a year.

One of the White Fathers of Africa (a Catholic missionary order) found the book in Rhodesia. . . .A gentleman from New Zealand found it in the ship's library when he sailed back to England. . . . A lawyer in Australia who had already translated "Jabberwocky" wired to London to get a copy.

Really, I had never felt lonesome. Loneliness is a feeling of city-dwellers, of people who never walk on earth unless they go to the cemetery. But letters really showed me that there are human relations other than those between doctor and patient, which, although important, have their limitations and tend to be less intimate when the pains subside.

The secret society of those who try to write about modern subjects in Latin, who play the game of exchanging Latin epistles, as if Bach and Voltaire were still in full activity, was not the only company aroused by the bear. The other was the fraternity of book collectors. Totally uninterested in the perfect and faultless editions of the real publishers, they wanted copies of the first one, the one without illustrations and with misprints. Human nature shows sympathy for imperfections and cherishes aberrations; I could have become a rich man if I hadn't given away my treasures. I could retrace but a very few—but I had found friends among the lovers of first editions, and they too joined the company of letter furnishers.

Letter writing has lost much of its romance nowadays. I do not think its excitement can ever be replaced by long-distance calls; telephones just kill a very particular type of human relations. Only one who has lived on an island where the mail arrives twice or three times a year really knows what letters mean, how much more written words weigh than spoken ones. My valley is a sort of island. I enjoy reading words that have not yet been pronounced in the forest, and that come from very far away. It is very much like sipping old wine from faraway countries, or tea from Darjeeling; it is good to overcome the distance between libraries and forests.

*Winnie ille Pu*, my hobby, has turned into "my success". Not one that can be measured in money. (To transform a book into a checkbook is a very primitive sort of success.) I gauge the amount of success by the names of the faraway friends who occasionally visit me with their letters, and who save me a dangerous journey into the outside world I prefer to know in their descriptions.

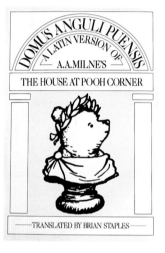

*Winnie ille Pu* was the first book in a foreign language to reach the bestseller list in New York. It sold 150,000 copies in five years and still sells. In 1980 it was joined by *Domus Anguli Puensis*.

In 1963 Dutton published *The Pooh Perplex*, in which Frederick Crews, a genuine academic, masqueraded as a number of fictitious literary critics. 'The Poisoned Paradise', which follows, purports to be by one Myron Masterson, mainstay of the English Department at the Colorado School of Mines.

## THE POOH PERPLEX

A STUDENT CASEBOOK

'A. A. Milne would have enjoyed this book; one can think of no higher praise'
*Daily Telegraph*

FREDERICK C. CREWS

Ignoring the superficial level of *Winnie-the-Pooh*, let us dive at once, like Melville's Catskill eagle, into the profundities and sub-profundities of the matter. It is not hard to dismiss the generally accepted impression of this book as a cheery, chins-up collection of anecdotes designed to educate Christopher Robin in the gentle virtues of English social life. Milne's chief spokesman, Eeyore, is a veritable Thersites, a malcontent who would have put Marston to shame. No pretense of "helpfulness" or "conviviality" escapes his wickedly incisive rebuttal. Nor, when we look around at the other characters, do we find a much rosier picture. The "lovable" Pooh is tragically fixated at the narcissistic stage of development. Rabbit and Owl are aging bachelors whose respective megalomania and fussiness are tempered only by their mutual friendship, of which the less said, the better. Kanga is the archetypal mawkish "Mom"-figure we see exemplified everywhere in America. And Piglet, Tigger, and Roo are such advanced cases that their problems must be analyzed separately below. As for Christopher Robin, his interest in these toy animals is undoubtedly "normal", if by normality we understand a neurotic effort to transfer onto one's furry dolls all the grievances and secret fantasies that characterize the onset of the latency period. "Aye, madam, it is common," as Hamlet remarked to his mother—but it isn't pretty!

The fact, indeed, that Christopher Robin has recently suffered the destruction and repression of his Oedipus Complex provides a key to the whole tone, as well as to many of the incidents, in *Winnie-the-Pooh*. The phase Christopher is entering is that of maximum repression, when toys, hobbies, games, and schoolwork hopefully will receive the libido that was previously lavished upon thoughts of "Mummy". Even in the most successful cases, however, the repression is incomplete; we can always see, if we try, a survival of the old incestuous wishes and a rather suspiciously overeager attempt to desexualize oneself and one's imaginary companions. Not without significance does Milne, who must be only too happy to see his little boy finally turning his conscious thoughts elsewhere, dedicate the book "To Her"—the mother who never appears *in propria persona*, but who lurks behind every page as the not-quite-relinquished goal, the secretly intended object of all Christopher Robin's "portentous little activity" (to quote *The Turn of the Screw*). The animals in *Winnie-the-Pooh* are lacking in genitalia, they seem to have no other activity in life beyond calling on one another and eating snacks—but the experienced critic need not be fooled. The real subject of the book is Christopher Robin's loss of his mother, which is alternately symbolized, accepted, protested against, denied, and homoerotically compensated for in the various "nursery" stories of the plot.

From the portrait of Christopher Robin himself, of course, we should expect the least enlightenment, since it is upon his toy animals that he attempts to project his forbidden fantasies. It is clear to the reader that Christopher knows what is off limits once one has entered the latency period in earnest. More revealing is the almost total absence of parents for the other characters in the story. Whenever Pooh and Piglet imagine that they are in danger they wish to be soothed, not by their own fathers and mothers, but by Christopher Robin; and the same holds true for the other animals. Surely this cannot be explained by saying that these dolls weren't *anyone's* children. *Winnie-the-Pooh* is virtually haunted by ancestral figures: Piglet's grandfather Trespassers William, Owl's revered Uncle Robert, Pooh's mysterious forebear Mr Sanders, and so on. The amazing fact is that there is no shortage of distant and dead relations but a severe want of immediate ones on the scene. And the point of it all is indisputable: Christopher Robin, still smarting under the paternal castration threat and the enforced renunciation of the mother, has decreed a ban on mothers and fathers in general. He has imagined for himself a blissful teddy-bearland in which no adult is permitted to intrude. He himself will be the sole father figure, and will "show up" his own severe parents by exercising only a gentle brotherly supervision of his charges.

Here, then, we have the rationale of the ideal world that Christopher Robin has hallucinated—a pastoral paradise, a garden of fun in which the danger of incest and punishment is nil. But like all such gardens, as Hawthorne was I believe the first to notice, something is likely to go awry sooner or later. In this case it is the entrance of Kanga that transforms *Winnie-the-Pooh*, with one brutal stroke, from the genre of bucolic idyll to that of depth-psychological Gothic tale of terror. The true meaning of Kanga's arrival—the installation of the emasculating Female as overseer of the doomed frolickers—is not lost on Rabbit, who does everything in his power to exclude her. All in vain! From the very moment of Kanga's appearance the pastoral playground is overshadowed by doubt and guilt, for the all-too-loving *anima*-Woman has pitched her temple here!

We should pay special attention to the fact that Baby Roo forms part of this invasion, for it is *as Roo's mother* that Kanga threatens the common happiness. All Christopher Robin's animals had, by his fiat, entered a kind of latency period of their own, never bothering themselves over the fundamental questions that small children want to ask their parents. Now Enter Kanga:

> Nobody seemed to know where they came from, but there they were in the Forest: Kanga and Baby Roo. When Pooh asked Christopher Robin, "How did they come here?" Christopher Robin said, "In the Usual Way, if you know what I mean, Pooh," and Pooh, who didn't, said "Oh!" Then he nodded his head twice and said, "In the Usual Way. Ah!"

No one, I think, will deny that these lines deal with the topic, "Where do babies come from?" No one can fail to draw the inference that Christopher Robin feels basically evasive on this subject; and no one will forget that this is entirely in keeping with my understanding of Kanga's role. The verification of my inspired guesswork, I confess, strengthens my resolution never to read the criticism of others but merely to rely on placing my unconscious in sympathetic rapport with that of the writer.

Kanga's corrosive effect on Christopher Robin's ideal society, like Margaret Fuller's on Brook Farm, stems from her desire to bring every male under her sway. I need hardly dwell on her treatment of Roo ("Later, Roo dear," "We'll see, Roo dear"); it is enough to make us all breathe a sigh of relief at having successfully crossed the border of puberty. More interesting thematically is her capture of Piglet. Piglet is, we may say, the very archetype of the sickly, nervous little boy who is terrified by father and mother alike. His fear of emasculation and his horror of intercourse converge in his abject quaking before the pit for Heffalumps, the "Cunning Trap" as he slyly calls it. He and King Lear agree entirely about this "sulphurous pit". And his misgivings turn out to have been all too justified. Piglet becomes Kanga's very first victim outside her immediate family. Instead of helping in the plan to blackmail Kanga into leaving, he finds himself stuffed into her womblike pouch, vigorously bathed and rubbed, and nearly made to swallow Roo's fulsome baby medicine. Ugh! It is a section of the book that I can scarcely stand to reread! Piglet's symbolic spaying is complete when Kanga, continuing the pretense that she is serving Roo, explains that the medicine is "to make you grow big and strong, dear. You don't want to grow up small and weak like Piglet, do you? Well, then!" From this moment onward Piglet, who certainly never showed much virility before, is fit only to try out for countertenor in a choir.

Kanga's role is raised to positively allegorical dimensions when she encounters Tigger in *The House at Pooh Corner*. Tigger is the one "intruder" in that volume, as Kanga and Roo were in the previous one, and this fact alone shows us how gutless the Pooh-world has become in the interim under Kanga's influence. For Tigger, the embodiment of pure Dionysiac energy, of sheer animal potency, appears strange and unwelcome to this melancholy band of castrati. Alas, poor Tigger! Nothing in the Forest is fit for him to eat but Roo's extract of malt, which must be administered by Kanga. And could we reasonably expect this matriarch to stand by idly and watch her household being overrun with sheer maleness? She sinks her hooks into Tigger at once:

> "Well, look in my cupboard, Tigger dear, and see what you'd like." Because she knew at once that, however big Tigger seemed to be, he wanted as much kindness as Roo.

As much kindness as Roo, forsooth! This is the beginning of the end. Sinclair Lewis, Wright Morris, and Evan S. Connell, Jr., all working together, could never nauseate us half so successfully as does the picture of

Kanga waving good-by to Roo and Tigger as they take their watercress and extract-of-malt sandwiches off for a sexless *déjeuner sur l'herbe*.

It is when things have reached this sorry pass that the inevitable homoerotic alternative to compulsory innocence suddenly offers itself to Kanga's victims. Already in *Winnie-the-Pooh* Piglet had reached a point comparable to Huckleberry Finn's satanic resolution to prefer hellfire to the female-dominated world he has thus far inhabited. Now, in the excitement over getting Tigger and Roo down from a heavily symbolic tree, Piglet flips:

> But Piglet wasn't listening, he was so agog at the thought of seeing Christopher Robin's blue braces again. He had only seen them once before, when he was much younger, and, being a little over-excited by them, had had to go to bed half an hour earlier than usual . . .

Christopher Robin is flattered and attracted by this fetishistic response to his little striptease, but he is naturally reluctant to enter into serious relations with a pig. Doubtless he has designs on one of the tiny scholars with whom he is now learning spelling and mathematics. Piglet, therefore, is thrown into the willing arms of Pooh, who at the end of the book welcomes him into his house as permanent roommate. Nor should we omit Tigger and Roo from this account. What, after all, did Roo have in mind ascending that tree on Tigger's back, squeaking, "Oo, Tigger—oo, Tigger—oo, Tigger"? What is the meaning of Tigger's compulsion to "bounce" upon all his male friends? Roo, at least, gets the point even if innocent readers have not done so: "Try bouncing *me*, Tigger," he passionately pleads.

Well then! This, within the limits of my volatile, intuitive temperament, is a sober and accurate account of *Winnie-the-Pooh*'s meaning. Were I to read other critics I would be sure to find that my interpretation has contradicted every threadbare cliché on the subject. I am sincerely sorry if this article must spread consternation in the ranks of four-eyed old professors and mooning Moms. But the truth, after all, must be told by someone; someone must bear the burden of demonstrating that English literature, since Shakespeare's day, has demoted itself continually from maturity down through pimply post-pubescence to the nervous sublimations of the latency period, and now stands on the brink of re-entry through the Oedipus and castration complexes. It is a fascinating, rewarding process to watch—particularly for myself, a simple, milk-fed boy of the Mesas, just glad to be a vigorous American critic in the middle of the twentieth century!

### QUESTIONS AND STUDY PROJECTS

1. Of the various authorities whom Masterson acknowledges as his literary and moral guides, which do you think influenced him the most? Perhaps one member of your class could look into St John of the Cross, another Sacco and Vanzetti, and so on. There may be a joint term-paper project here!

2. Masterson's conclusions are bound to arouse some disagreement, but we can all grant his point that Kanga is a "Mom" figure, as he puts it. Write an essay on the importance of the American Mother in the home, in the community and nation, and on the international scene today.

As Alison Lurie put it, Frederick Crews managed 'to stifle almost all critical comment on *Winnie-the-Pooh* for a decade'. After 'the Hierarchy of Heroism in *Winnie-the-Pooh* and "A la recherche du Pooh perdu"' (*Weltschmerz*, alienation and the rest), one begins to wonder if perhaps the great Heffalump expedition really is a paradigm of colonialism and Eeyore the spokesman for the disillusioned post-war generation. Not everyone has been deterred. An apparently genuine paper by Geoffrey Cocks presented to the Southern California Pyschoanalytic Society on 29 January 1973 included some comments on the 'orality further expressed in Milne's depiction and animation of bears in his children's stories. Bears are a symbol for the good mother and also the good parents who in the depressive phase are conceived of as one and the same and introjected as such.'

At a symposium on children's literature in Cologne in 1987, a Swedish scholar, Anna-Karin Blomstrand, presented among other ideas about *Winnie-the-Pooh* a suggestion that the book encourages children to 'trust in the invisible hierarchy of a society, built upon the assumption that there will always be a good father – Christopher Robin – in the background, leading to confidence in the welfare state or a Christian saviour, neither of which may deserve adult confidence.'


In 1966 the brilliant career of Winnie-the-Pooh was deeply affected by the first appearance of a Walt Disney film. Disney's original idea was for a full-length feature to be directed by Woolie Reitherman. In their book, *The Disney Studio Story* (1988), Richard Hollis and Brian Sibley suggest that it was problems over the 'Britishness' of the subject matter which resulted in the first film, *Winnie-the-Pooh and the Honey Tree*, emerging as a twenty-minute short. Shepard called the film 'a complete travesty', but Daphne Milne said in an interview in *Woman*, from which the pictures and caption above right are taken, 'Ever since I sold the film rights of the Pooh books to Mr Walt Disney, I had been wondering with some anxiety what he would make of them in a cartoon. I had confidence in Mr Disney's genius for handling imaginative themes – yet, one never knows whether one is going to agree! On an evening last August I turned on the television in my London flat to see a brief advance excerpt of the Pooh cartoon being shown in a programme about Walt Disney films. I was nervous. If I did not like this version of Pooh I would feel deeply disappointed and hurt. Pooh is part of my life, part of my cherished memories. I leaned forward. There was a nursery scene and a glimpse of Christopher Robin as a child in cartoon. There was the tree in the 100 Aker Wood with bees buzzing about it, and Pooh, attached to a balloon, sailing upwards in search of honey, his favourite food. . . . I relaxed. It was all right. Nothing jarred. I was very relieved.'

A. A. Milne himself had admired Walt Disney back in the thirties. In 1938 he wrote to Kenneth Grahame's widow about *Toad of Toad Hall*: 'I expect you have heard that Disney is interested in it? It is just the thing for him, of course, and he

THE ANIMALS "IN CONFERENCE" WITH CHRISTOPHER
ROBIN. HERE'S HOW THE FAMOUS ILLUSTRATOR
ERNEST SHEPARD SAW THE SCENE IN THE ORIGINAL
DRAWINGS HE MADE FOR *HOUSE AT POOH CORNER*

AND HERE'S HOW WALT DISNEY, IN THIS
SEQUENCE FROM THE FILM CARTOON
VERSION, CATCHES THE IMAGINARY
ATMOSPHERE OF THE TABLEAU EXACTLY

would do it beautifully.' Disney's *Mr Toad* – also a short film –
was not made until 1949 and we don't know what Milne thought
of it.

Further Pooh short features followed the first: *Winnie the Pooh and
the Blustery Day* (1968) includes the sequence when Pooh has to
rescue Piglet from the flood. Piglet was certainly not entirely
ousted by the gopher. *Winnie the Pooh and Tigger Too* came out in
1974. The first three were combined as *The Many Adventures of
Winnie the Pooh*. A fourth short film, *Winnie the Pooh and a Day for
Eeyore* (1983), was actually made outside the Disney Studio and
directed by Rick Reinert. A popular children's series on the
Disney TV Channel used the characters in new stories and it is
these and the often ugly spin-off merchandise which, however
popular with the American public generally, are thought by many
people to have had a regrettable effect on Pooh's image and
career. There are many Pooh books in existence – some marketed
by the Golden Press and Nelson – which have no mention of or
relationship with either Milne or Shepard. A friend of mine
overheard someone in a south London supermarket saying, 'Oh,
I didn't know Walt Disney wrote *Winnie-the-Pooh*.'

In terms of merchandising, Pooh proved one of Disney's most
successful characters since Mickey Mouse. Tied in with the
release of the first film were 169 items from 49 different licensed
manufacturers. In addition to soft toys, children's clothes, games
and puzzles, there were no fewer than 19 different publications.
There is still a great deal of Disney-based merchandise about and
some particularly unattractive Poohs, which bear no resemblance
to the real thing, but the situation has improved since Disney
realized the value of the Shepard material itself. Disney now
authorizes the marketing of a great many attractive bits and
pieces with the authentic Shepard images (see page 186).

This article appeared in the *Daily Mail* on 16 April 1966 and perhaps reflected a more general British reaction than Daphne Milne's to the first Disney film. In the *Evening News*, Felix Barker had been waging a campaign to have Christopher Robin's voice re-dubbed with a 'standard southern English' accent.

# MASSACRE

## ... OR HOW DIS

THIS is an exercise in gunboat journalism. An attempt to defend against an extraordinary attack one of the last proud remnants of the British Empire—Winnie the Pooh.

For 41 years A. A. Milne's four slender volumes of stories of the bear, his friend Christopher Robin and their acquaintances in Hundred Aker Wood—such as Eeyore the Donkey, Piglet, Rabbit, Kanga and Roo—have delighted children and parents.

OUT goes Winnie, Milne style... IN comes Winnie, Disney style

They have their own language, songs and games. Milne's characterisations — complemented by a series of charming illustrations by E. H. Shepard—gave them a unique quality among fairy tales.

The books are among the world's best-sellers and came through all translations with their Britishness intact.

But on June 16, 1961, they fell into the hands of a Mr. Walt Disney.

For the past three years a director, six writers, eleven animators, nine "voices," three background artists, four layout designers and two composers have been rewriting, redrawing and resinging the first two chapters of one Milne book. All told no fewer than 150 Disney men have been involved.

OUT goes the Milne Piglet... IN comes the new character, Gopher

The result is a 26-minute film, *Winnie the Pooh and the Honey Tree*, now going on to general release in Britain.

It is little short of a massacre.

One trace of Britishness *does* remain—the voice of Christopher Robin. This was conceded only after a brave stand by a British film critic, Mr. Felix Barker, of the London *Evening News*. Hearing of the Hollywood massacre, he dispatched a fusillade of cables of protest and apparently as a result the boy's voice was redubbed with an English accent.

Otherwise victory for the Hollywood hordes **s e e m s** complete.

### Sincere

MR. WOLFGANG "Woolie" Reitherman directed the Dis-

**WOLFGANG REITHERMAN**

ney operation. He looks not unlike a Pentagon general from *Dr. Strangelove*.

He had never heard of Pooh until 1961 (not one of the senior men on the film had read it as a child or parent).

Reitherman believes firmly that he has done nothing wrong : " I'm satisfied," he said. And he added, aglow with sincerity : " As far as Pooh is concerned, we stayed closer to the original story than we'd ever done on anything before."

It all depends, as Pooh would say, what you mean by Closer. The *Daily Mail's* American staff subjected Reitherman to a barrage of questions.

*1. Who killed Piglet—and why ?*

OUT goes Rabbit, Milne style... IN comes Rabbit, Disney style

# IN 100 AKER WOOD

## THE WALT SAID POOH TO WINNIE

### BY IAIN SMITH AND JERRY LEBLANC

Piglet, a shy creature, Pooh's constant companion and one of the most charming characters in the story, does not appear in the film. "As far as Piglet is concerned, we're all guilty," said Reitherman, chewing his cigar a little harder. "I'm not shielding anyone."

He claimed there simply wasn't *room* for Piglet in the film. When the film was cut down from a full-length feature to a short, Piglet was left on the cutting-room floor.

But Reitherman's defence of the assassination of Piglet does not bear examination. For room has been found in the film for an entirely new character — a gopher, a burrowing rodent peculiar to America.

*2. Who, what, why, when, how is a gopher in the film?*

It appears that, in the Very Unenchanted Forest of film commerce, a gopher is *worth more than a Piglet.*

It was felt that the gopher had a "folksy, all-American, grass-roots image" which Americans would go for.

Pressed, Reitherman admitted that the rodent had been introduced because Disney was worried by the "Britishness" of the original.

*3. Why were most of the characters given Mid-West accents?*

"The Mid-West accent is the generally neutral accent at which we aim as it is acceptable to the whole American market," said Reitherman.

Britain, you notice, is apparently nothing to do with it.

*4. Why was Christopher Robin Americanised?*

(The answers to this question are not considered suitable for British Pooh children over the age of 70.)

In the E. H. Shepard drawings, he has long hair and wears smocks. *You* may love him like that. All his other

millions of admirers may love him like that. But, as one of Reitherman's animating artists, a Mr. Hal King, put it without a qualm : " Christopher Robin came out too *sissified*. So we gave him a haircut and some decent clothes."

He now looks rather like Pinocchio.

*5. What happened to A. A. Milne's songs?*

The sheer nuttiness of Milne's songs seems to have been too much of a challenge for Reitherman and Co. So they ignored them completely and introduced their own (composed at vast expense by the Oscar-winning Robert and Richard Sherman).

Readers are asked to judge for themselves the various qualities of the following examples of Sherman-Pooh and Milne-Pooh :

MILNE:
" *It's a very funny thought that, if Bears were Bees, They'd build their nests at the bottom of trees. And that being so (if the Bees were Bears), We shouldn't have to climb up all these stairs.*"

SHERMAN BROS.:
" *Winnie the Pooh, Winnie the Pooh. Tubby little cubby all stuffed with fluff. He's Winnie the Pooh, Winnie the Pooh Willy nilly silly ole bear.*"

## Sensible

THESE examples are the stretcher-cases. But Reitherman and his gang have inflicted many smaller wounds. Rabbit, for instance —a nice little animal in Milne, sensibly drawn by Shepard on the lines of a real rabbit—

becomes a maniacal Bugs Bunny figure in the film.

One consolation for Pooh-mourners is that the effort of recreating Winnie has cost Mr. Walt Disney one million dollars. Not so gratifying are the methods being used to recoup it.

Many American manufacturers are involved in a degrading race to buy the rights to exploit a series of Pooh products. The list of items so far allowed by the Disney " merchandising division "—in return for 5 p.c. of the profits—runs to two-and-a-half typewritten pages.

There are to be Pooh schoolbags, pencil cases, luggage, towels, bibs, wallpaper, mattresses, and games.

None of this wheeler-dealering with a part of the British heritage disturbs Reitherman and his cohorts. To them, it appears, Winnie the Pooh is not really all that different from Mickey Mouse.

As Reitherman said : " We've got the spirit of Milne and Shepard—but it's Disney too ! "

---

Barker's efforts drew a letter of support from Christopher Milne himself and the following telegram from Barry Norman, Bernard Levin ('part Lithuanian') and Julian Holland, who at that time shared a room as feature writers on the *Daily Mail*.

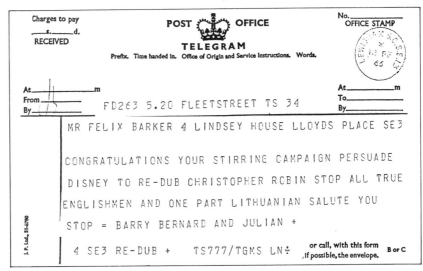

**POST OFFICE TELEGRAM**

Charges to pay — s. — d. RECEIVED

Prefix. Time handed in. Office of Origin and Service Instructions. Words.

No. OFFICE STAMP

At___m From___ By___

At___m To___ By___

FD263 5.20 FLEETSTREET TS 34

MR FELIX BARKER 4 LINDSEY HOUSE LLOYDS PLACE SE3

CONGRATULATIONS YOUR STIRRING CAMPAIGN PERSUADE

DISNEY TO RE-DUB CHRISTOPHER ROBIN STOP ALL TRUE

ENGLISHMEN AND ONE PART LITHUANIAN SALUTE YOU

STOP = BARRY BERNARD AND JULIAN +

4 SE3 RE-DUB + TS777/TGMS LN+

or call, with this form ,if possible, the envelope. B or C

**A. A. Milne's niece Angela explodes a myth about Winnie the Pooh**

# "POOH" REVELATION VINDICATES DISNEY FILM

IT MAKES ME FURIOUS the way people are grumbling over Walt Disney's version of Winnie the Pooh as if he had gone and ruined a masterpiece.

For it seems to me, as the niece of the man who wrote the book, that an injustice is being done; that the facts behind the case are unknown, and it is time to reveal them.

I think this especially when I hear it said that the gopher in the film *Winnie the Pooh and the Honey Tree* is an out-of-key intrusion. An intrusion! Hear the story of A. A. Milne's original writing of "Pooh," from the beginning.

## Buck teeth

It was on a fine May morning in 1925 that Christopher Robin came home from a walk in Ashdown Forest to tell excitedly how he had seen a perfectly extraordinary little animal frisking round an elm-bole.

Nobody then believed the child's incoherent description, but next day when my uncle was sitting in the garden reading a *Mid-Sussex Herald* headline: GOPHER ESCAPES FROM CHEWING-GUM CRATE IN BRIGHTON DOCK, across the lawn ran a small, dropsical, kangaroo-shaped creature with a sagging stomach, buck teeth and an expression somehow combining sophisticated decadence with congenital dementia . . . an animal which, my uncle saw in an inspirational flash, held the very spirit of youth and innocence at play on a summer morning in an English forest.

So the gopher was born. And about time too, for the Pooh stories, which their author had just begun, were hanging fire.

## Telegram

I never saw the whole Gopher Draft, as we called it. But from fragments it is clear how far flagging invention was revitalised — for example in "Eeyore's Birthday," where the gopher delivers a Western Union singing telegram; or in "Expotition to the North Pole," where this helpful little fellow drives up in a provision-laden truck only to be snatched by a vulture and dropped over a cliff into the English Channel and blown back on land by a whale. No wonder my uncle realised, as he worked on this gopher, that Pooh and Piglet and the rest of them now sounded stiff and British by comparison!

The next step was to get them to talk American too, like the red-blooded woodland denizens they were. So, instead of clumsy lines like "'But, Eeyore, was it a Joke, or an Accident?'" he wrote "'Say, Eeyore bud, was it a Gag, or the Way It Happened?'" Of course to write authentic American dialogue my uncle had to read any amount of Scott Fitzgerald and Mark Twain and back copies of *Movie Moments*, but it was worth it as the work took on a simple, safe, classless, generally acceptable Mid-West flavour that gradually permeated even Christopher Robin's voice.

## Dodgers

Only in the books, of course, for in real life in those days you couldn't get a British boy to talk or even dress like an American; facts which irked my uncle as the new Pooh concept gripped him ever more firmly.

"Whyncha talk gutsy, Butch?" and "How come you ain't wearin' ya paper Brooklyn Dodgers cap?" were remarks which rang round the Sussex farmhouse at this period.

But on the creative level all went well as the great outdoor saga, folksy to its grass roots, unrolled on paper. Soon the first instalment of the manuscript was posted and on its way to fame.

## Hamburgers

Of what happened next I have some more documentary evidence which is incomplete; scraps of letters, whether from agent or publisher we do not know. But their content is hideously clear:

". . . . The stories are very pretty, and admirably convey what goes on if you take a lot of stuffed toy animals into a wood these days. But frankly the MS needs revision . . ."

". . . . We fully believe that you did see this gopher, as confirmed by the newspaper cutting you now send. But alas, in the book world what matters is to reach the widest public. We aim not only (as your gibe suggests) at the Kensington nannies but ultimately at the world. We see "Pooh" translated into French, Latin, Urdu, shorthand, reformed spelling and Morse. As things are, you will confine the appeal to a handful of illiterates munching hamburgers in Kalamazoo . . ."

". . . . Thank you for your accommodating letter. We are glad you see our point of view. Could you, while you are at it, take out all references to Rabbit's cross-eyes and red nose, as we are asking Mr. Shepard to draw him like a real rabbit . . ."

". . . . YOU MENTIONED ON TELEPHONE THAT GOPHER HAD REPLACED A QUOTE DURNED LITTLE NO HYPHEN GOOD HOG CALLED PIGLET UNQUOTE STOP WHY NOT BRING HIM BACK TO PLUG GOPHER GAP QUERY . . ."

## Ill-scanning

My uncle did what was required. Bitterly, and with his high sense of purpose gone, he took out the gopher and fitted Piglet in somehow. The antics of the characters were flattened, the pace was reduced, the narrative style down-graded to impeccable scholarly English, the dialogue peppered with British upper-class in-joke slang of the most blatant appeal to Lancashire slum-dwellers and Turkish primary schools. But he didn't care by now. He didn't even care, really,

that the songs had to be rewritten.

These little verses scattered through the stories had originally given my uncle more trouble than anything. He had sat up all night fashioning stanzas for this demanding art-form:

*See*
*This tree?*
*It usedta be*
*A tree where a great big furry purry*
*churry ole Owl-bird could sit*
*Like he was enjoyin' it.*

Now they had to be changed. Angrily he jotted any ill-scanning lines that came into his head:

*Here lies a tree which Owl (a bird)*
*Was fond of when it stood on end . . .*

"If that's what they want in Helsinki," said my uncle, "they can have it."

Little did he guess that forty years later there would come along the one man who could put things right—who, with an almost clairvoyant grasp of what had been wrong with "Pooh" all those years, and working with a team including no more than six writers, would in one short film succeed so magnificently in restoring the missing magic!

## Fuss

A pity that, thanks to that *Evening News* film critic kicking up a fuss beforehand, Christopher Robin's voice has been dubbed in upper-class British; but you can hardly expect an American film company filming a British classic not to slip up *somewhere*, can you.

The caption on this postcard from Walt Disney World in Orlando, Florida, reads: 'A happy-go-lucky Tigger and Pooh might even cheer up Eeyore when the trio visits Fantasyland . . . the entrance marked by the towering Cinderella Castle.' Enormous representations of the characters are popular in Disney's theme parks.

Serious collectors should try to get hold of *A. A. Milne: a hand list of his writings for children* by Brian Sibley (The Henry Pootle Press, 1976) and *A. A. Milne: a Critical Bibliography* by Tori Haring-Smith (Garland, N.Y., 1982). There is also a selected bibliography in *A. A. Milne: His Life* (Faber, 1990).

Children's books are notoriously difficult to find in mint condition and that is how it should be. A battered first edition of *Winnie-the-Pooh*, which has long lost its dustjacket (such as the one I have, given to my mother by my father when it came out in 1926), has no commercial value but is a witness to more than sixty years of enjoyment by succeeding generations of a family. When I did radio phone-ins on the subject of Milne (both in East Anglia and Washington, D.C.), one of the most popular questions was about the value of family copies of the books. I encouraged the callers to enjoy having them and not to think of selling them. But *fine* copies of early editions do, of course, have considerable commercial value and there is a great deal of pleasure to be had in acquiring copies of the four great books as they looked when they first came out.

The early editions have lettering and Shepard designs blocked in gilt on the cloth and T.E.G. (top edges gilt). *When We Were Very Young* was bound in blue (some in navy, some in kingfisher – the fifth edition, December 1924, used both colours), *Winnie-the-Pooh* in dark green, *Now We Are Six* in dark red and *The House at Pooh Corner* in salmon pink. Even in their ordinary editions (they were also bound in leather), they are very fine compared with the regular trade editions today or the cheap editions which came onto the market in 1934. My own copy of *The House at Pooh Corner*, given to me when I was five in 1937 (at just the right age), is a ninth edition in the blue cloth common to the cheaper version.

Prices of the ordinary first editions in good condition have rocketed in recent years. In 1977 J. J. Rigden of Canterbury had them 'most with dust wrappers, top price £14', but prices around £50 were already being recorded for the two *Pooh* books. In the 1980s, even without jackets, they climbed up through prices around £35 to double that for the least popular, *Now We Are Six*, and correspondingly more for the others. The value of a second-hand book is, of course, what someone is prepared to pay for it and there have been some extraordinary (and to me ridiculous) prices paid at auction recently. One always hopes that people are buying out of love; one fears that they are buying for investment. It is sad if prices go so high that it is impossible to buy an early edition as a special present for a christening, for instance.

*When We Were Very Young* is the rarest of the four books, as its first edition was much smaller than the others. The first dustjackets in cream paper with blue lettering advertised on the back flap *Fourteen Songs*; later ones *The King's Breakfast*. I have seen it recently for sale at £750. A set of all four books in first edition with dustjackets can be offered at over £2,000. One set sold recently at Sotheby's in New York for $2,500. Marchpane, the London dealer (in Cecil Court), called them 'perhaps the most influential children's books of the twentieth century'. He says it is difficult to keep *Winnie-the-Pooh* in the shop; it is sold as soon as he acquires it.

With inscriptions, of course, prices are much higher. The limited editions, signed by both Milne and Shepard, have been sold for over $8,000. One out of series copy, signed by Milne for Shepard, went for £12,100 at Christie's in December 1990, though the estimate had been only £1,500–£2,500. The record seems, as I write, to be the £16,500 paid at Christie's for Shepard's own copy of an American first edition of *Pooh*, inscribed for him by Milne (see page 151). A remarkable price, $12,000, was paid in New York for J. M. Barrie's copy from Milne of *Winnie-the-Pooh* (see page 98). Even more was paid for a copy of *When We Were Very Young* inscribed by Milne for his nephew, Jock, which was sold for $16,000 to a 'famous American professional footballer', with Daley Thompson the under-bidder.

Other rather expensive Milne titles are the limited edition of *Toad of Toad Hall*, signed by both Milne and Kenneth Grahame (recently offered for £350) and the rare *When I Was Very Young*, published in limited editions in both New York and London in 1930. It has sold for several hundred pounds. The more modest book collector should look for *Once on a Time*, both in the first edition (1917) and in the 1922/1925 editions illustrated by Charles Robinson. The five books of Milne's verses (see page 61), set to music by Fraser-Simson, are also well worth collecting. Particularly attractive is *The King's Breakfast*, smaller than the others and with a good dustjacket. Prices are nearly always above £50, but of course much depends on condition. The early Pooh Calendars are hard to find, inevitably, because calendars are generally thrown away. The earliest was for 1929. One for 1930 sold in the 1980s for £60. The 1930 *Christopher Robin Birthday Book* (4th edition 1938) is less rare and is particularly attractive when filled in with birthdays sixty years ago (see page 118). Other early books worth looking out for are the *Christopher Robin Story Book* (1929) and *Verses* (1932). They are amalgamations of the earlier books but with some new illustrations.

In 1986 Sotheby's sold a remarkable collection of early material related to *When We Were Very Young*, which had been put together by the American collector Carl Pforzheimer over a long period (including both drawings and holograph poems, as well as a typescript and first editions of the related books and letters) for £120,000. This material is now in the Pierpont Morgan Library in New York.

E. H. Shepard's drawings fetch higher and higher prices as the years pass, particularly, of course, those of Pooh and Christopher Robin. In 1970, just after Shepard's generous donation of three hundred drawings to the Victoria and Albert Museum, the Poohsticks Bridge drawing sold for £1,700. At Sotheby's in 1989 the drawing of Pooh sitting on a stepping-stone in the stream sold for £16,000. The first illustration in *Winnie-the-Pooh* of Christopher Robin pulling Pooh downstairs sold in December 1991 for £18,700.

Christie's sold Shepard's preparatory drawing for the endpapers of *Winnie-the-Pooh* for £12,100 in December 1990. The estimate had been for £3,000—£5,000. A particularly high price was paid for a pair of bathroom drawings from the beginning of *Winnie-the-Pooh*, which went for £22,000. A very rough pencil sketch, a preliminary drawing for Christopher Robin saying his prayers, went for £2,200 (twice the estimate) in the same sale, and the original black-and-white drawing of Christopher Robin climbing a tree from page 49 of *The House at Pooh Corner* (see page 101) went for £5,500. An unfamiliar image (in colour) of Christopher Robin and the animals carol singing (see page 6) – which was possibly for a Shepard Christmas card – went for £5,280. A late colour rough for a German edition showing Pooh conducting the animals reached £7,700.

What follows is part of a paper, of considerable interest to collectors, by John R. Payne. It appeared in *Studies in Bibliography* (Virginia), Vol. 23, 1970. It included a table showing the total number of copies sold by Methuen up to July 1968. Once sales passed a million, it seems that people stopped counting. Sales of the paperback have presumably by now overtaken the hardback. Overall sales of the English edition average around half a million copies annually, with 30 per cent of them selling in South Africa, Australia and New Zealand. The books are equally popular in Canada and the States, where they are published by Dutton.

| Sales to 1968 | Hardback | Paperback |
|---|---|---|
| *When We Were Very Young* | 967,000 | 450,000 |
| *Winnie-the-Pooh* | 959,000 | 600,000 |
| *Now We Are Six* | 649,000 | 450,000 |
| *The House at Pooh Corner* | 764,000 | 500,000 |

Printing orders were given for *When We Were Very Young* on 17 September 1924 for 110 large paper copies on hand-made paper and 5,140 regular trade copies. The printing of the trade copies was completed by 5 November (with 35 overs) and bound, along with 10 traveller's samples, between 21 October and 2 December 1924.[1] One hundred thirteen copies on hand-made paper were printed by 3 October. Publication date was 6 November 1924, and a copy of the limited printing was registered for copyright in the British Museum on 11 November.

Of importance to collectors is the presence or absence of printed endpapers in copies of this first printing. It is often quoted that printed endpapers are present in some regular trade copies and absent in others, the inference being that those copies with plain endpapers are an earlier issue. The records show, however, that printed endpapers were not ordered until 18 November, six days after the second trade impression had been ordered, and were first used in copies of the second impression. Thus the complete first impression has plain white endpapers, and the use of printed endpapers began only with the second impression.

*When We Were Very Young* was enthusiastically received, and on 7 November electroplates were made for further printings. On 12 November a second trade impression of 5,182 copies was ordered, and this was followed by four additional printings during 1924 totalling 43,843 copies. These same plates were used through the 15th printing of 7 December 1926. On 2 June 1927 and again on 13 December 1940, type was reset and new electroplates were made.

The publishers have not distinguished between 'edition' and 'impression' in their production records; each new printing is called a new 'edition'. By McKerrow's definitions of edition and impression[2] the printing of 12 November 1924 is actually the second impression of the first edition, even though it is the first printing from the first set of electroplates. Likewise, those books of the '16th edition' are actually the first impression of the second edition, printed from the second set of electroplates prepared on 2 June 1927. And books designated as '32nd edition' are the first impression of the third edition, printed from the third set of electroplates prepared on 13 December 1940.

A summary of the printing of each of the four books under discussion will be found in the table at the end. Information includes: 1) title and edition; 2) dates of the original setting of type and subsequent electroplates; 3) dates printing was ordered; 4) number of copies printed.

The success of *When We Were Very Young* resulted in a second children's book, *Winnie-the-Pooh*. Methuen's confidence in *Winnie* is evidenced by their ordering two sets of electroplates before printing had begun. This was on 13 August 1926. Three days later, printing orders were given for 365 large paper copies on hand-made paper and 24 copies on Japanese vellum. These were advertised as 350 on hand-made paper and 20 on Japanese vellum. 35,000 regular trade copies were ordered printed on 17 August. Of these, 30,000 were printed by 31 August and ordered bound the same day. These were received from the binder, along with 11 traveller's samples, between 3 September and 13 October 1926. They were placed on sale 14 October 1926, and one of the 24 copies on Japanese vellum was registered for copyright in the British Museum on 3 November.

An additional 3,000 copies of the first trade impression were printed by 11 September and ordered bound in red, blue and green leather by Burn the same day. It was not until 8 October 1926 that printing was completed for the remaining 2,000 trade copies (with 67 overs), along with the 365 copies on hand-made paper (with 7 overs), and the 24 copies on Japanese vellum (with 3 overs). Binding was completed for the regular trade copies by 20 October; the copies on hand-made paper by 29 October; and the copies on Japanese vellum by 18 November.

The same set of electroplates was used through the 27th impression of 26 November 1941. Type was reset, new electroplates made, and the first impression of the second edition was ordered printed on 9 March 1942. This is called the '28th edition' by Methuen. The old electroplates were melted down on 23 March and the second setting of type was distributed on 28 September 1942.

*Now We Are Six* was Milne's next children's book. Electroplates were made of the first type setting on 21 July 1927. On 3 August printing orders were given for 50,000 regular trade copies, 218 large paper copies on hand-made paper and 26 copies on Japanese vellum. By 23 August printing was completed for 40,000 trade copies and the complete impressions on vellum and hand-made paper.[3] On the same day all copies were ordered bound. The trade copies were bound and returned to Methuen between 28 May and 6 October 1927. The copies on hand-made paper were bound between 1 September and 7 October, and the copies on Japanese vellum between 14 September and 1 October. Publication date was 13 October 1927, and one of the 26 copies on Japanese vellum was registered for copyright at the British Museum on the same day.

Of the remaining 10,000 regular trade copies, 5,048 were ordered bound in cloth on 10 September and were received from the binder between 6 October and 15 October. The final 5,000 trade copies were ordered bound in leather by Ship Binding Company on 13 September: 1,500 copies each in blue and green leather, and 2,000 copies in red. Binding was completed between 17 September 1927 and 2 November 1928.

The same set of electroplates was used through the 18th impression of 9 March 1942. Type was reset, new electroplates made, and the first impression of the second edition was ordered printed on 9 June 1942. This is called the '19th edition' by Methuen. Type was distributed on 28 September 1942, and the old electroplates were melted down on 8 October 1942.

The last of Milne's books to be discussed is *The House at Pooh Corner*. Electroplates were made of the first type setting on 14 August 1928. Printing orders were given the same day for 75,000 regular trade copies, 360 copies on hand-made paper and 28 copies on Japanese vellum. 45,177 trade copies were printed by 23 August and ordered bound the same day. The binding of these, along with 300 traveller's samples, was completed between 23 June and 31 October.

By 7 September, 25,100 additonal trade copies had been printed. 20,000 of these were ordered bound the same day by Ship Binding Company and were completed by 27 November. Also on 7 September an additional binding order went out to Ship for 4,000 trade copies to be bound in leather: 1,200 in blue, 1,200 in green, and 1,600 in red. Binding of these 4,000 copies was completed by 3 October 1929.

By 10 September the 28 special copies on Japanese vellum and the 360 copies on hand-made paper (with 13 overs) had been printed and ordered bound. The Japanese vellum copies were bound by 10 October and the copies on hand-made paper by 11 October. Publication date was 11 October 1928, and one of the 28 copies on Japanese vellum was registered for copyright at the British Museum on 17 October.

On 11 October an additional binding order for 4,524 trade copies was given to Ship. These were returned by 4 January 1929. A final binding order was given on 4 January 1929 for 150 trade copies to be bound in blue leather. These were completed by 12 February 1929.

The same set of electroplates was used through the 16th impression of 9 March 1942. Type was reset, new electroplates made and the first impression of the second edition was ordered printed on 9 June 1942. This is called the '17th edition' by Methuen.

1. Printing was completed as follows: 3 October, 3,000 copies; 13 October, 1,000 copies; 5 November, 1,175 copies.

2. Edition—the whole number of copies of a book printed at any time or times from one setting-up of type (including copies printed from the stereotype or electrotype plates made from that setting-up of type).

Impression—the whole number of copies printed at one time.

3. Printing of the regular trade copies was completed as follows: 23 August, 40,000 copies; 8 September, 5,000 copies; 10 September, 5,000 copies (with 48 overs).

| Title and Edition | Dates of type setting and/or preparation of electroplates | Date of printing order | Number of copies |
|---|---|---|---|
| **_When We Were Very Young_** <br> first edition <br> large paper copies | Original type setting <br> 17 September 1924 | 17 September 1924 | 113 |
| first edition <br> regular trade copies | | 17 September 1924 | 5,175 |
| first edition, second impression <br> (first impression from plates) <br> regular trade copies | Electroplates prepared from original setting, 7 November 1924 | 12 November 1924 | 5,182 |
| second edition | Type reset, new electroplates prepared 2 June 1927 | 2 June 1927 | 30,750 |
| third edition | Type reset, new electroplates prepared 13 December 1940 | 13 December 1940 | 10,112 |
| **_Winnie-the-Pooh_** <br> first edition <br> large paper copies | Two sets of electroplates prepared 13 August 1926 | 16 August 1926 | 372 |
| first edition <br> Japanese vellum copies | | 16 August 1926 | 27 |
| first edition <br> regular trade copies | | 17 August 1926 | 35,067 |
| second edition | Type reset, new electroplates prepared 9 March 1942 | 9 March 1942 | 12,663 |
| **_Now We Are Six_** <br> first edition <br> large paper copies | Electroplates prepared 21 July 1927 | 3 August 1927 | 218 |
| first edition <br> Japanese vellum copies | | 3 August 1927 | 26 |
| first edition <br> regular trade copies | | 3 August 1927 | 50,048 |
| second edition | Type reset, new electroplates prepared 9 June 1942 | 9 June 1942 | 12,710 |
| **_The House at Pooh Corner_** <br> first edition <br> large paper copies | Electroplates prepared 14 August 1928 | 14 August 1928 | 373 |
| first edition <br> Japanese vellum copies | | 14 August 1928 | 28 |
| first edition <br> regular trade copies | | 14 August 1928 | 75,204 |
| second edition | Type reset, new electroplates prepared 9 June 1942 | 9 June 1942 | 12,734 |

174 In this article (right), Herrmann explains how Shepard worked at an extremely advanced age on the later very satisfactory coloured illustrations for the Pooh books, which first appeared in 1973, the year Shepard was ninety-four. They are now widely used in all sorts of ways. Shepard never gave this treatment to the poems, but in 1989 Mark Burgess was given permission to colour Shepard's line drawings. Herrmann also mentions Shepard's earlier coloured plates, which were described by Russell Davies in the *Times Literary Supplement* in 1991 like this: 'Around eighty he developed a simplified "modern" style, which, bathetic after his best stuff, is adequate to its task.'

The illustration here is an example of this – bathetic indeed compared with its black and white equivalent. It first appeared in *The World of Christopher Robin* (1959).

*Frank Herrmann, author and publisher, creator of the benevolent Giant Alexander, has contributed to the archive of children's literature in this piece written for Margery Fisher's magazine* Growing Point.

I joined Methuen's as a production manager in 1956. This meant a great leap forward, both in responsibility and salary (from £800 to a princely £1,250 p.a.). I had started my working life in publishing at Faber & Faber in Russell Square nine years earlier and it had been the best of all possible training grounds in every aspect of book production and design, for Faber's standards under the eagle eye of Richard de la Mare were immensely high.

The emphasis of Methuen's publishing activities was directed much more towards education both in schools and universities than Fabers', but the firm had a small general list, largely books on humour and travel, and there was, of course, a famous backlist of children's books headed by Kenneth Grahame's *The Wind in the Willows* and A. A. Milne's books about Pooh and Christopher Robin, all illustrated by Ernest (E.H.) Shepard.

My brief from the management on joining the firm was to modernize the essentially traditional and rather dowdy look of Methuen books with their bulking featherweight papers and uninspired typography of the twenties and thirties. It posed a wonderful opportunity, the more so as Alan White, the managing director, promised me a completely free hand and indeed never once interfered in my activities over many years.

It was the beginning of a long friendship and a very happy working relationship with Shepard. He was known to his friends and intimates as 'Kipper' and it was thus that I addressed him for twenty years. With a little encouragement he soon produced, among other work, colour plates for *The World of Pooh, The World of Christopher Robin* and a special edition of *The Wind in the Willows*. It had long been my dream to put the four famous A. A. Milne titles into paperback, but there had been strong opposition from the traditionalists within the firm because they feared that it might reduce the hardback sales. At long last, at an editorial meeting in 1964, I got my way and Shepard soon produced four charming jackets for the paperback editions. They were issued early in 1965 at 2/6d (12½p!) each with the four titles banded together with a bright yellow band (a new marketing idea then) proudly proclaiming 'The Whole of A. A. Milne's Work for 10/-'.

The paperback launch was a success from the word go. It precipitated a great revival of interest in Pooh. I recall that many universities started Pooh Clubs and we sold an amazing 2¼ million copies of the paperbacks in eighteen months – and the hardback versions continued to sell at precisely the same rate as previously, of about 11,000 copies each year.

When the excitement had died down after some years, I began to nag Shepard about producing colour versions of all the Milne illustrations, but he was well into his eighties by then and his wife very much opposed the suggestion. But at lunch at Simpson's I explained to Shepard how I would make it really easy for him to introduce the colour, and he became quite enthusiastic about the idea. I remember he gave me one of his puckish smiles and said, 'I'll do it, but it'll cost you!'

So we selected the very best and least used of the many sets of line blocks (electro types) of the illustrations we had at the printer. We proofed them up with the most careful inking on a very fine paper. We then made a new set of line blocks from these proofs *twice the original size* and pulled these up on the most expensive watercolour paper we could find. They were then hand-delivered by me to Shepard with suggestions on how he could colour them quite simply with watercolour washes. His wife was furious. 'The work will kill him,' she said. 'And it will take him years.' Curtis Brown, the agents, had already told us that Shepard wanted the unheard-of sum of £5,000 for the work, but everyone at Methuen's had agreed that it was worth it, and Shepard was dead keen to make a start. It took him less than six weeks to finish the work. Sadly his wife died soon afterwards. He, however, survived her for many more years.

It took some time to translate all the colour work into print. It also involved a massive capital outlay. Shepard had finished his work around 1970 and the first complete colour edition didn't appear until early in 1973 (nearly fifty years after he had first illustrated the books). The colour plates have now been reprinted innumerable times in many different forms and have given pleasure to thousands of children brought up to expect colour in books in an age when they see colour on television as of right for hours each day.

**Shepard, like Milne, sometimes got tired of his identification with that 'silly old bear', as he once called him, and he looks suitably stern in this Norman Mansbridge drawing from a** *Punch* **dinner menu in 1960.**

In 1974 Christopher Milne, nearly twenty years after his father's death and not long after his mother's, published his own memoir of his childhood, an essential document for anyone interested in the brilliant career of Winnie-the-Pooh. Later he would follow it with *The Path Through the Trees*. The act of writing these books helped Christopher Milne to come to terms with his father's biography.

Pendennis in the *Observer* on 22 September 1974 looked forward to publication of *The Enchanted Places* and Charles Causley was one of many who welcomed it when it first came out.

## Bear facts

Christopher R. Milne has spent over forty years trying to get off his knees from saying his prayers. Perhaps the most famous of all tiny boys (by comparison, Little Lord Fauntleroy was a mere starlet), A. A. Milne's golden-curled son grew up loathing the Pooh books, 'Vespers' (especially Vera Lynn's sentimental rendering) and, sometimes, his father for—as he puts it—'climbing on my infant shoulders and filching my good name.'

After years of silence, the middle-aged Milne has finally written his autobiography, *The Enchanted Places* (for Methuen, who sell over a quarter of a million Pooh books a year). It is a delightful book—the tender tale of the aloof father excluded from his only son by their mutual shyness, and a ring of love the child drew around his nanny, with mother (who wished he had been a girl) getting the odd look-in.

Christopher Milne today is a skinny, shy, pigeon-toed man rather confused by the healing process of finally writing about 'his murky past'. He still uses schoolboy words and hops from one foot to the other, owlishly blinking through his spectacles. In 1951 he and his wife moved to Devon, where they run a successful, rambling bookshop on Dartmouth harbour front and live in a blacksmith's forge in the country, sharing everything together—including the care of their only, 18-year-old, daughter, a spastic.

Under his father's will he shares the royalties of the Pooh books with the Royal Literary Fund, the Garrick Club and Westminster School. The considerable income does not affect him: 'I loathe money–I just don't know what to do with the stuff.'

And yet, the small boy still shows in the man (although now as an integrated part rather than a hated black shadow dogging his adult independence). Seeing Mr Milne off at Paddington induced a protective worry about whether he had his ticket, a book—some chocolate perhaps? He even looks more like Christopher Robin than a 54-year-old bookseller, and at last that can be said about him without hurting him. ('Oh, the agony of mothers saying to children in my shop, "Come and shake hands with the real Christopher Robin."')

*Enchanted Places* comes out in November; Milne Jnr is almost looking forward to it. 'When at last you've pulled the bandages off the sore place, you don't mind rolling up your sleeves to show the scars.'

*Pendennis*

# The shadow of Pooh
## The Enchanted Places by Christopher Milne (*Eyre Methuen*, £3.50)

" Do you know who you are walking with? " a stranger once asked the son of a famous poet. " My father," was the reply. " Nonsense ! " came the startling response. " You are walking with the Poet Tennyson."

Even more daunting than the inheritance of a great name must be the imprisonment, like a fly in amber, of a clearly recognizable childhood portrait of oneself within a popular work of fiction. To do the late A. A. Milne justice, his son Christopher, in *The Enchanted Places*, makes the important point—perhaps too easily forgotten in the life of a working writer—that although his father had made him a name, possibly it was " more of a name than he had really intended".

At all events, the name was made. Mr Milne here describes how, finally, a child by nature shy and withdrawn came to terms with a near-lifetime of such greetings as, " Hullo, Christopher Robin ! Still saying your prayers ? " That his father was an Unbeliever, Christopher Robin never christened, and whatever else the child was doing in " Vespers " he wasn't saying his prayers, were all, apparently, irrelevant.

*The Enchanted Places* is an autobiography of extraordinary tact as well as candour. It contains a cool appraisal of the author's parents, and also a deeply sympathetic and understanding account of their somewhat guarded relationship with him. There is a memorable portrait of the Milnes' Nanny: the near mother-substitute figure with whom the little boy really did go to Buckingham Palace to watch the changing of the guard. Mr Milne, " an only child, oddly dressed, odd hair style, odd name, the hero of a nursery story ", bade her goodbye at the age of nine and set off for boarding school, when the love-hate relationship with his fictional namesake really began.

It was to last for decades. He writes, terrifyingly, of pessimistic moments after the Second World War, searching for some suitable job: "it seemed to me, almost, that my father had got to where he was by climbing upon my infant shoulders, that he had filched from me my good name and had left me with nothing but the empty fame of being his son ".

But in this moving, and often amusing, account of his retreat from the long shadow of Christopher Robin, Mr Milne recognizes that this was also what his father longed to do: and in his case, with a complete lack of success. After the four brilliant children's books, A. A. Milne felt that for him "the mode was outmoded", and in his autobiography *It's Too Late Now* (written in 1938 at the age of 56) declared: "I wanted to escape from them. . . . In vain. . . . As a discerning critic pointed out: the hero of my latest play, God help it, was ' just Christopher Robin grown up '."

With the writing of *The Enchanted Places*, Christopher Milne succeeds remarkably in disentangling himself, as much as a man in his position is ever able, or—one might add—ever really desires, from the tentacles of a myth.

## Charles Causley

In 1976 Brian Alderson, children's books editor of *The Times* and often a tough critic, celebrated Pooh's 50th birthday, or rather the 50th anniversary of the publication of *Winnie-the-Pooh*, with this piece.

# Why Pooh lovers should stick to the Bear essentials

In a glass case somewhere in the middle of New York there resides a Bear of Very Little Brain. A few years ago he temporarily exchanged his case for a similar one at the Victoria and Albert Museum, where he was revealed as also a Bear of Very Little Fur, a Bear of Singularly Battered Frame and altogether a creature much ill-used by time. His first appearance fifty years ago: "Coming downstairs now, bump, bump, bump, on the back of his head" did not bode well for his survival, and if he had not there and then been transformed into Winnie-ther-Pooh ("Don't you know what *ther* means?") it is hard to think of him reaching any sort of majority, let alone figuring in the present fiftieth birthday celebrations.

Perhaps one might also hazard that Pooh's fame would be a good deal more restricted if A. A. Milne had recounted his adventures in the vein of their earliest chapter: "In Which", you may remember, "We Are Introduced to Winnie-the-Pooh and Some Bees, and the Stories Begin". For although the tale at the centre, and its attendant rhymes ("Isn't it funny, how a bear likes honey") are known by everyone, the way it is told is today an embarrassment. Milne is here easing the reader into a private colloquy—first telling him what is going on and then turning to Christopher Robin to bring him into the story too. Christopher Robin asks questions (some of them italicized in parenthesis in the middle of the action: "'*Was that me?*' said Christopher Robin *in an awed voice*") and he is constantly being addressed as "you", even at such dramatic moments as the shooting down of Pooh and his balloon with the pop-gun.

Fortunately Milne realized how gauche and confusing this style of address was in a children's story, and once the introduction is over, he does not revert to it until the very end of the last chapter "In Which Christopher Robin Gives Pooh a Party and We Say Good-bye". This enables him to exploit to the full the qualities that have made *Winnie-the-Pooh* (and of course *The House at Pooh Corner*) so famous: the neatly turned stories, the felicitous humour, which works so well at adult-level and child-level alike, and above all, the dialogue—the changing tones and phrases which body out the characters of Pooh-and-Piglet-and-Owl-and-Rabbit, and lugubrious, sarcastical Eeyore.

While one cannot speak for the vast audiences for *Winnie-the-Pooh* in the 22 languages into which he has been translated (but *is* there an audience for it in Esperanto?) one cannot help seeing the fluent *tellability* of these stories as the cause of their immediate, continuous and apparently never-ending success. Unlike many other contributions to what may be called "the Sussex school of children's literature", which reached its apogee in the 1920s and 1930s, *Winnie-the-Pooh* has a robustness of storytelling that raises it above the level of the merely comfortable.

Those clever social commentators who would condemn the Sussex school to perdition for being middle class in fact miss the salient point, which is that fey or sentimental writing weakens so many of these books; but when, as in Enid Bagnold's gorgeous *Alice and Thomas and Jane*, or in *Pooh* itself, the writer shows such complete command of his material then class considerations become irrelevant. "Read it doing the voices" cry the children of every family—and every family knows that, for it alone, these voices will be authentic ones.

Because of the naturalness of Milne's original stories—and not forgetting the spontaneous accompaniment of Shepard's drawings—it is difficult to credit that anyone should ever wish to meet *Winnie-the-Pooh* in anything but his original guise. (Excellent bound and paperback editions have been produced for his fiftieth anniversary, published by his traditional impresario, Methuen, at £1.35 and 40p.) And yet on top of these modest and near-perfect little books there has been piled such a plethora of selections and other fancifications that new generations of readers, discovering Pooh for the first time, may be at a loss to distinguish the Bear from his public exhortations.

While one forbears to speak of the terrible things that occurred during the Boom Times of the Disney film, you may still meet with Winnie-the-Pooh in coloured compendia, or chopped up into single-story "flats", or boxed up to imitate Maurice Sendak's "Nutshell Library", or even employed as a basis for painting books, song books, cookery books and Christmas cards. (A fairly exhaustive run-down of the themes and variations can be found in Brian Sibley's *A. A. Milne; a handlist of his writings for children*—limited edition, from The Henry Pootle Press, 55 Heath Cottages, Chislehurst Common. Two guineas.)

Such peripheral entertainments may say much for the bon-hommy ("French word meaning bonhommy") of the Pooh industry. They may also attract bibliographers and social historians, for whom the proliferating editions of a popular text provide fodder for "research". They may even represent that quality of enthusiasm which "spreads knowledge sideways among equals"—words which come from Christopher Milne's autobiography *The Enchanted Places* (Methuen, L.), which is also something of a biography of Pooh himself. Even so—if I were setting off with a child for the first time to the Hundred Acre Wood, or introducing him to that doleful inhabitant of the Gloomy Place—I know which route I would take and I know that it would be the true original route, the least affected and the simplest. Moreover, with no great drawback, it may still be travelled for only 40p.

**Brian Alderson**

The invitation to Pooh's party in New York represents many celebrations which were held on both sides of the Atlantic and indeed in the Antipodes. There were Pooh Corners in bookshops and Poohsticks competitions wherever there was a handy bridge. New Zealand had a 'Write a Hum for Pooh' contest and Pooh helped to raise money for the Save the Children Fund. A Pooh Calendar came out shaped like a honeypot.

E. P. Dutton & Company cordially invites you to help us celebrate the 50th birthday of Winnie-the-Pooh at a luncheon on Thursday, October fourteenth.

The incomparable Winnie looks forward to welcoming you on this special occasion at the Tavern-on-the-Green, Central Park West at 67th Street, at 12:30 P.M.

R S V P
Elliott Graham
(212) 674-5900

178

178

Three years later, in the Year of the Child, Pooh crowned his
career by appearing (with Christopher Robin, Piglet and Eeyore)
on a British postage stamp. In May of that same year, 1979,
Christopher Milne celebrated rather uncomfortably the restoration
of Poohsticks Bridge and in September the unveiling of a
memorial to his father and E. H. Shepard. The Conservators of
Ashdown Forest agreed that 'five rough stones' should be dotted
about in a sheltered spot just below Gill's Lap. There is no
signpost. The memorial is meant to be found only by those who
are looking for it. It is, as C. R. Milne put it, 'a place where he or
she can spend a few moments alone, away from the outside
world'. In 1981 a further memorial was erected at London Zoo.
The bear cub represents the original Winnie (as in Winnipeg),
who gave her name to Pooh.

Daily Mail, Wednesday, May 16, 1979                                                      PAGE 9

## KEEP THAT RUDDY BEAR AWAY FROM ME SAYS CHRISTOPHER ROBIN

# Twigs sail again at Pooh's bridge

POOHSTICKS floated peacefully down at Pooh's Bridge yesterday. The fur, we are afraid, tended to fly.

But to begin at the beginning....

The sun was delightfully warm. It shone on the bluebells in Hundred Acre Wood and on to a bridge which went nowhere in particular.

Christopher Robin came down from nowhere and thought that, if he watched the river slipping away beneath him, he would know everything there was to be known.

It was only when he saw a lot of men with expansive cameras that he realised it wasn't going to be quite his day.

### Winces

To make matters worse, there was a man from a TV company who kept brandishing a toy bear, which looked remarkably like Pooh.

'I'm not having my picture taken with that ruddy bear,' said Christopher Robin, who at 58 is not so young as he once was.

Truth to tell, he even winces slightly when people refer to him as Christopher Robin instead of Mr Milne, son of the author, A. A.

His challenger at Poohsticks — w h i c h involves dropping sticks into the stream and seeing which one appears on the other side of the bridge first — was Mrs Pat Drake, of

the East Sussex County Council's highway committee.

It seemed an appropriate way of celebrating the restoration of the bridge at Hartfield Farm, Sussex, by the council and the publishers Methuen, who print the Pooh stories.

Mr Milne won the game.

Then everyone went back to the council's offices in Lewes.

There the chairman, Mr Robert Mitchell, talked of Pooh Bridge in the same breath as San Francisco's Golden Gate.

'It is as important a bridge as any in the world,' he said.

'The local people don't mind pilgrims visiting it, but they don't want a massive cavalcade of cars parking on the grass outside their houses.'

Mr Mitchell was referring to the Hartfield people's refusal to put up a signpost to direct tourists to the bridge.

They prefer Hundred Acre Wood to be a little peaceful.

Mr Milne, who now runs a bookshop in Devon, spoke affectionately of the 70-year-old bridge.

'I know this was part of my father's imagination,' he said, 'and I had hoped that someone would fall in love with the bridge and save it from ruin.

Story by
ANN KENT

Christopher and Pooh

Christopher without Pooh yesterday                    Picture by JOHN GOULDER

"and by and by they came to an enchanted place
on the very top of the Forest called Galleons Lap"

HERE AT GILLS LAP ARE COMMEMORATED
A·A·MILNE 1882-1956
AND
E·H·SHEPARD 1879-1976
WHO COLLABORATED IN THE CREATION OF
"WINNIE-THE-POOH"
AND SO CAPTURED THE MAGIC
OF ASHDOWN FOREST
AND GAVE IT TO THE WORLD

The Zoological Society of London
and the
Trustees of Pooh Properties
invite you to attend the unveiling by

Christopher Milne

of a bear statue to commemorate
Winnie-the-Pooh
and his creators

AA Milne and Ernest Shepard

at 11 am on Wednesday 23 September 1981
Coffee 10.30 am

RSVP Press Office, London Zoo, Regent's Park, London NW1 4RY

Please come to the East Service Gate opposite the
Main Office of the Zoo on the Outer Circle of Regent's Park.

**THE TRUSTEES OF THE POOH PROPERTIES**

request the pleasure of your company at
The Unveiling of the Memorial to
**A A MILNE and E H SHEPARD**

at Gills Lap, Hartfield, Sussex
on Thursday, 20th September 1979 at 3.00 pm
and for tea afterwards at Hartfield Village Hall

See reverse for map of
the Hartfield area.
(Nearest BR station is
East Grinstead – 8 miles
from Gills Lap, via Forest
Row)

"I was talking to Christopher Robin," said Piglet,
fidgeting a bit, "and he said that a Kanga was
Generally Regarded as one of the Fiercer Animals.
In which case 'Aha!' is perhaps a *foolish* thing to say."

(Left) The 'last great thematic series' of the political cartoonist Vicky arose from Harold Wilson's reported habit of humming when he was worried. Vicky naturally cast Wilson as Pooh. This cartoon appeared in the *Evening Standard* on 25 February 1965.

Nicholas Garland has often used Shepard's drawings and Milne's characters as an inspiration. In this group, Pooh appears variously as George Brown (with Harold Wilson as Christopher Robin), Denis Healey and Neil Kinnock.

The earliest appeared in the *Daily Telegraph* on 13 March 1966, Denis Healey as Chancellor of the Exchequer in the *Daily Telegraph* on 1 November 1977 and Kinnock's declining showing in the polls in the *Independent* on 15 May 1987.

"... and Pooh Bear floated up into the sky, and stayed there — level with the top of the tree and about twenty feet from it ..."

(Winnie-the-Pooh)

"HERE IS EDWARD BEAR, COMING DOWNSTAIRS NOW, BUMP, BUMP, BUMP..."  (WINNIE-THE-POOH)

182 Pooh has also appeared over the years in a great many non-political cartoons, often syndicated, so that it is not always possible to trace their origin. Of this group, Poohsticks Bridge was in *Private Eye* on 13 November 1987, two were in the *New Yorker* and John Donegan's 'Winnie the What? –' appeared in *Punch*, also in 1987. 'Footrot Flats' comes from New Zealand.

"For Pete's sake, can't we talk about something besides 'Winnie-the-Pooh'?"

"That's the fourth time I've read 'Winnie the Pooh' and I still don't know what the hell it's getting at."

"He hums in his sleep."

183

*"I'm fed up of Poohsticks. Let's go down the arcade and get ourselves tattooed"*

"Winnie the _what_ ? "

**184** In 1986 the *Sunday Times* organized a competititon to celebrate the 60th birthday of 'the grand old bear of English letters'. Among the entries received the most amusing had actually been written some time earlier, not by the competitor but by Alan Coren in *Punch*. Here it is:

*From Christopher Robin Milne's recent autobiography, it turns out that life in the Milne household was very different from what millions of little readers have been led to believe. But if it was grim for him, what must it have been like for some of the others involved? I went down to Pooh Corner – it is now a tower block, above a discount warehouse - for this exclusive interview.*

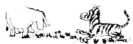

WINNIE-THE-POOH is sixty now, but looks far older. His eyes dangle, and he suffers from terminal moth. He walks into things a lot. I asked him about that, as we sat in the pitiful dinginess which has surrounded him for almost half a century.

'Punchy,' said Winnie-the-Pooh, 'is what I am. I've been to some of the best people, Hamley's, Mothercare, they all say the same thing: there's nothing you can do about it, it's all that hammering you took in the old days.'

Bitterly, he flicked open a well-thumbed copy of *Winnie-the-Pooh*, and read the opening lines aloud:

" 'Here is Edward Bear, coming downstairs now, bump, bump, bump, on the back of his head, behind Christopher Robin. It is, as far as he knows, the only way of coming downstairs''.' He looked at me. 'The hell it was !' he muttered. 'You think I didn't want to walk down, like normal people ? But what chance did I stand ? Every morning, it was the same story, this brat comes in and grabs me and next thing I know the old skull is bouncing on the lousy lino. Also,' he barked a short bitter laugh, 'that was the last time anyone called me Edward Bear. A distinguished name, Edward. A name with *class*. After the king, you know.'

I nodded. 'I know,' I said.

'But did it suit the Milnes ?' Pooh hurled the book into the grate, savagely. 'Did it suit the itsy-bitsy, mumsy-wumsy, ooze-daddy's-ickle-boy-den Milnes ? So I was Winnie-the-Pooh. You want to know what it was like when the Milnes hit the sack and I got chucked in the toy-cupboard for the night ?'

'What?' I said.

'It was "Hello, sailor!" and "Give us a kiss, Winifred!" and "Watch out, Golly, I think he fancies you!", not to mention,' and here he clenched his sad, mangy little fists, 'the standard "Oy, anyone else notice there's a peculiar poo in here, ha, ha, ha !"'

'I sympathise,' I said, 'but surely there were compensations ? Your other life, in the wood, the wonderful stories of ......'

'Yeah,' said Pooh, heavily, 'the wood, the stories. The tales of Winnie-the-Schmuck, you mean? Which is your favourite ? The one where I fall in the gorse bush ? The one where I go up in the balloon and the kid shoots me down ? Or maybe you prefer where I get stuck in the rabbit hole ?'

'Well, I –'

'Hanging from a bloody balloon,' muttered Pooh, 'singing the kind of song you get put in the funny farm for ! Remember ?'

"How sweet to be a cloud,
Floating in the blue !
Every little cloud
*Always* sings aloud."
That kind of junk," said Pooh, 'may suit Rolf Harris. Not me.'

'Did you never sing it, then ?' I enquired.

'Oh, I sang it,' said Pooh. 'I sand it all right. It was in the script. *Dumb bear comes on and sings.* It was in the big Milne scenario. But you know what *I* wanted to sing ?'

'I have no idea,' I said.

His little asymmetrical eyes grew even glassier, with a sadness that made me look away.

'*Body and Soul*,' murmured Pooh, 'is what I wanted to sing. *Smoke Gets In Your Eyes.* Or play the trumpet, possibly. It was,' he sighed, '1926. Jazz, short skirts, nightingales singing in Berkeley Square, angels dancing at the Ritz, know what I mean ? A world full of excitement, sex, fun, Frazer-Nash two-seaters and everyone going to Le Touquet ! And where was I ? Hanging around with Piglet and passing my wild evening in the heady company of Eeyore ! *The Great Gatsby* came out that year,' said Pooh, bitterly. 'The same year as *Winnie-the-Pooh.*'

'I begin to understand,' I said.

'Why couldn't he write that kind of thing about *me* ?' cried the anguished Pooh. 'Why didn't I get the breaks ? Why wasn't I a great tragic hero, gazing at the green light on the end of Daisy's dock ? Why didn't Fitzgerald write *Gatsby meets a Heffalump* and Milne *The Great Gatsby.*'

'But surely it was fun, if nothing else?' I said, 'Wasn't the Milne household full of laughter and gaiety and –'

"A.A. Milne,' Pooh interrupted, 'was an Assistant Editor of *Punch.* He used to come home like Bela Lugosi. I tell you, if we wanted a laugh, we used to take a stroll round Hampstead cemetery.'

Desperately, for the heartbreak of seeing this tattered toy slumped among his emotional debris was becoming unendurable, I sought an alternative tack.

'But think,' I said cheerily, 'of all the millions of children you have made happy !'

He was not to be shaken from his gloom.

'I'd rather,' he grunted, think of all the bears I've made miserable. After the Pooh books, the industry went mad. My people came off the assembly line like sausages. Millions of little bears marching towards the exact same fate as my own. into the hands of kids who'd digest the Milne rubbish, millions of nursery tea-parties where they were forced to sit around propped against a stuffed piglet in front of a little plastic plate and have some lousy infant smear their faces with jam. "O look, nurse, Pooh's ate up all his cake !" Have you any idea what it's like, he said, 'having marmalade on your fur? It never,' and his voice dropped an octave, 'happened to Bulldog Drummond.'

'I'm sorry ?'

Pooh reached for a grubby notebook, and flipped it open.

Suddenly the door burst from its hinges, and the doorway filled with a huge and terrible shape.

"Get away from that girl, you filthy Hun swine !" it cried.

"The black-hearted fiend who had been crouched over the lovely Phyllis turned and thrust a fist into his evil mouth.

"Mein Gott!" he shrieked, "Es ist Edward Bear, MC, DSO!"

"With one bound, our hero ....."

Pooh snapped the notebook shut.

'What's the use ?' he said. '*I* wrote that, you know. After Milne packed it in, I said to myself, it's not too late, I know where the Pooh corner is, I shall come back like Sherlock Holmes, a new image, a ...... I took it to every publisher in London.'

"Yes, very interesting," they said, "what about putting in a bit where he gets his paw stuck in a honey jar, how would it be if he went off with Roo and fell in a swamp, and while you're at it, could he sing a couple of songs about bathnight ?"

He fell silent. I cleared my throat a couple of times. Far off, a dog barked, a lift clanged. I stood up, at last, since there seemed nothing more to say.

'Is there anything you need ?' I said, somewhat lamely.

'That's all right,' said Winnie-the-Pooh. 'I get by. No slice of the royalties, of course, oh dear me no, well, I'm only the bloody bear, aren't I ? Tell you what, though, if you're going past an off-licence, you might have them send up a bottle of gin.'

'I'd be delighted to,' I said.

He saw me to the door.

'Funny thing,' he said, 'I could never stand honey.'

As in 1976, there were celebrations all over the world. There was a huge party at the London Zoo, with what *The Times* called 'a heffalump of a cake'.

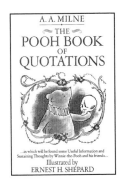

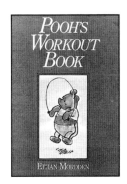

Sales of the real books soared and there were innumerable spin-offs, including *The Pooh Book of Quotations*, edited by Brian Sibley, *The Pooh Journal* (with plenty of space for your own special thoughts), Katie Stewart's Pooh cookery books, the *Pooh Workout Book* and Pooh sticker books. Also available were the *Pooh Craft Book*, the *Pooh Recorder Book* and the *Pooh Get-Well Book*. In the current list from Methuen Children's Books there are 120 different Pooh items – including pop-up books, colouring books and alphabet and counting friezes and this, of course, is not including all the available merchandise from other firms, some of it shown on the next page, together with a hand-carved set from New Zealand. By now the paperbacks are more expensive than when Brian Alderson wrote in 1976, but it is worth reminding readers of his advice to introduce children to 'the true original route'. The original two story-books are, of course, the corner-stone of Pooh's brilliant career, what made him, as *Today* newspaper once put it in a headline, 'POOH, MEGASTAR, ON A PAR WITH JAMES BOND, PRINCE AND JOAN COLLINS' – but likely, I would say, to last a good deal longer than the others.

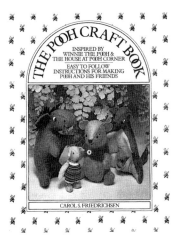

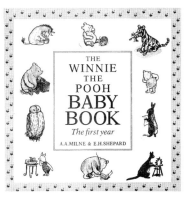

Milne was a success on radio from the very beginning. The BBC archives reveal that the songs from *When We Were Very Young* (music by Fraser-Simson) were sung over and over again in the early days of broadcasting. Often they were late at night – at 10.30 p.m. before the 11 o'clock close-down. On 7 November 1925 Dale Smith, the baritone, who seemed to have a monopoly, sang some, including 'The King's Breakfast', on 'Children's Hour' at 5.15 for the first time. The songs made regular appearances on the programme throughout the 1920s, but it seems not to have been until 1929 that the stories were read as regularly as the songs were sung. The reader was usually Ronald Simpson.

In his autobiography, Christopher Milne says that his father himself made a record of Chapter 3 of *Winnie-the-Pooh*, reading in 'a dry monotonous voice. No ups and downs.' You will have found some comments on poetry reading from Milne on page 65 of this book. 'No expression', that was how he liked it, and poetry readers would do well to remember this. Christopher himself, aged seven, made a record – singing three songs and reciting one. His cousin felt that 'the poor child was being exploited', but the record that caused the boy more problems was one made, he thinks, by George Baker which included a rendering of 'Vespers'. Christopher recalled 'how intensely painful it was to me to sit in my study at Stowe while my neighbours played the famous – and now cursed – gramophone record remorselessly over and over again.'

George Baker sang Milne songs on the radio several times in the early thirties, as did Dale Smith. There were no fewer than eight Milne programmes on 'Children's Hour' in 1933 and 1934 but then it seems as if there must have been a change of controller; hardly anything by Milne was heard again until 1939.

It was in 1939 that Norman Shelley, lovingly associated with Milne by many people, was first heard as Winnie-the-Pooh. Instalments were heard every Friday from 7 July until 29 September, over the period when war was declared – a sure point in a disintegrating world. The following year, during Dunkirk and the fall of France, stories from *The House at Pooh Corner* were regularly broadcast. After the war, hardly a year passed without series of readings from the two Pooh books, which had totally supplanted the poems and songs as far as radio was concerned. Ian Carmichael was heard as Pooh in the 1960s and Bernard Cribbins seems to have been first heard in 1969. Alan Bennett's readings are now probably the most popular of all and have been heard regularly in recent years.

Pooh's first appearance on TV was probably as a rather crude puppet in a week-long series by the Commedia Puppets, for which the BBC paid thirty-five guineas an episode. The BBC had to provide only 'voices', a framework for the sets and 'a few rostrums for the operators to stand on'. The first performance went out on 30 January 1952. The experiment does not seem to have been repeated. More successful on TV was William Rushton, whose *Jackanory* readings from the books were regularly

188 repeated after 1975. In 1976 the Weston Woods film *Mr Shepard and Mr Milne*, made by Andrew Holmes, was shown to celebrate the 50th birthday of *Winnie-the-Pooh*. Other celebratory programmes on radio have been Brian Sibley's *Three Cheers for Pooh* and *Now We Are Sixty* presented by Barry Norman and produced by Roger Macdonald.

In the theatre, *Winnie-the-Pooh* has often disappointed. Undoubtedly Milne would have dramatized it himself if he had thought it were possible. There was apparently a musical comedy version – with music by Allan Jay Friedman and lyrics by Milne and Kristin Sergel in Chicago in the 1960s. In 1971 Julian Slade's musical was shown in London and the BBC sent the novelist A. S. Byatt and her children to report on it. After saying how much she liked the books ('Even from being a very small child I liked the language'), Antonia Byatt described how angry her children got when Pooh was stuck in Rabbit's hole. 'They said anyone could see he wasn't stuck. Even a child of three could see he wasn't stuck. And this offended them. And then they were offended by the character of Piglet, who was played by a man large enough to be a lot larger than Christopher Robin.' However, I am told the musical continues to be performed from time to time and is particularly popular in Australia, South Africa and Hungary. In 1987 I myself saw a huge Christopher Robin and an ungainly Pooh in a later adaptation by Glyn Robbins and felt glad I had not taken any children to it. A musical by Julian Slade and Gyles Brandreth, called *Now We Are Sixty*, was more about Milne than Pooh. I saw it with a packed, happy audience at Cambridge, but the critics were not impressed and it did not move to London. Peter Dennis has had more success – on both sides of the Atlantic – with his one-man show *Bother!*

In 1986 some newspapers printed a rumour that Steven Spielberg had his eye on Pooh: 'the final glorious posthumous accolade.' But nothing recently has been heard of the scheme. Pooh and friends functioning as E. T. functioned in a real Forest: it's a beguiling thought.

## The Career Continues

Sometimes it seems to me quite difficult to get away from Pooh. On a morning in 1991 when I was coming down to London to work on the final stages of this book, I walked into the waiting-room at Diss station and saw a poster of Pooh and his friends advertizing BR's new family railcard, with a joke about saving mhoney. In W. H. Smith's new advertisement there are Winnie-the-Pooh Christmas cards, unfamiliar designs, somewhere between Shepard and Disney, exclusive to Smith's. Someone sends me a card: 'What do Guy the Gorilla and Winnie the Pooh have in common?' Answer: 'The same middle name.' I've heard it before with Attila the Hun. Pooh appears in unexpected places: on special postcards designed to be sent to the Canadian Prime Minister: 'Tax Pooh? Bother! A tax on books is a tax on learning.' And, again in Canada, in both English and French, at petrol stations: '*Collectionez les huits livres à seulement 50c chacun.*' In Japan, students use Pooh pencil-cases and tote bags. Often *Winnie-the-Pooh* is the first book they read in English, having met it earlier in Japanese. Pooh Clubs have been sighted as far away as the University of Otago, Dunedin, New Zealand. In the 1980s a Poohsticks Society in Oxford was second in size only to the Union.

The Woodland Trust launched a project with Walt Disney using Winnie-the-Pooh to 'raise awareness of the need for the conservation of

Britain's woodland'. The campaign was called Planet-Pooh. In Kashmir, in northern India, a women's cooperative used the image of Christopher Robin, Pooh and Piglet on a namdha. Hand embroidered in wool on a felt background, it appeared in the Oxfam catalogue. In New Plymouth, New Zealand, a young woman swimmer was spotted with a neat tattoo of Pooh, Eeyore and Tigger on her shoulder. A report of the Royal Society for Nature Conservation in 1991, examining the effect of building an East Grinstead by-pass, called itself *Death at Pooh Corner*, because of the threat to Ashdown Forest. In the States, Pooh appeared on the cover of *People* magazine when it was reputed that he helped to rescue the Texan toddler who spent fifty-eight hours trapped in a well. Familiar hums calmed the child during her long ordeal.

The world of Pooh and his friends has become so familiar that adults quote from it with a fair degree of certainty that their readers or listeners will pick up the reference. I give a few examples among many. Philip Larkin was referred to in the New Zealand *Listener* as 'the Eeyore of English poetry' and Robert Maxwell in the *Spectator*, just after his death, as 'the bouncy Tigger' of British business. Lynn Barber in the *Independent on Sunday* wrote of Ken Russell, the film director, 'still complaining in his Eeyore voice'. The whole of the New Zealand cabinet was characterized under the heading 'The party at Pooh Corner' in the *Listener*, with Jim Bolger as Eeyore, trying not to be bounced on by Ruth Richardson as Tigger and Robert Muldoon, the former Prime Minister, appearing as Piglet, his powers sadly diminished.

No journalist seems to be able to mention nannies without bringing in Christopher Robin, and stairs are also inextricably linked to both the boy and his bear. Heffalump traps make frequent appearances in the newspapers. In fiction, there is a particularly nice Milne reference in Jan Mark's *Zeno was Here*: 'On all sides she is betrayed, the betrayals related in a tone not of acute outrage but of chronic disgruntlement; she comes on like Eeyore rather than Margaret of Anjou.' Tom Stoppard in *Hapgood* throws off: 'In Paris you bounced around like Tigger', and Clive James sums up the British in distress:

> Like fearful Pooh and Piglet they keep humming
> But few believe a cure will be forthcoming . . .

I mentioned to a man from the South Norfolk District Council that at times of flood I put a marking stick in, 'like Christopher Robin', as the river approaches my back door – and he came back immediately with, 'Well, I hope you never have to take to a honey-jar.'

In *The Times* a headline 'A HOARD SWEETER THAN POOH'S HONEYPOT' referred to Milne's legacy to the Royal Literary Fund. Pooh's brilliant career provides wonderfully for 'needy authors and their dependants'. Pooh is the largest benefactor of the Fund, year after year contributing over £100,000. He certainly deserves to be called the twentieth century's most famous bear, and in the *Guardian* recently, Milne's *Winnie-the-Pooh* stories were nominated as the greatest children's books of the century. There seems every reason to suppose that Pooh's brilliant career will continue for as long as children, and their elders, go on reading.

Ulica
Kubusia
Puchatka

Pooh is in no way an insular bear. His appeal is universal and there is interest in him all over the world – but, as far as I know, there is only one street named after the famous characters. This plaque, celebrating Pooh and Piglet, is a street-sign in Warsaw.

The list of languages into which Pooh has been translated now runs to thirty-one: Afrikaans, Breton, Bulgarian, Castilian, Catalan, Chinese, Czech, Danish, Dutch, Finnish, French, Frisian, German, Greek, Hebrew, Hungarian, Icelandic, Italian, Japanese, Macedonian, Norwegian, Polish, Portuguese, Romanian, Serbo-Croat, Slovak, Slovene, Swedish, Thai, Esperanto and Latin.

The author and publisher have taken all possible care to trace the copyright holders of all the materials used in this book, and to make acknowledgement of their use. We apologise for any omissions which may have occurred; they will be corrected in subsequent editions provided notification is sent to the publisher.

Particular acknowledgement is due to C. R. Milne, The Trustees of the Pooh Properties, the Executors of the Estate of E. H. Shepard, the E. H. Shepard Trust and Mrs Minette Hunt for permission to reproduce much Milne and Shepard material; and to Dutton Children's Books, a division of Penguin Books USA, Inc., for permission to reproduce much of the Milne and Shepard material in Canada. Specific copyright notices for this material are listed at the front of this book.

It will be understood that those to whom acknowledgements are given below are the copyright holders of the material referred to, with the exception of all Milne and Shepard material, and that there can be no further reproduction without their permission.

For permission to reproduce other material in this book, acknowledgement is due to the following:

Brian Alderson and *The Times* for his article on **p 177**; Felix Barker for his telegram on **p 165**; the Beinecke Rare Books Collection, Yale University Library, for letters on **pp 68, 79** and **136**, photographs on **p 68** and the Drinkwater rhyme on **p 136**; Andrew Birkin for the photograph on **p 180**; Caroline Bott for the Bestall illustrations on **p 51**; the British Library for articles on **pp 16–17, 27, 66, 76–7, 89–95, 108, 119, 145–6**, illustrations on **p 179**; the Syndics of Cambridge University Library for the cover of *Granta* on **p 20**; the Camden Registrar for the birth certificate on **pp 8/9**; Charles Causley for his review on **p 176**; Christie's, London, for the picture on **p 6** and Christie's, New York, for the catalogue page on **p 98** and title page on **p 169**; Fred Colebourn for the photographs on **pp 34** and **35**; the late Jane Grigson for Geoffrey Grigson's article on **pp 72–4**; the *Daily Mail* for articles on **pp 164** and **178**; Dorling Kindersley, publishers, for Roland Kemp's photograph of the Farrell bear on **p 36**, taken from *The Ultimate Teddy Bear Book* by Pauline Cockrill; Dutton Children's Books for book jackets on **pp 57** and **105**, list of printings on **p 109**, article on **pp 116–17**, brochure on **p 253**, 'birth certificate' on **p 255**, invitation on **p 177** (and see Methuen); the *Evening Standard* for the Vicky cartoon on **p 180**; Nicholas Garland and the *Independent* and *Telegraph* newspapers for his cartoons on **pp 180** and **181**; Gollancz, publishers, for *The Valley of the Latin Bear* on **pp 153–8**; the Harry Ransom Humanities Research Center, the University of Texas at Austin, for letters on **pp 12, 13** and **67**, MS on **p 40**; Susan Hitch for the street-sign photograph on **p 190**; Iwanami Shoten Ltd for the map endpapers from their Japanese

edition of *Winnie-the-Pooh* (reprinted on the endpapers at the back of this book), *Life* magazine for the photographs on **pp 100, 101** and **151**; Robin Llywelyn and Alan Crumlish, photographer, for photographs of Plas Brondanw on **p 47**; Methuen Children's Books, London and Dutton Children's Books, New York, for drawings from *Drawn from Memory* on **p 8**, 'Vespers' on **p 46**, 'The Dormouse and the Doctor' on **p 48**, 'Sneezles' on **p 52**, 'The Invaders' on **p 55**, 'Teddy Bear' on **p 59**, 'The King's Breakfast' on **p 60**, Introduction to *The King's Breakfast* on **pp 62–5**, 'Eeyore Has A Birthday' from *Winnie-the-Pooh* on **pp 89–95**, 'Dinkie' ('Binker') from *Now We Are Six* on **pp 102–3**, Introduction to *The Hums of Pooh* on **pp 127–8**; the Milne family for photographs on **pp 9, 13, 18, 19, 21, 22, 24, 27, 29, 32, 86, 87, 137** and **152**, letters on **pp 29** and **37**; the National Portrait Gallery for Howard Coster's photograph on **p 87**; the *New York Herald Tribune* for the article on **p 150**; the New York Public Library for photographs on **pp 54, 79, 100, 101, 143** and **151**, articles on **pp 132, 136, 150, 152**; the *Observer* for the Pendennis article on **p 176**; the Opie Collection, Bodleian Library, Oxford, for the title page on **p 57**; the Osborne Collection of Early Children's Books, Toronto Public Library, for the Reginald Birch illustration on **p 11** and 'Vespers' card on **p 46**; *Private Eye* for the cartoon on **p 182**; *Punch* for material on **pp 22, 23, 26, 31, 49, 51, 59, 60, 166, 175, 183** and **184**; the Royal Collection, St James's Palace, for the photograph of *Vespers* from Queen Mary's Dolls House on **p 46**, © Her Majesty the Queen; the Royal Mail for the first-day cover on **p 178**; the Royal Photographic Society, Bath, for Horace Nicholls' photograph of Henley Station, 1912, on **p 28**; Peter Ryde for inscriptions to Anne Darlington on **pp 56** and **100**; Bill Sanderson for photographs on **pp 55, 80, 83, 110, 113, 136, 138, 139, 179, 185, 189, 190** and others;

Charles Scribner's Sons, a division of Macmillan Inc., New York, for permission to reproduce in Canada the words from the MS of *Toad of Toad Hall*, the Introduction to this play and the coloured Shepard picture of Toad, **pp 40–43**; Brian Sibley for photographs on **pp 61, 71, 75, 81, 86, 87** and **135**; Diane Smart for the photograph of the boxed ceramic figures on **p 138**; Vanessa Strong and Andy Ewan for the 'King's Breakfast' loaf on **p 61**; Trinity College Library, Cambridge, for MSS on **pp 77, 84, 85** and **112**, cast list and photograph on **p 21**; the Board of Trustees of the Victoria and Albert Museum for *Pears' Annual* on **pp 102–3**, 'Tiggers Can't' on **p 114**, Race Game on **p 138**; the Zoological Society of London for the record card on **p 35**; the Walt Disney Corporation for the Disney illustrations on **pp 163–7** and **186**, © Disney; W. H. Smith for their Christmas cards on **p 186** and R. John Wright Dolls, Inc., Cambridge, New York, for the teddy bear on **p 189**.

The author would also like to thank:

the Bear Museum, Petersfield, the Bethnal Green Museum of Childhood, the British Library (Bloomsbury and Colindale), Kenneth Fuller of E. W. Marchpane (Books), the Library of the Lincoln Center for the Performing Arts, New York and the Written Archives Centre of the BBC

and the following:

J. E. Brunskill, Margery Fisher, Arthur Freeman, Joy Hallam, Michael Hearn, Norman Jaehrling, Alistair Johns, Rawle Knox, Bernice Makepeace, Michael Millgate (the friend referred to on **p 7**), Barbara Milne, James Morrison, Anne Powell, Rona Selby, Michael Shaw, Elizabeth Stevens, Anthony Thwaite, Jeanette White and Lena Young.

This brief index is designed to help you find your way round the book; it is not intended to be comprehensive. References to the characters who appear over and over again throughout the book (i.e. Milne and his son, E. H. Shepard, Pooh himself and the other toys) are not indexed and you will be directed only to the major references to the four main books.